International Architecture
YEARBOOK

International Architecture
Yearbook

The Images Publishing Group Pty Ltd

McGraw-Hill
New York Washington D.C. San Francisco
Montreal Toronto

ISBN 0 07 031841-7

Projects that are going to be completed within the period
January 1997 to June 1998 are now being accepted for the
next volume of the *International Architecture Yearbook*.

Projects to be considered should be submitted to:
International Architecture Yearbook
The Images Publishing Group Pty Ltd
6 Bastow Place
Mulgrave, Victoria 3170
Australia
Telephone: +(61 3) 9561 5544
Facsimile: +(61 3) 9561 4860
E-mail: books@images.com.au

Printed by South China Printing Co (1988) Ltd, Hong Kong

Contents

6

EDUCATIONAL

INSTITUTIONAL

PUBLIC

RECREATIONAL

RESIDENTIAL

RETAIL

OTHER

Critiques

Architecture's Three Realms

By Michael J. Crosbie

We spend most of our lives in buildings. This simple fact, so obvious that we rarely ponder it, gives architects and the buildings that they create an incredible power over how our lives are shaped. While many of the buildings we use everyday may not have benefited from an architect's involvement, this volume is filled with examples of architecture that rises to our needs, dreams, and aspirations in three realms: living, working, and playing.

Living

Houses are our most intimate buildings. And they achieve that intimacy in myriad ways. They can also be sweeping manifestations of our egos, private places where we invite no-one, recollections of time and architecture long gone. If we examine the Dietz House in Williamstown, Massachusetts, USA, it is hard not to be transported back to a time when agrarian buildings dotted the sparse New England countryside. Designed by Burr & McCallum Architects, this house is a wish for a simpler, perhaps slower time. Such a wish is highly appropriate for the place we go to escape—a house as a refuge. The architects have adopted not only the forms of rural buildings, but carry the imagery through in their placement on the site, simple detailing, colours, and fenestration. This is a house that appears as if it has always been here.

A similar approach is taken by the same architect in the Plehn/Marple House in Wothington, Massachusetts, USA, which appears to have been built over a lifetime. Here is a rural house that is like a marriage: an agreement to accommodate different tastes: she likes Modern clean lines, he'd rather live in a rambling old farmhouse; and like a good marriage, the architecture is more than the sum of its parts.

A radical departure in architectural style, but no less an inner sanctum, is the Stone Cloud House in Seoul, Korea, designed by Kyu Sung Woo Architects. Here, the house seems to turn in on itself, creating a protected stronghold from which one can survey the surroundings from a variety of vantage points: elevated walkways, rooftop terraces, landings, and stairways. The house's concrete and stone detailing add to the sense that this is indeed a private castle. Materials are used in their natural state.

A pair of houses, both by Arbonies King Vlock Architects, and both in the same coastal town in Connecticut, USA, demonstrates the role of the house as castle. The Indian Point Residence appears quite literally to be such a stronghold, a shingle-clad fortress crowned with dormers, chimneys, and a widow's walk. On the waterside, this re-creation of a great manor offers a virtual veranda on its interior, allowing an unimpeded promenade from one end of the mansion to the other.

At a third the size of this rambling castle, the Vorio Residence offers a tight wrapper of vernacular materials, and explodes inside with light and space. The interior follows the roofline, while the centre of this soaring volume is occupied by a heavy, timber aedicule that hoists a roof monitor to the heavens. In a certain way, this house seems more spacious than its Indian Point neighbour—a sun-filled tent with views to a thick wood.

Simple forms and their connections is the theme of the Great Island Residence, designed by William Kite Architects, which occupies a spot overlooking the water in Cape Cod, Massachusetts, USA. Like many rural buildings, this one employs a linkage of forms that meander through the landscape. The linkages between the shingle and stone forms, virtually transparent metal and glass, suggest a collision of new and old material sensibilities.

A similar approach is taken in a House in Surry, Maine, USA by Peter Forbes and Associates. Here, the house stretches out along the sea coastal site, creating a concrete raft for the house to virtually float like an ark. While the muscular concrete columns anchor this house to its wind-swept locale, they also express the need to extend long, lasting roots in the shifting sands. The rough stone fireplace appears to anchor the ark to its site, while the decks provide vantage points for the water views.

For his own home in Boston, architect Peter Forbes created a *'tabula rasa'* with free-flowing space and elegantly detailed surfaces. The architect ingeniously uses a curved translucent glass wall to shield a bedroom while delivering natural light deep into the plan. A place for everything and everything it its place, Forbes' apartment is so free of any evidence of human habitation that it approaches LeCorbusier's definition of a machine for living.

Working

Great architecture can elevate the daily grind. Some of the greatest works of the 20th century have been houses of commerce: Frank Lloyd Wright's Larkin Building and Gordon Bunshaft's Lever House for years served as the settings where paper was pushed and gossip was swapped at the water cooler. Today, architecture can function as an amenity to attract talent in a competitive labour market, or as a landmark on the corporate skyline.

For example, Tai Soo Kim Partners' LG Research and Development Park in Daeduck, Korea, was designed as a Mecca for a world-class research staff, and a place that would inspire reflection, interaction, and creativity. Stretching out across a tree-filled campus, inside the building is a veritable cathedral for research, distinguished by a nave-like, light-filled circulation spine that encourages informal interaction among the scientists.

Another building in Korea by the same architects reveals a playful dimension in the work environment. The Kook Min Corporate Training Center assumes the profiles of nearby rolling hills, while other curved elements echo the mountains beyond. This reflection of the topographic landscape makes it familiar and timeless. The architect broke the dormitory and instruction programs into two separate buildings which allow the former to be leased during periods when it is not used to serve educational needs.

Yet another Korean building, the Shinhan in Boon Dahng, designed by Kyu Sung Woo Architect, was built to serve a newly planned city. A reflection of the growth of Asia, the building appears to take the urban grid as inspiration for its rigid facade. It also makes a different facade gesture on four sides, acknowledging the different streets and urban demands that surround it.

Work of another sort is housed in the Royalston Community School in Royalston, Massachusetts, USA, designed by TAMS Consultants. The building is pushed deep into the site and oriented to allow sweeping views of the trees surrounding it, particularly from a tower that houses the art program. The school is scaled to the buildings in this rural community, and suggests some of its historical architecture. The dormered classroom wing recalls the form of the one-room schoolhouses that were common in the town during the 18th and 19th centuries.

TAMS has created another New England landmark in the Ventilation Building #7 of the Ted Williams Tunnel in Boston. This elegantly detailed structure of civic proportions serves the needs of huge machines that remove automobile exhaust from the tunnel and supply fresh air. This exquisite shroud takes its place at the heart of the city, and demonstrates that a building as a machine, dedicated to pure function, can still be a work of architecture.

Playing

The word recreate is an apt term for play. As adults, we play in the obvious places: sports' stadiums, casinos, and resorts. But we also 'recreate' through exposure to new ideas and artefacts—as we enjoy them in museums, concert halls, and theatres. Architecture for play helps us to charge our batteries and civilise our lives and our communities.

Three addition/renovation projects by the firm of Ann Beha Associates not only provide new space for recreation, but literally recreate the original buildings. At the New England Conservatory of Music's Jordan Hall, Beha's work is essentially invisible: the restoration of architectural details that had become lost or covered over the past century. This restoration has burnished an old jewel to reveal the brilliance of its ornate architectural features. The hall's acoustical characteristics have been enhanced, while improved climate control systems allow greater use of the landmark building throughout the year. Improved patron services now accommodate a greater number of concert goers.

Beha is as comfortable working with Modern buildings as she is with Neo-classical ones. Her design for additions to the Sterling and Francine Clark Art Institute in Williamstown, Massachusetts, USA, deftly inserts new gallery space, dining and reception areas, library, classrooms, and office space in and around former courtyards. Honouring the 25-year-old museum by Modern master Pietro Belluschi, Beha's additions to the Clark's rooftop appear to have always been there, with materials that resonate with those of the existing building.

Across the continent from her base in Boston, Beha has sensitively renovated and added to a congeries of Belluschi buildings that includes the Portland Museum of Art. Again, the younger architect shows mature restraint, working easily within Belluschi's 1930s Moderne vocabulary and incorporating an adjacent Masonic Temple as the new site for arts' organisations and museum operations. Beha's designs for museum exhibits themselves show an ease with working at a variety of scales.

A flexible setting for the play might best describe the new Miller Performing Arts Center at Alfred University in Alfred, New York, USA. Designed by Kallman McKinnell & Wood Architects, the Miller displays a commanding presence on the campus and is a local landmark in the small town. It establishes a heroic scale for the performing arts, with fenestration that reinforces the Miller's acute geometry. The ample windows allow the building to glow as a campus beacon by night, and maximise views across the valley by day.

Within its historic urban context, the Kum Ho Art Gallery in Seoul, Korea uses a Modern language to make connections with nearby landmarks. Architect Tai Soo Kim has created a veritable jewel box for art, much of it submerged below grade to keep its height below that of the Imperial Palace across the street. With its granite and metal exterior, the gallery is in keeping with the materials and colour of the Palace. Deferential to the older structure, it nonetheless establishes an appropriately civic posture.

Demonstrating that an architecture for play can be a powerful tool for urban regeneration and growth, Schwartz/Silver Architects' design for Two Rivers Landing in Easton, Pennsylvania, USA, contains a rich mixture of uses. The various contents of visitors' centre, shops, museum, and activity centre is revealed to passers-by through new large glazed openings that entice others to explore the building. A measured use of materials and colours, Two Rivers Landing has energised downtown Easton's surrounding older structures and has brought new life to an old city through the power of architecture.

Michael J. Crosbie is a senior architect with Steven Winter Associates and an adjunct professor of architecture at Roger Williams University. The author of several books on architecture and hundreds of articles in various professional journals, Dr. Crosbie lives with his family in the small New England village of Essex, Connecticut, USA.

Defining Design
By Greg G. Hall

Dynamic economic growth in the Asian region has provided generous opportunities for both foreign and local architects. However, recent economic fluctuations have caused many to question the long-term stability of the region, particularly (its ability to support) the large-scale infrastructure and development projects that characterise planning in most cities.

Yet economic growth in the region, even if it slows, continues to be dynamic. And the demand for buildings is constant. Visitors to the region are impressed by its energy, its *creative energy*—an energy that seeks to create relentlessly. This energy is evident in the character of projects. Until recently these were predominantly speculative office and commercial projects. However, the scope of projects is changing and giving way to a greater variety of building types.

The change in the character of projects is accompanied by a change in issues with which architects in Asia are confronted. Clients are intent upon building faster and cheaper versions of American skyscrapers and shopping malls. Choices for materials are limited to costly imports or, more often, locally produced imitations. Environmental issues that have ramifications for the building industry are increasingly high on regional and national agendas. And equally critical, cultural and social issues are becoming a focus for regions that see their identities lost in the face of widespread economic development.

All this comes at a time when architects worldwide are expected and called on to be environmentally, socially and culturally responsible. While many architects are responsive to and sympathetic with these needs, many people in Asia feel that it is unreasonable for the region to suddenly be held accountable for standards it has taken the rest of the world a century to develop.

In response to the growing complexity of constraints, many architects are taking an increasingly dominant role to define and shape projects. They do this not only to increase their effectiveness, but to ensure the success of the project. This is critical because the way in which the project is defined determines, to a large extent, the success of the project. And many architects are finding that involving the client with the definition of the project ensures its success.

Tonkin Design, in Hong Kong, was charged with developing an image to unify a series of cinemas and help it compete with other new cinemas in the city. The design for the first in the series, Broadway Mongkok, establishes colour and lighting as key elements that were carried through to subsequent Broadway projects. In the Mongkok project, the entrance to the theatre is through an alleyway—building codes required that the enclosure be classified as a temporary structure. The architects covered this space with a red fabric 'roof' that undulates in the breeze as the shadows of numbers taken from a movie countdown fall in and out of focus on backlit screens. A similar kinetic drama is the focus of the design for the Broadway Yuen Long. Here the same intense theme of red and light is played against changes in scale.

In these projects as well as others, Mike Tonkin explains that they sought to develop a visual language that relates to the city and the culture of Hong Kong as well as to the unique character of the individual project—a methodology he explains as "trying to find the primary origins." To say that the Broadway projects are Chinese in character is oversimplistic. Yet the theatres have an identity that is undeniably Hong Kong. By subtly reflecting some of the more exciting aspects of Hong Kong and allowing these to direct the design, the Broadway projects have, quite unselfconsciously, become a part of the city and its neighbourhoods to an extent that few projects can claim.

Just as design problems are not inherently defined as cultural problems, neither are they inherently defined as climatic problems. Concern for environmental issues is not widespread in Asia. Architect Ken Yeang remarks that, although the recent pollution from the fires in Indonesia have caused many people in southeast Asia to realise that environmental issues do not respect political or economic boundaries, developers are still indifferent to environmental issues. Market competition does not encourage the additional investment of either time or capital that is often necessary to realise environmentally responsive buildings.

Hamzah and Yeang's practice shows a concern for development of buildings in relation to specific environments. In their design for Central Plaza, a 30-floor office tower in Kuala Lumpur, Hamzah and Yeang sought to increase the project's environmental responsiveness through the incorporation of natural ventilation for public areas. One of the most unique features of the building is the most straightforward; the form of the building responds to solar orientation—a response still rarely employed in high-rise building design. The building form and structure are articulated to create sunshades and terraces in contrast to the sheer curtain wall on the north. While these features are appreciated by the users and increase the building's potential value, their presence is due to the architect's emphasis of environmental issues along with the client's requirements in the definition of the project.

Hamzah and Yeang's attention to environmental issues and concern for the user are equally evident in two other recent projects. In the design of Megan Corporate Park, a business development in Kuala Lumpur, individual building units are separated to facilitate natural ventilation and lighting to circulation spaces. Similar issues are addressed in the design of the Casa del Sol. The section of the building increases in width at the upper floors to provide shading to lower floors. Ventilation is enhanced by the division of the building into blocks and separation of the circulation corridor from the facade which increases privacy for the housing units. In both projects the form of the building responds to the topography as well as the solar orientation.

Hong Kong is typical of many Asian regions as well as many Western countries in the absence of a modern building tradition that addresses environmental issues. Both developers and the government have consistently taken a short-term view and favoured economy and expediency of construction over other issues. Housing in Hong Kong is a case-in-point. Constant demand for housing, complicated by a shortage of land suitable for housing projects, places priority upon density. Although Hong Kong has achieved record housing construction over the last 20 years, population growth and economic growth contribute to an increasing demand for more housing of higher quality.

Verbena Heights is one of several new high-rise housing projects built in Hong Kong. The project, however, stands apart from the majority of housing projects in Hong Kong as the first to address environmental concerns. Although this was not a requirement, Anthony Ng Architects included detailed consideration of environmental issues with their design proposal to the Hong Kong Housing Society's design competition.

Design standards and prices for public housing in Hong Kong are regulated by the government. Although consideration of environmental design issues increases the value of housing and reduces long-term operating costs, housing sale prices are not able to reflect the cost of such extra amenities. Despite this restriction, the architects were able to include environmental issues in their design with only minimal cost increases.

In contrast to most high-rise housing projects in Hong Kong which are easily recognised by a standard repetitive floor plan arranged without consideration of site conditions, the orientation of Verbena Heights was based on detailed studies of the immediate area as well as solar orientation and prevailing wind patterns. Balconies and a variety of sun-shades were designed to reduce solar gain. Interior courtyards and gardens located on different levels throughout the project encourage natural ventilation and reduce

heat gain. In addition to these passive measures, several active measures were introduced to conserve water and promote recycling. A range of demonstration projects within the complex encourage an awareness of environmental issues among residents and visitors.

Although economic constraints are always present, they become dominant factors in periods of economic change. Anderson Anderson Architects' project for a panelised prototype house near Kanazawa, Japan builds upon their extensive project experience with both large- and small-scale residential work in Japan and the U.S. Their prototype addresses high labour costs in Japan through the utilisation of an open-panel wall system that is prefabricated in the U.S. and constructed on site in Japan.

Peter Anderson explains that they wanted to develop a system that exploited the potential of prefabricated panels to minimise labour-intensive and costly on-site construction. In addition they wanted to avoid the appearance of a prefabricated house as well as conservative U.S. suburban models which Japanese homes often follow. The design shows an understanding of traditional Japanese craftsmanship and modern Japanese building technology as well as Japanese aesthetic sensibilities. It satisfies the need for affordable housing and adapts to changing lifestyle patterns in Japan such as an increase in the elderly living with young families. The ability of the prototype to create and enclose exterior space—an aspect that is neglected by most Japanese home builders—is well-suited to the severe constraints of Japanese lots.

Redefinition of the project, in some cases, can overcome economic restrictions. Stephanie Smith and Ken McBryde of *innovarchi pty ltd* found the congregation of St. Andrews Anglican Church in Queensland to be preoccupied with maximising the number of seats and minimising the building costs. Working with the congregation they developed a building program that transcended the building committee's preconception of a concrete block shed with a tin roof. They encouraged the congregation to retain the existing building and use it both as a focal point in the design and as an enclosure for a courtyard between it and the new building. They likewise encouraged the congregation to rebuild on the same site rather than move to a suburban site. In this way the new building maintains its relationship with the town and contributes to its urban character.

Smith and McBryde sought to develop a design that was culturally, climatically and environmentally suited to the locale. Equally important for them was the division of the building into distinct elements—a visual hierarchy that allowed them to focus attention as well as resources upon the design, detailing and construction of elements that were most important to the project. This is evident in the articulation of elements such as the timber portals, partitions, paneling, windows and ceiling panels as well as the roof beams and cladding that are exposed at the eaves of the generous ambulatory that surrounds the building. The simplicity of the church, its siting and its relationship with the original building and the community reflect the values of the architects and the aspirations of the religious community.

The constraints surrounding a building project are often considered to be predetermined and fixed. However, this view of the constraints is at odds with the fundamental meaning of design. The definition of the building design problem is rarely taken to the extreme to determine the project's development.

The success of a building is subjective. It may be defined by a variety of criteria. However, the architect ultimately establishes the criteria through definition of the project—a combination of the client's needs and wishes complemented with the architect's unique view of the project.

Greg G. Hall is an architect whose academic and professional work focuses on design management of building resources. Hall was educated at the University of Texas at Austin (BArch) and the University of Hong Kong (PhD), where he was a Fulbright Fellow (1993-1994). Hall has lived in Japan, China, Hong Kong, Europe, Africa and the U.S. where he has worked on a variety of international building projects.

Towards a Sustainable Aesthetic
By Dennis Sharp

Much is heard today of the adverse effects of human activities on global and local issues. The debate reflects a constant battle between homo sapiens and nature. It is a battle that has had repercussive effects too on architecture and city planning. So much so that many cities have grown out of control and a great deal of attention is being given to their expansion and urban development programmes.

The universal migration of rural peoples to urban areas has a long history but the catastrophic problems of dealing with cars in historical city centres is much more recent. Design solutions that ignore local environmental conditions or cultures is another constant problem facing architects and planners. Harnessing technology for 'sustainable' growth in the development of human settlements has become one of the most pressing challenges for architects and urban designers today. This challenge is reflected in many of the projects illustrated in this Yearbook, a number of which show that a new sustainable aesthetic is emerging if not as yet, fully articulated into a family of forms or a style.

Eco Technology

The current buzz word 'sustainability' is often misused or misunderstood. It is applied widely across a whole spectrum of human settlement issues. Its use in an ecological sense often refers to global concerns about bio-diversity and pollution and technology as well as to energy efficiency and renewable sources. However, both these areas seem to have neglected to provide a follow-through into the world of appearances thus neglecting a basic human and cultural need for a clearly stated aesthetic.

In order to reflect upon and offer some pointers towards a specifically eco-friendly and environmental architectural language the table needs to be cleared more often, and recourse made to architectural ideas. In today's period of Eco-Technology simple, confused and overt references are made in a building's design to mechanical and natural processes and inadequate visual solutions to the appearance of these kind of projects are proffered.

A design solution that offers a full frontal display of the energy-efficient entrails of the building—the bits and bobs of external services, solar panels and light shelves, bold and repetitive louvres, huge ventilation shafts, and shiny fresh air chimneys—is not an answer. These expressions are simply symbols of designer display. These elements are seen as architectural features on the outside of buildings while internally much play is made of coloured service ducts, exposed ceilings and displays of open and filigree structural elements, often in themselves rather decorative. The architects concerned with this type of design may well be building on the functional tradition of Modern Architecture which allowed the domination of the utilitarian parts of a building to reduce or negate the symbolical and expressive side of the architecture.

The desire for a clear expression of sustainability alters our existing values at all levels. It challenges economic and political values as well as those values of comfort, space, scale and formal means of expression and current aesthetics.

In architecture and city planning there is both a fundamental need and a challenge to architecture although almost every architect will question what their building projects look like. For some designers of course, aesthetic expression provides a vehicle for idiosyncratic schemes and passionate ego-trips oft creating novelty for themes and passionate ego-trips often creating novelty for novelty's sake.

Essential Sustainability

Sustainability is an essential goal in the architectural design process. It cannot be divorced from utility, technology, physical and psychological comfort, construction, or the development of architectectonic forms. It is not an excuse for design anonymity but rather encourages an awareness and excitement in form giving opportunities, incorporating a sensitivity to creative expression which is in keeping with time, scale and place.

Technology and the City

Technology needs to be harnessed to the production of systems that are reliable, economic to run, easy to maintain and which are sustainable in terms of their use of resources and their environmental impact. It was an argument mooted by Richard Buckminster Fuller with his Design Science Decade programme in the 1960s when he argued for a new synergy between the designer, nature and the universe frequently warning of the fate that awaits a reckless disregard of such matters. Bucky's message about survival and haplessness is little different today. At Habitat 11 last year in Istanbul the problem of the rapid growth of cities and their future sustainability was addressed as part of a globally involved programme.

The Habitat deliberations were proactive and in the light of their application to architecture we can pose the question: "by what creative means can architect, urban planners and designers deal with challenges caused by mans greed, exploitation ineptitude, cruelty, wastefulness and naiveté and turn it to good effect"? How can architects exploit the interaction between environmental issues through the pursuit of the best possible conditions for people by employing technical and environmental filters for heating, ventilation, lighting, cooling, shading and luminosity? How can homo sapiens live in harmony with nature and use modern technologies?

These issues are concerned with doing the right thing at the right time in the right place—an act that Habitat called *good practice*. The Habitat initiative has examined various models drawing upon examples of the way cities and buildings can be transformed territorially by natural means but using modern technologies.

One particularly apt example, a major model initiative, is in the USA; a 22-mile river park at Chattanooga. There, a new greenway connects new housing, commercial developments and parks and the river becomes, in what was a former slum-ridden and industrially derelict city, its new, stimulated lifeblood—providing a stream of cultural and civic consciousness that has galvanised action to create new theatres, schools, restaurants and businesses.

Three other examples, all in Europe, had somewhat similar problems including unemployment, disused or abandoned riverfronts and a need for urban transformation. They can be found in Barcelona, Glasgow and Bilbao. The former was partly rejuvenated by the Olympic Games and the redevelopment of the seafront of Barcolenetta. Glasgow, with a huge publicity campaign—MILES AHEAD was seemingly transformed by its rediscovery of its own fine building heritage and public parks, its commercial good sense and cultural pedigree (it is surprising what the rekindled memory of one architect, admittedly of the calibre of Charles Rennie Mackintosh, can do).

In Bilbao a new triumphalism prevails, through which a desire of the city to redefine itself in modern terms saw the introduction of major capital cost projects by world renowned architects—supported by finance from the whole Basque region, providing the

opportunity for an immediate and consistent revitalisation of the city. Foster, Stirling and Wilford, Calatrava, and Gehry whose creation of the new Guggenheim Museum is already producing a sensational new image for the city as effective in its transformation of status as the Opera House was for Sydney—these architects have contributed effectively to the remaking of a place that had lost its raison d'être as a major maritime port. It will sustain its future through culture and community initiatives anchored to good design.

A number of other smaller European examples, in most cases individual buildings concerned with sustainable issues of technology and cultural identity, have been included in this Yearbook. The British based projects explore aspects of sustainability in what Stephen Hodder has called: a fusion of design and technology. With their major award-winning Centenary Building for Salford University (which won the prestigious Stirling Prize for Architecture 1996), Hodder Associates have developed a distinct aesthetic for a building that serves not only as a functional University building but one that also serves the city. Through its varied and clearly articulated facades it has proved to be an important component as part of a city that is pursuing an all out attempt to revive its fortunes and vying for attention with its distinguished and almost overwhelming neighbour, Manchester. It is renewing its life from within the framework of its 19th century plan and by adventurous redevelopment programmes for the sites vacated by the now derelict industrial and shipping industries. This has enabled Salford to commission architects like Santiago Calatrava, James Stirling and Michael Wilford and more recently Daniel Libeskind to design key feature buildings in the city which will sit side by side with the competent work of local architects such as Hodder Associates.

The London-based architects Allford Hall Monaghan Morris in contrast have worked on the micro-scale. Small school buildings are notoriously difficult to design, particularly placed in the context of an existing school in a tough, urban neighbourhood surrounded by a mixture of high buildings and school prefabs. St Marys Infant School in Kilburn puts a high priority on providing a special environment for young children meeting an unusual challenge for sustainable growth but an essential one in any community: a protected realm for the infants. Through their curved-shaped building they have emphasised the importance of the interior of the school providing a sense of privacy yet allowing through high-level windows, southerly light to penetrate the building mass. As a contrast to this there is also a group of low-level windows which allows the youngsters to look out onto nature.

Sustainability also influences the way designs develop, particularly in relation to existing site conditions. What appears to be a traditional two-storey rectangular building the SINC for the University of Sussex in Brighton, is in fact an innovative and sustainable research building by Eric Parry Architects. Completed in 1996 it is a naturally ventilated and passively controlled structure which has enabled a design solution to be developed with the use of a wide plan. The normal dimensions for this kind of building have been increased three times.

Another area of research, this time in the commercial world of computers, has been developed by the London based practice Studio Downie. Their Executive Studio, Hounslow, West London is an up-to-date on-line business facility. Inside the facility there is an office-of-the-future and a learning centre located as adjuncts to the demonstration space. The purpose of the project is to enable business people to experience Information Technology (IT) in a high performance environment.

Will it be by individual projects such as these designed by firms with talent and reputation, by skill and artistic methods, or by the use of the computer and the accumulation of information that the city will be transformed by individual structures that will encourage and absorb change? Certainly questions like these need to be asked:

Question one is that of the TIME Scale : What is the life cycle of a building project? Few people would have any difficulty assessing the life cycle of their car and attributing values to it. The consumer asks whether it has a viable existence after say 200,000 kms., or whether it should be sold at 100,000. Whether it needs a new engine or a new body or after five years becomes entirely out-of-date aesthetically (or stylistically) and needs to be replaced by a new model with a new shape! Now ask yourself: How many of this same group of car owners have even the slightest idea of how long a building could or should be expected to last or indeed whether it needs a new service system, is uneconomical in use, out-of-date or aesthetically reprehensible! Another further question refers to *wearability* or what used to be called *weathering*. When is a building worn out? When its original use has ended or, as in the case of the Georges Pompidou Centre in Paris, where so many people have passed through it that it needs a complete overhaul at present?

The short fuse of practical politics is often broken by such short-term expediencies and the demand for quick financial returns. They provide every antithesis to the arguments about long life and the sustainable aspects of materials used in construction processes. Where short life buildings need a temporary appearance and the employment of reusable materials; longer term heavier uses require a range of materials and finishes needing less maintenance and servicing than the temporary examples but requiring higher capital investment in the first place.

The architects of the Modern Movement from whom much has still to be learned, were interested in the expediency of prefabrication and ease of construction (which produced its own kind of temporary building aesthetic) as well as in new synthetic materials. These architects knew that expendable and extensible types of building were capable of development and change. More traditional architecture was seen as static and often monumental. Such Modern Movement matters were pertinent at a time deeply concerned with machines, the machine aesthetic and machine production and one can understand how tempting and desirous it was to think of the house as a prefab, or a machine for living in and the city, at least in the Italian Futurists' science-fiction sense, as a place of geometrical splendour devoted to speed and giant, dynamic power stations. Marinetti's famous Messagio was specific on this point: The problem of modern architecture...has nothing to do with defining formalistic differences between the new buildings and the old ones. The prophetic key to the current position envisaged by Marinetti was, as he said, the need to create new buildings on sane plans gleaning every benefit of science and technology, settling nobly every demand of our habits (culture) and our spirits...establishing new forms, new lines, new reasons for existence, solely out of the special conditions of Modern Living, and its projection as aesthetic value.

The Areas of Change

There is a need to define areas of change in order to achieve sustainable environments. The areas of concern include the use and reuse of materials, methods of design and planning, spatial and form characteristics as well as other factors such as mobility, transportation and constructional methods. Then there is the ever present political,

economic and cultural considerations which are influenced by international, national, regional and local considerations, ethnicity and languages and expressions of identity.

Changes in technology—which mark the way in which we shall live and work—are fundamental, for although we may well have lost the urge to use the Machine as a Modern Age symbol, we cannot ever escape the power of science and technology.

Form on the other hand is a found, yet unspoken, language. Sensitively accumulated over the years through a series of styles all expressive of aesthetic and cultural values, architectures creative forms emerge in order to express new conditions, new facts and to show a new face. Classical forms have had there place so have modern ones. What then are the characteristics of a sustainable aesthetic?

As designers we can recommend that attention is paid to the way that new forms may arise. The processes of design that enable new forms to be generated are as important as attending to the technical, scientific and political motivations that fuel the need for change. New forms to need to work in tandem with the old, although clearly the new is never old. But the conjunction of old and new can itself result in an aesthetic adventure.

The Teylers Museum, Haarlem shown in the Yearbook has been renovated by the Hubert-Jan Henket's Dutch architectural practice which examined the question of sustainability posed by placing the new parts of the scheme in close conjunction with the old. The architects bring in to play modern details and new materials that contrast with the intentions of the original architects but without losing the integrity or accommodations served in a charming old building that has fossilised over decades. Now its future life is assured.

In marked contrast to this approach the Cairo-based practice of Dr Farouk Elgohary Architectural Consultants' attempt to combine the new with the old through a fusion of traditional Islamic motifs and modern western imagery and designer sales methods. This approach is be found in the recently opened Horreya Mall in Heliopolis. Situated on a tight high-density urban site it employs simple geometric forms to produce an eye-catching and popular building with a multiple of uses. The concentration and complexity of these uses is impressive and ranges from the two generous cinemas, to restaurants and fast-food outlets and retail outlets situated around the central atrium space.

Symbiosis and Syncretism

Many technical changes in architecture find expressive for derived creativity from nature but it also needs to symbolise the aspirations of community and the settlement. The Japanese architect Kisho Kurokawa has called this a Symbiotic process. Others have referred to it as a Syncretic process reflecting a belief in the relationship of artistic endeavour and architectural design. Sustainability is about energy, about social responsibility, human needs, hot-desking and home-working as well as efficiency. Its systemic definitions could not have been more appropriately timed when society itself is changing so fundamentally. It may well tell us that big buildings are efficient and that the bigger the individual space the greater the efficiency due to less air fluctuations. It tells us too that individual units that use a solar heater are running up a greater expense than a group of houses. More generally most commercial, public and institutional buildings need cooling while most housing needs heating. The social implications of change range from problems created by the growing proportion of elderly people, lower birth rates, increasing world population, unemployment, high divorce rates and singles' needs.

The Role of Nature

What so often is left out of definitions of sustainability is the aspect of *nature*, the part it plays, its integrity, power and inviolable character. For many city-dwellers nature is known mostly—apart from the weather and the sky—through the parks or the banks of a river that may bisect a city heart often from where the present conglomeration itself began.

It is easy to speak knowingly about *nature*. Homo sapiens have for centuries treated nature with fear, wonder, awe and contempt, creating a paradoxical situation harnessing nature for the good in energy efficient and social experiments like TVA yet condoning the destruction of the world's rain forests, setting precious woodlands alight and causing urban catastrophes through traffic and pollution.

Clearly there is no paradise to be found around the corner. Around each bend is another environment and another opportunity to design a new place with all the creative energy and passion that homo sapiens share. But who determines the form and nature of the built environment? Through which decision making process is it determined? Could it be through inspiration by nature? By technological and ecological analysis? We are all concerned with the design of human settlements that are sustainable and uplifting.

One of the main arguments for a modern architectural approach to form has concerned itself with what I call the *Time Space Continuum*. But this cannot be done without understanding the evolution of forms. Architectural forms are a direct result of meeting a problem. Expressive forms are hard to develop and new and innovative forms on which much effort is expended by architects are even more difficult to originate. Indeed, originality (which so many designers strive for) is hard to come by, as every plagiarist knows. There is nothing plagiaristic in say Santiago Calatrava's TGV and Airport Terminal at Lyons Satolas which achieves its ingenious and satisfying aesthetic from drawing upon the natural shapes of birds in flight or in Frank Gehry's new Guggenheim Museum recently opened in Bilbao. Subjecting Bilbao to a quick rule of thumb investigation on sustainable issues, it is surprisingly supportive. Although an 'unusual' and original building, it derives its characteristics from natural sources including fishes and flowers, the great atrium itself the stamen of a giant flower whose petals burst out with the walls of the building. Neither building could have been developed as designs without the computer technology we now all use. Faced with a really long-lasting material the *'Guggy'* can be easily maintained. It has been designed to last for a long time and is one of the most acceptable models so far, of the aesthetics of sustainability.

Dennis Sharp, senior partner, writer and director, has published many books on modern architecture and was named Special Professor of Architecture at the University of Nottingham.

Contemporary Trends in Architecture and Their Impact on the Future

By James Steele

During the past year the frenetic pace of globilisation has seemed to increase exponentially as digitisation increases its inexorable reach. The tendency to specialise at every level from new nation states formed to protect ethnic identity to entrepreneurial individuals hoping to capitalise on the new trend toward outsourcing, has been an obvious antidote to such homogenisation and it has noticeably affected architecture, as well.

A far cry from the uniformity of the 'International Style' that prevailed for the two decades after World War II, the architectural scene today is diverse and becomes more complex daily. The inclusiveness used as a battle-cry in the rebellion against the restrictiveness of modernism in the mid-1960s remaining the only recognisable common denominator throughout. As the most effective legacy of the failed initiative of Postmodernism, which even co-founder Robert Venturi accused of degenerating into superficiality and the same cliquishness as its predecessor, inclusiveness has continued to successfully coincide with an irrepressible trend toward popular expression that is discernible in each of the increasing number of movements that are extant today.

The New Urbanists, who have issued the first manifesto since the polemics of the Congress Internationale d'Architecture Modern (CIAM), are the most obvious and most well organised proponents of such popular inclusiveness. The signatories of this initiative to make cities as habitable and memorable as the formative communities of the past, Andreas Duany and Elizabeth Plater Zyberk, Stefanos Polyzoides and Elizabeth Moule, Peter Calthorpe and David Solomon, have conscientiously spread their gospel through the practical application of new legal, rather than physical constructs that have slowly been replacing the existing zoning regulations in the United States. By attacking institutional instruments, rather than singular formal issues, they have managed to substantially change urban patterns and have attracted a loyal following among architects, city planners, social scientists, and others concerned about the present disintegration and future improvement of the city.

Many of the principles adopted by the New Urbanists in their manifesto deliberately coincide with a heightened environmental awareness now being formulated under the heading of sustainability. The sustainable ethos dovetails nicely with New Urbanist principles because the impetus toward more closely configured communities that encourage pedestrian movement and traditional construction methods, using local materials, coincides exactly with the wider ranging environmental sensibilities extant today, which are more socially conscious than the singular solar strategies that emerged after the oil shocks of the 1970s.

The University of Arizona Residence Halls, which are Moule and Polyzoides largest project to date, defines the approach. While for an academic, rather than purely residential community, the design displays the same integrated approach used in

New Urbanist projects. Combining tactics of clustering and mixed-use with environmental strategies based on traditional indigenous patterns and materials, the complex not only provides a rational, atypical solution to a difficult design problem, but intends to establish a prototype in the process.

Courtyards, which have played an important historical role in the American southwest, but have been eclipsed in the post-war suburban rush, have been re-introduced as the primary typology by Moule and Polyzoides, providing a startlingly fresh alternative to the anonymous residence halls typically found on American college campuses. The architects describe their function as providing a "memorable figure of open space." The direct result is a more protective and intimate environment for the residents that is far cooler due to natural evaporative action and the thermal massing provided by concrete, brick and block structure.

James Stirling and Michael Wilford have also attempted to change the rules in the design of Temasek Polytechnic in Singapore. They equally imply a prototype in this case intended to inform the frenetic growth still going on in the region and have particularly targeted a model for housing that breaks the vertical slab block or point block profile usually seen on the island. Singapore's housing program, which has gone through several refinements over the last three decades, has been recognised and adopted as a model of efficiency throughout southeast Asia, but the monotony of its sterile appearance has been an unfortunate legacy

that has prompted sharp criticism. William Lim, who has been one of the few local architects with the prescience to protest at the beginning of the process while it was still possible to change it and has subsequently been marginalised as a result, was trained at the Architectural Association in London during the Brutalist phase in the 1960s. There are striking similarities between his early proposals for a more measured and humane development of Singapore and the strategies employed by Stirling-Wilford at Temasek Polytechnic that go beyond the coincidence of the formal training of each firm.

Temasek is a reminder of what Singapore could have been, as well as a predictor for the future with regional implications that are as potentially influential as the Singapore housing program itself has been as a development model. The lessons provided by Temasek are that the requisites of density can be satisfied without verticality and that efficiency can be achieved without uniformity and that environmental factors can be successfully incorporated into large projects. Nature need not be sacrificed on the altar of growth. Stirling-Wilford have achieved this through a flexible hierarchy in which scale is broken down through clustering. A student and staff population equivalent to that of a small city is effortlessly and elegantly accommodated in four village-like groupings along a central spine interrupted by a horseshoe-shaped plaza. The groupings related to the four individual schools at the Polytechnic and the Spine is a sometimes open/sometimes enclosed promenade created by carving out a slot in the curved band of housing above. While highly stylised, the integration of landscaping along the edges of the linear spine and inside the horseshoe also fulfils Lim's vision of architecture co-existing in the verdant paradise made possible by the tropical climate of Singapore.

If any criticism may be offered of Temasek, it must relate to the formality of the planting and the underestimation of the heat and humidity in the region that outsiders typically seem to have when designing there. Circulation spines such as those used as the organising device here, as a Cumbernauld New Town derivative that can be traced in Stirling-Wilford's work through the iconic, but unrealised Derby Civic Centre, St. Andrews University and the Olivetti Headquarters are not as practical when they are open in this climate. Details such as this, however, need not significantly detract from the important contribution of Temasek as a model for the future, not only in Singapore, but in other parts of Asia, as well.

History comes around full circle in an elegant New York townhouse completed last year by Tod Williams, Billie Tsien and Associates. Occupying a lot made vacant by the earlier demolition of two brownstones, the house has a street facade that is descriptive of the distance that has been travelled between the culturally and contextually anonymous International Style that peaked in the late 1950s and early 1960s and the New Modernism which Williams and Tsien represent. Their trademark minimalism and

judicious application of materials, evident in such landmark projects as the La Jolla Neuroscience Laboratory, are refined here to both react to and interpret the busy street that the house faces. A monolithic slab of limestone, which dominates the facade, is strategically positioned to direct views from the interior, regulate natural light during the day and modulate entry from the sidewalk so that there is a place of decompression between outside and in.

This calculated restraint continues inside, as the sense of progression begun at the front door is amplified in a path of discovery, from public to private that culminates with a terraced back garden. This sense is also expressed vertically. A lightwell opening up from the first floor *piano nobile* receives borrowed light from a clerestory on the roof and a stepping series of floors above this level, which end in a high loft, benefits from this light, as well. They mirror the garden terraces at a larger scale, setting up an interior-exterior point and counterpoint in section that is palpably recognisable in the third dimension as the central spatial experience of the house, as a private haven from a hectic city life.

The spectrum represented by these three projects, from New Urbanism in Arizona to determining a new prototype for regional interpretation in Singapore and ending with the renewed sensitivity of a New Modernist interpretation of a classic urban design problem, is indicative of the way architecture is now moving. Each example shows a recognition of the fact that it is no longer possible to ignore society, tradition, culture, and climate and that appropriate responses to each or all of these result in buildings that are far richer. As the myriad directions that the profession seems to be taking continue to fragment even further, this is the common denominator in each. The heated debates of the last 30 years have, at least, had this result. The upshot is that the task of the architect has greatly expanded to encompass a greater understanding of history, an appreciation of ethnic diversity and the past patterns that this has created, popular tastes, geopolitics and the intricate network of environmental resources that underpins it, in addition to the new digital skills required to remain competitive today. This has the potential to greatly enrich, rather than damage the profession, to finally and definitively open up the field to additional interpretations of these values.

James Steele is an associate professor in the School of Architecture at the University of Southern California and the author of 30 books and monographs as well as numerous articles published internationally.

Competitions and the Internationalisation of Japanese Architecture
By Hiroshi Watanabe

In Japan, during the period covered by this volume, two public projects that were the subject of major competitions in the 1980s were at last completed and a third competition was held for a new national library facility to be built north of Nara. Competitions occasionally become showcases for avant-garde ideas, but the winning proposals for these competitions were more indicative of mainstream thought and thus enable us to track the priorities of a large segment of the architectural world. Though it would be hazardous to read too much into a few projects, they suggest a sustained interest in modernism. The most recent of these events also seems to reflect the current trend toward increased solicitousness for the environment as well as simpler forms and materials.

The competition for the New National Theater, to be located in Tokyo and used for opera, ballet and other Western-style performances, was held in 1986 in the early part of the bubble era. The Japanese architectural world was just emerging from its parochialism. It was in that year that Arata Isozaki completed the Museum of Contemporary Art in Los Angeles. While a few Japanese architects had earlier done work abroad, MOCA was arguably the breakthrough project. (The recent announcement that Tadao Ando had been commissioned to design the Modern Art Museum in Fort Worth, Texas, was noted in publications here without much comment, so inured have they become to Japanese working abroad). As for works by foreign architects in Japan, there was as yet only the occasional restaurant interior or golf clubhouse. The National Theater competition brief was at first available exclusively in Japanese, and an English-language version was distributed only after several months had passed and complaints voiced. Moreover, the jurors were all Japanese. Though circumstances were far from favourable, Isozaki, who happened to be on the jury, persuaded Hans Hollein, Bernard Tschumi and Peter Eisenman to submit proposals. The foreign contingent responded with strong design ideas and images, while many Japanese entrants, by comparison, seemed preoccupied with functional minutiae. In the end, the jury opted for a safe Japanese proposal, competently designed by a former member of the design department at a major construction company. A number of critics, disappointed at the result, dismissed the whole event as a 'pseudo-international' competition. The project itself, long delayed by problems with the site, was completed only in February 1997.

The 1989 competition for Tokyo International Forum, a cultural complex to be built in the Marunouchi business district, took place at the height of the bubble era, a year after the competition for the Kansai International Airport Passenger Terminal Building and shortly before the completion of some of the private-sector projects most closely identified with that period, such as the Hotel Il Palazzo by Aldo Rossi. This time, the organiser, the Tokyo Metropolitan Government, took care to abide by UIA rules for international competitions. The architects on the jury were modernists, and not surprisingly the winning scheme was essentially modernist in conception. The logistical problems involved in holding an international competition were nothing to the challenges that had to be met during design and construction by the U.S. architect, Rafael Vinoly, who divided his time between his Tokyo and New York offices, and his Japanese client, who had practically no previous experience in working with a foreign designer. Completed in May 1996 at a cost well in excess of a billion dollars, the Forum consists of four halls of different sizes designed for everything from experimental theatre to international conferences, an underground exhibition area and an enormous glass hall that has little obvious purpose other than to look splendid, which it does. An exemplary building in many respects, the Forum suffers from a problem common to many public works built primarily for the sake of prestige: under-use. There is little pedestrian traffic around the site, and the open-air plaza in the middle is empty for much of the day. The semi-public organisation now administering the facility will have to work diligently to compete with similar facilities in the metropolitan region and to draw visitors to this cultural outpost.

The national library competition, the results of which were announced in August 1996, was for a computer-oriented facility to be located in the Kansai district and intended to complement the main library (ie. the National Diet Library) in Tokyo. The jury, which again included architects of modernist persuasion—in fact many of the same jurors as in the two above-mentioned competitions—chose a modernist scheme by a relatively young Japanese architect about whom little was previously known. This event was unlike the earlier competitions in that the site was not in a built-up urban area of the sort found throughout the world but in a

district in the early stages of development. That may have made it more difficult to picture for overseas entrants and account for their generally poor showing. Many of the Japanese finalists attempted to adapt their schemes to the natural environment surviving in the neighbourhood. The winning design was especially self-effacing and environment-friendly, with its volume half-buried in the ground and topped with greenery.

Tadao Ando in Osaka and Shin Takamatsu in Kyoto may be the best-known architects in the Kansai region—if indeed they are still to be counted among designers based in Kansai, so widespread have their practices become—but many others merit attention. Waro Kishi in Kyoto is the designer of elegantly detailed modernist buildings. Like Ando, he has often had to deal with urban sites with narrow frontages that are typical of the region. (Indeed, one early work was a steel-frame version of Ando's famous Rowhouse in Sumiyoshi.) The House in Higashi-Nada, a reinforced concrete structure, may seem quite slim, standing on a site 4.2 metres wide, but in fact in the past he has had to deal with sites that are even more cramped. What is interesting about his work, as can be seen in this house and the steel-frame House in Higashi-Osaka, is that he has not simply overcome the difficulties of the site but turned constraints into opportunities to create distinctive spaces. The vocabulary is that of modern architecture, but the solutions have been rendered site-specific. A nearby green space is acknowledged, a view of the cityscape is offered, and an extra tall ceiling is provided where available amid an otherwise tightly-knit environment. These serve to differentiate what might have been a uniform set of spaces.

It is probably safe to characterise the work of Akira Kuryu too as essentially modernist. Okazaki City, for which he designed an art and historical museum, is known as the birthplace of Tokugawa Ieyasu, the feudal warlord who unified Japan. The building is intended to be an auxiliary facility for the main museum building to be constructed in the future and serves as a storehouse for historical artefacts. As it has a storage capacity larger than is initially required, a part of it has been turned into an exhibition area. The architect has chosen to bury much of the storage area in order to make the building volume less conspicuous. As a result, visitors approaching the facility see above-ground only the entrance foyer and a restaurant. On the opposite side, the building has been conceived as an extension of the hillside and steps down in stages to a pond. Various devices such as wind-driven sculptures, a mist-producing mechanism and a waterfall create environmental 'events', and these help to blur the distinction between the work of architecture and the park in which it is situated. Kuryu shows considerable skill in marshalling disparate forms and spaces into a coherent and dramatic whole.

Riken Yamamoto has, in the past, undertaken field trips to study indigenous villages in various parts of the globe. That background is reflected in his interest, not so much in the final form of a building, as in spatial relationships and the way they reflect family and community relationships. Iwadeyama Junior High School is a facility consolidating several existing schools, and its educational program is based on five courses of study that are meant to suit the needs and interests of each student. Yamamoto has conceived the school as a system of spatial layers, with a great deal of visual and verbal communication made possible between people in different layers. Views into classrooms are offered, and places where students can gather are provided. This generates a certain amount of noise and restlessness, but the interaction seems to create a sense of community. The school as a whole may lack a readily imageable form, but a large curved wall, ostensibly installed to screen the school from strong seasonal winds, serves as an identifying feature and helps to pull the design together.

It is difficult to categorise the work of Kengo Kuma. Not so long ago, he was producing what seemed standard post-modernist works, complete with classical columns. More lately he has created stripped-down, dematerialised designs of glass and water. His versatility is not in doubt. (He was recently named one of the architects for Expo 2005 in Seto City, Aichi Prefecture, an event whose theme is to be 'Beyond Development: Rediscovering Nature's Wisdom'). His Stage in the Forest is a facility dedicated to Noh. The district in Miyagi Prefecture in which the work is located is known for its strong interest in that traditional Japanese dramatic form. A Noh stage is always constructed with a pitched roof, a sign of its origins as a freestanding building. However, since the Meiji era, a Noh stage and its spectator area have normally been housed inside a larger, reinforced concrete box. Kuma's idea was to restore the setting for Noh to its original form and to construct the stage as a structure standing in the woods. Doing away with the larger building envelope was also intended to produce savings in cost. Locally produced stone and wood were used. The result is a work of simplicity and dignity that enhances the performance of ritual dramas.

Totoro Kindergarten by Katsuhiro Kobayashi is in a newly-developed residential suburb of Yokohama. The site is half-surrounded by one-family houses built on hillsides and by an embankment and local railway line. The building is divided into two rooms, an enclosed, semi-elliptical room for events and gatherings and a second room that can be completely opened to the outdoor playground. The architecture itself has been conceived as a play area, with a jungle gym-like structure, a catwalk joining the two rooms, and alcoves in which children can hide. The spaces have been scaled to the proportions of children, but there is no attempt at cuteness. They have a spare, primary character that is in sharp and pleasing contrast to the cosy domesticity of the houses all around the kindergarten.

Hiroshi Watanabe is a writer and translator based in Tokyo. His most recent book is on the Marugame-Hirai Museum by Alfredo Arribas.

...And Now For The Good News

By Michael Webb

This is the best and worst of times for the architectural profession. Masters as different as Frank Gehry, Renzo Piano, Norman Foster, Richard Rogers, and Richard Meier are creating large-scale work of extraordinary quality that has captured the attention of a mass public. Innovative buildings are analysed and debated in the popular media, and there is a lively response to architectural exhibitions. Post-modernism has been recognised for what it is—a slick veneer of historicism that is as irrelevant to a building's purpose as the surface ornament of art deco—and is now dismissed with the contempt it deserves. The deconstructivist fad is also in eclipse, and architects are increasingly concerned with the performance of their buildings.

Despite these encouraging signs, many practitioners feel increasingly marginalised, and far too many talented firms are short of work. Bold initiatives are frustrated and mediocrity flourishes. Nowhere is this more evident than in Los Angeles, a hub of experiment in the 1980s, which has recovered from recession without regaining its nerve. Commercial and public commissions have dwindled, and private clients are reluctant to take chances. Eric Owen Moss is dependent on a single enlightened developer. Coop Himmelblau arrived full of anticipation from Vienna, and departed empty-handed. The construction of Walt Disney Concert Hall is still on hold, 10 years after Frank Gehry won a competition for its design and this architect, acclaimed around the world, has no current work in the city he moved to 50 years ago.

Some American architects have found profitable employment abroad, but that may change if the economic boom in southeast Asia falters, and the economies of Japan and continental Europe remain stagnant. Adventurous architects from Finland to Japan have been even harder hit by the downturn in construction. Meanwhile, hopeful graduates continue to pour out of architectural schools with little prospect of building anything more substantial than a web site. Supply and demand are gravely out of balance, and too few potential clients appreciate what a good architect can do to enrich the environment.

However, the purpose of this Yearbook is not to lament shortcomings, but to chronicle achievement world-wide, and there are some notable examples to celebrate. Moshe Safdie, the Israel-born architect who won fame and fortune in Canada while struggling against the odds to enhance Jerusalem, has finally completed his first major public building in the United States. The Skirball Museum and Cultural Center is located in a pass through the Santa Monica Mountains in west Los Angeles. It comprises a cool, smooth-skinned complex of poured concrete, banded in pink granite, with rounded vaults clad in stainless steel that stand out boldly against a backdrop of dark hills. The buildings reach out to embrace the landscape. Walkways are shaded by vine-clad pergolas, and classrooms open onto courtyards, blurring the division between interior and exterior, and reminding one that Israel and southern California share a benign Mediterranean climate. Like Safdie's Hebrew

Union College in Jerusalem, the Skirball is designed to bring people together, and encourage visitors to explore a wide range of cultural offerings and chance encounters. In this way, it makes an important contribution to Los Angeles' meagre public realm.

The Skirball celebrates the 4,000-year history of the Jewish people and the story of their struggle and success in the United States. Safdie notes that there is no Jewish architectural vocabulary, for Jews appropriated local traditions during the Diaspora. His work, and particularly this structure, embodies strong cultural values—of continuity, community, and respect for learning—but they are expressed abstractly, in contrast to the familiar, and often debased language of Moslem architecture.

Safdie's public buildings in Canada have tended to be far more exuberant and expressive, and a fierce debate has raged over the competition-winning Library Square in downtown Vancouver. An elliptical office block steps down and is wrapped around one side of an oval public library to define a plaza. Library Square establishes a sense of place in a loose grid of freestanding steel and glass towers. With no street line or established architectural order to respect, Safdie was free to create his own grand urban scale, and to allow the program to generate the architectural forms.

Vancouver is a wet and windy city in an active seismic zone. Thus, a massive structure with generous interior spaces was required. The architect looked back to Habitat (the precast megastructure in Montreal that launched his career, 30 years ago) to devise a system of construction that would allow the precast concrete and sandstone columns to be moulded on site and rapidly assembled. As a result, the complex was designed and built in just three years. There are no suspended ceilings; services are housed beneath each floor, and can easily be accessed for maintenance and upgrading. Safdie claims that the resemblance of the Library to the Colosseum in Rome is fortuitous. Each library floor has a rectilinear core of stacks with perimeter reading areas contained within the oval wall. Only after this plan was fully developed did the architect discover how close he had come to the form and scale of the Colosseum.

A second Vancouver commission, for a site across the street from Library Square, allowed Safdie another opportunity to combine practicality and drama. The Ford Centre for the Performing Arts was constructed on a tight schedule and budget, but provides patrons with an exhilarating facade, faceted lobby, and boldly modelled auditorium that accommodates Broadway musicals and other popular entertainments.

A few miles west of the Skirball, in the hills above Malibu, is Frank Israel's Dan House, 'one of the last and best works' by the prodigiously talented architect, whose life abruptly ended before he could realise his full potential. The clients commissioned a remodel of their conventional ranch house, and Israel, with project architect Steven Shortridge, devised a plan in which angular pavilions would open out of the extended box. They were about to begin construction when a devastating brush fire wiped out the neighbourhood. To avoid further delay, it was decided to recreate the form of the old house and build the planned additions around the existing footprint.

Israel's last years were spent exploring the concept of folded planes that would fuse walls and roof. Here, a zinc-clad roof tilts, juts, and is folded down over the angular pavilions like origami, almost concealing the linear plan of the original core. Inside and out, glulam fir beams are exposed to suggest constructivist sculptures and to impart a dynamism to each part of the house. Inside, every space flows into the next, with few divisions. There is an intricate play of diagonal and orthogonal geometries, and of ceiling heights—from the low entry to the soaring vault above the living room, and within the master bedroom where beams radiate from a steel column like the spokes of a wheel.

The Dan House is made to seem more spacious than it is. For architects Gunther Domenig and Hermann Eisenköck the challenge was to minimise the impact of the five-storey, 300 metre-long RESOWI Centre on the historic south Austrian city of Graz. Their competition-winning design for the faculties of Social Sciences, Economics and Law at Karl Franzens University occupies a site along the eastern edge of the campus that is bordered on three sides by handsome, turn-of-the-century apartment buildings. The strategy was to set the new block back behind a screen of trees, and to articulate its

component elements to break up the bulk. Offices are suspended from a massive steel frame; lecture theatres jut from the west facade, a library curves out like a separate limb, and an elliptical cafeteria projects out to canopy the entry portal. The interior is divided into seven self-contained sections with elevator lobbies between. In each section, perimeter rooms flank a skylit atrium, drawing natural light from both sides, and opening onto galleries and coffee stations that project into the void of the atrium. Together with the new university plant physiology building of Klaus Kada, RESOWI demonstrates a mastery of scale and a mature restraint that mark a new direction in a city long dedicated to architectural experimentation.

Frank Gehry has been demonstrating his mastery of scale and form over the past decade and his Bilbao Guggenheim Museum should be a highlight of the next Yearbook. The Nationale-Nederlanden Building occupies a site at the edge of Prague's historic centre that was cleared by a stray American bomb in 1945 and has remained empty until now. For the first four decades of this century, Prague was a hotbed of architectural innovation, and wonderful examples of art nouveau, cubism, and international modernism are scattered among the Gothic and baroque treasures. During the sclerotic years of Soviet domination, originality was sternly discouraged, and the city became, like Venice, a backwards-looking museum.

The return of capitalism has generated a mix of sleazy and overbearing new construction; Gehry's building, commissioned by an enlightened Dutch company, shows how old and new can enhance each other. The design (developed in collaboration with the Prague-based architect Vlado Milunic) provoked bitter controversy and was realised only through the intervention of President Have, who used to live next door in an apartment building his father designed.

Prague is a city of delightful surprises, and this addition is squarely in that tradition. It rises eight storeys from a narrow site, anchors the corner of two busy streets and a bridge across the Vlatava river, and animates an irregular public plaza. Square window frames seem to bob like rafts in the wave forms that are modelled into the cement plaster riverfront facade. Twin cylindrical towers, one extruded from the facade, another of double-skinned glass, turn the corner. A 'Medusa's head' of silvery mesh strips, designed to catch the light, spins from the top of the first tower; a glass canopy flares from the second like an overskirt. The building was quickly dubbed Fred and Ginger, in reference to the dance team of Astaire-Rogers, and it's an apt comparison, for the two forms seem about to glide away or to perform a spectacular leap. An advertising agency has made inventive use of two office floors, regrettably, the penthouse is occupied, not by a public gallery as Havel had wished, but by a vulgar, overpriced French restaurant.

Michael Webb is the author of Architects House Themselves: Breaking New Ground, and eight other books on architecture and design. He is currently preparing a new series of monographs to be published by IMAGES.

Corporate

Abdulrahim Place

Interdesign Company Limited
in association with Wong and Tung International Ltd

Completion: July 1996

Location: Bangkok, Thailand

Client: DS Management Co., Ltd.

Area: 95,000 square metres; 1.2 million square feet

Structure: Reinforced concrete

Materials: Ceramic tile veneer; glass; stone

Cost: 1,400 million BAHT

1   Northeast elevation
2   Night view from Lumpini Park
3   Site plan
4   Elavator lobby
5   Main entrance
Photography: Image Focal

Commanding a superb location where Bangkok's central business district meets the city's largest park, Abdulrahim Place has attained immediate landmark status. The building's pyramidal-topped profile, strikingly lit after sunset, is a highly visible presence on the skyline of one of the world's nightlife capitals.

The 34-storey tower has been set back 100 metres (328 feet) from the site's frontage on one of the city's most heavily-trafficked arteries. The first-class office accommodation commences above the 10-level, concealed parking podium, freeing the remainder of the site for a landscaped linkage toward the park.

The massing is segmented by a series of setbacks and corner permutations, creating numerous opportunities for sky terraces and dual-view offices. Intersecting vertical and horizontal ribbons of masonry envelop the glass curtain wall and provide a lively dimensionality to the shaft.

The space efficient, flexible floor plate and open views have enhanced the building's desirablity to a full roster of well-known international corporate tenants.

1

0   20   40m

2

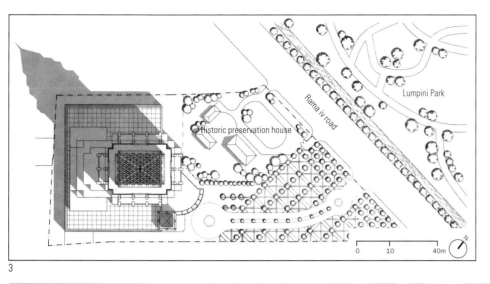

3

4

5

Bay Networks Regional Offices and Executive Briefing Center

Fox & Fowle Architects
in association with David J. Spector & Associates; Jaros Baum & Bolles

Completion: July 1996
Location: New York, New York, USA
Client: Bay Networks
Area: 6,224 square metres; 67,000 square feet
Materials: Ceramic tile; patterned glass; pearwood

Fox & Fowle Architects was selected by Bay Networks to design its regional offices in Manhattan. Bay Networks is one of the world's leading suppliers of computer networking solutions, offering equipment, service, training and certification programs.

Bay Networks' new offices consist of three floors at 320 Park Avenue, totalling 6,224 square metres (67,000 square feet), in area. The installation houses Bay Networks' New York City-based staff as well as a 1,300 square metre (14,000 square foot), executive briefing centre for providing customers with product demonstrations and training. This sales centre makes extensive use of current computer and video technologies in support of its customer oriented function.

The new offices took advantage of accelerated design and construction techniques, allowing the project to be designed and built in just under seven months. For this assignment, Fox & Fowle Architects worked with the project consulting firm of David J. Spector & Associates and Jaros Baum & Bolles, consulting engineers.

1   Conference room waiting area
2   Elevator lobby and reception
3   Stairway
4   16th floor plan
5   Main conference room
6   Product demonstration room
Photography: Marco Lorenzetti /Hedrich-Blessing (7)

1

2

3

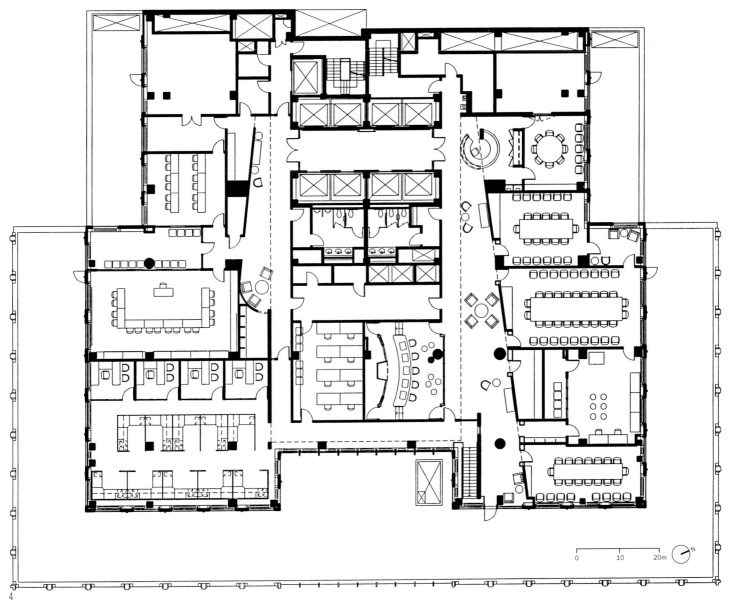

4

5

6

Bayer Corporation, North American Pharmaceutical Division
Flad & Associates

Completion: September 1996
Location: West Haven, Connecticut, USA
Client: Bayer Corporation
Area: 23,225 square metres; 250,000 square feet
Structure: Steel
Materials: Precast concrete; tinted glass
Cost: US$24 million

The North American Pharmaceutical Division Headquarters was designed to serve as the centrepiece of Bayer's multi-million dollar campus expansion. The building's architecture serves as the 'gateway' to the existing collection of buildings on the 100-acre complex.

With its completion, more than 700 Bayer employees in leased space were relocated to the central campus. The primary purpose for the facility was to consolidate the administrative functions for the Pharmaceutical division to improve inter-departmental efficiencies; unify site functions; promote communication, interaction, and efficient and effective work processes; and reduce operational costs. In addition, the building's image needed to provide an environment capable of attracting and retaining qualified staff. The building (floor plates) needed to be designed with a high degree of flexibility and adaptability to meet Bayer's need for future change. The design by Flad & Associates achieves and exceeds all of these objectives. The master plan created a contemporary image along the Interstate 95 corridor which passes by the facility. The concept for the plan is a series of working neighbourhoods which typically support 24-30 people and are located along the perimeter of the building to optimise access to daylight and views of the natural areas.

1   Elevation
2   Front entry at night
3   Long view of courtyard
4   View of main entry
5   Connecting bridge and lobby
6   Sculptural stair is focal point of lobby
Photography: Steve Hall/Hedrich-Blessing

1

2

3

4

5

6

Central Plaza

T.R. Hamzah & Yeang Sdn Bhd

Completion: June 1996

Location: Kualu Lumpur, Malaysia

Client: Malview Sdn Bhd

Area: 22,371 square metres; 240,807 square feet

Structure: Reinforced concrete frame; brick infill

Materials: Aluminium; granite; glass; ceramic tiles

Completed in 1996, Central Plaza is situated within Kualu Lumpur's 'Golden Triangle'. The brief called for a landmark office building for rental, maximising the plot ratio (1:7.5).

The rectangular site has an ideal east–west orientation with the 'wafer thin' office floors sitting on a plinth of seven car parking floors with a naturally ventilated entrance ground floor lobby, together with retail facilities at the lower ground level.

As a marketing requirement, the client requested the typical office floor to be column free. This arrangement initiated the need for structural bracing at the end columns of the east and west facades. Recessing the facade glazing on the west face offered the opportunity to use this structural feature as sunshade, allowing marketable

windows on this hot facade to view out into the main street below.

A curved fully-glazed curtain wall on the north face gives an uninterrupted view of the distant hills. The sunshade-free elevation is compensated by use of solar-reflective glass, and becomes a geographical indicator of the northerly direction.

Terraces and an extensive roof-garden offer building users the opportunity to relax in pleasant surroundings, while the perimeter service core, which consists of the lift lobby, stairways and toilets, has natural ventilation and natural lighting.

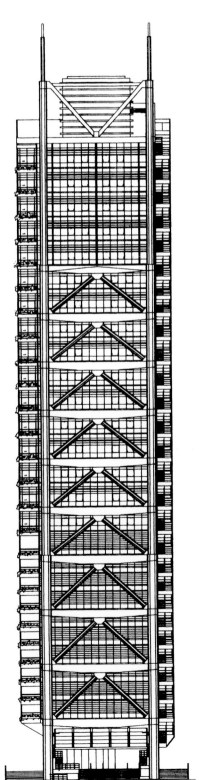

1

2

1 West elevation
2 Main facade, facing west
3 Rear elevation
4 Entrance canopy
5 Site plan

3

4

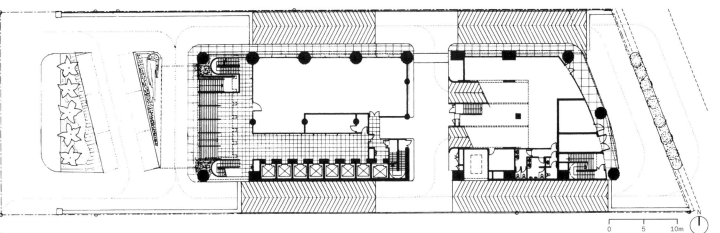

5

0   5   10m

6

7

6 Entrance canopy
7 Rooftop swimming pool
8 Ground floor entrance lobby
9 Typical first floor plan
Photography: K.L. Ng

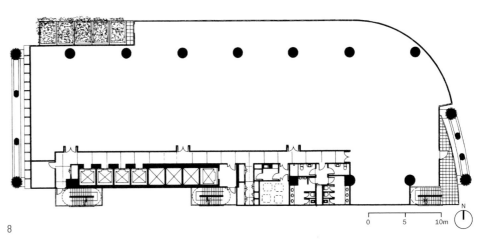

8

9

Chancery Building, United States Embassy, Singapore
The Stubbins Associates, Inc.

Completion: November 1996

Location: Singapore

Client: U.S. Department of State, Office of Foreign Buildings

Area: 10,683 square metres; 115,000 square feet

Structure: Granite; metal

Materials: Stainless steel, marble; black metal

The U.S. Embassy office building is located in the heart of the garden district of Singapore. The design features a formal courtyard defining the building entry, and a landscaped colonnade providing covered access from the site entrance to the building front door.

The five-storey structure fronts Napier Road, a busy urban parkway, and is flanked by the British and Australian High Commissions. In addition to Consular Services, a U.S. Information Services Library and Agricultural Trade Office, Marine Security Guard Quarters and an adjacent swimming pool, the building houses conference facilities, a cafeteria and offices for a 200-person staff.

The Embassy plays two roles: guest in the host country and host to the citizens of that country. Its architecture must symbolise the virtues of American culture while being differential to the local culture. Its plan must be secure, while creating an atmosphere of hospitality. This was achieved firstly by projecting an entry pavilion forward to receive visitors while establishing a long, closed block in the background to contain secure functions. Secondly by creating a courtyard; 'common ground' that mediates between the host country and the extra-territorial presence of America and finally by developing an architectural vocabulary and pallet of materials that suggests both the formal orders of western, classical architecture and the poetic shapes of the East.

1

2

1   Main elevation
2   Courtyard view at night
3   Elevator lobby
4   Main entry
5   Atrium
Photography: Hans Schlupp

3

4

5

Corporate Head Office: Irvin & Johnson Ltd

Douglas Roberts Peter Loebenberg Architects cc

Completion: December 1996

Location: Victoria Junction, Cape Town, South Africa

Client: Irvin & Johnson

Area: 10,000 square metres; 107,642 square feet

Structure: Reinforced concrete; steel

Materials: Precast concrete finished in grey granite and white marble chip; stainless steel

Cost: 20 million rand

Irvin & Johnson Ltd (I&J), owns one of the largest fishing fleets in the southern hemisphere. The company not only prepares and freezes fish products but also other prepared foods and fresh vegetables.

Situated in Victoria Junction, an old warehouse area alongside the harbour, the building comprises a double-volume top-lit space housing predominantly open office planning. Lower levels house computers and parking.

Specialised cellular spaces are grouped at the front and rear of the double volume: boardroom, dining room, experimental kitchen and juice bar and meeting rooms at the front and toilet, storage and plant rooms at the rear.

500 watt Halophane industrial glazed fittings supplement good natural light created by traditional vertical skylights, protected by overhanging curved roofs. Interior finishes have an industrial quality echoing the company business.

The robust exterior is created with suspended walkways, stainless steel bracing, green-coloured vertical steel columns, horizontal piping and modulated red brick. The red clay brick and dark green metal and wood are popular Victorian industrial building elements in Cape Town.

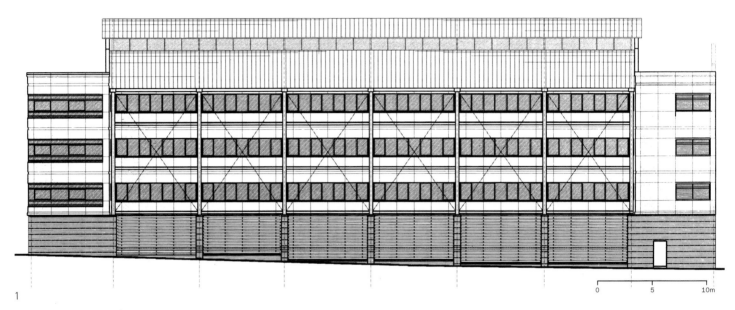

0   5   10m

1

2

1   Side/east elevation
2   Form, material and colours complement environment
3   Front elevation
4   Cross section
5   Open planned workstations surround double-volume
6   Double-volumed entrance view from first floor lift landing
7   Entrance reception desk

Photography: courtesy Douglas Roberts Peter Loebenberg Architects cc

3

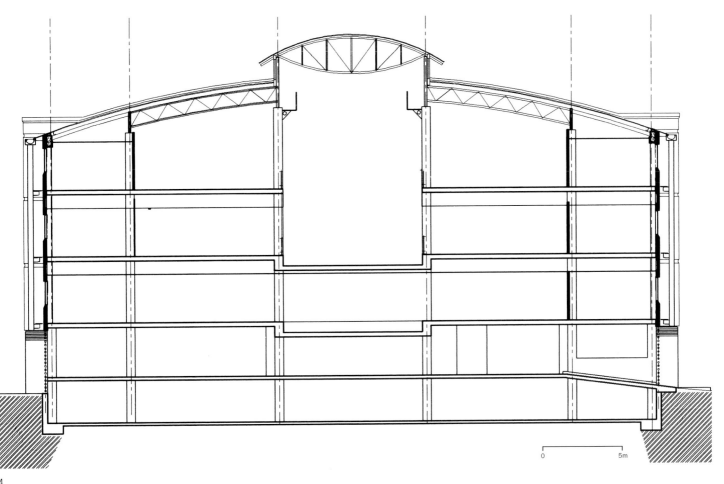

4

5

6

7

Generale Bank Tower
Murphy/Jahn

Completion: July 1996
Location: Rotterdam, The Netherlands
Client: Generale Bank Nederland
Area: 28,334 square metres; 305,000 square feet
Structure: Precast/cast-in-place concrete
Materials: Steel; glass; granite spandrels

Typologically the Tower can be described as a centre core slab-type building. This building type maximises the amount of perimeter offices and provides for open offices at each end. Through the addition of the wing the required building density and area are achieved.

On the city side, an urban square is developed as a forecourt to the Schielandshuis, the Hoogstraat and the Tower. A formal garden, as an extension of the Schielandshuis, provides a focus for the square. This garden overlays the plaza and extends to the adjacent buildings, drawing these separate elements together as a single composition. The location of the auto-ramp and drop-off below the raised wing provide protected access to the building and closure to the urban space while having minimum impact on the square.

To the east, the curved glass bay extends from the canal to the Blaak, opening views to the harbour from the office floors.

The geometry of the Tower accepts the difficult site conditions. Urbanistically, the wedge shape which results further emphasises the edge of the canal and minimises the impact of sight lines to the canal. The garden side of the project responds to the daylight requirements of the adjacent apartment building through the use of a stepped liner. Raising the wing above the plaza maintains the visual connection to the Maritime Museum while providing closure to the square. Sloping the bussel results in a more refined shape as a gate to the Korte Hoogstraat. The two elements, the wedge and liner along with the wing are connected at the wall which bisects the building.

1

2

3

1 Stepped liner responding to daylight requirements
2 View front canal
3 Wedge shaped tower maximises harbour views
4 Sloping wing above plaza
5&6 Elevations

4

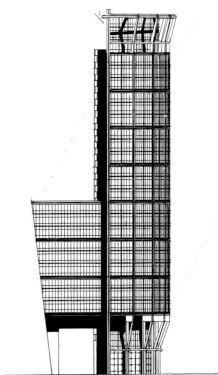

5

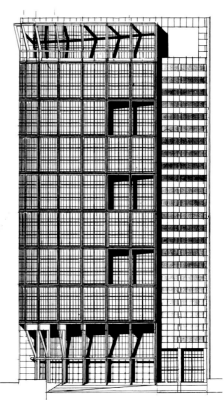

6

7 Typical high-rise plan
8 Raised wing above plaza
9 Auto-ramp drop off
10 Lobby/reception
11 Reception
Photography: Brian Rose

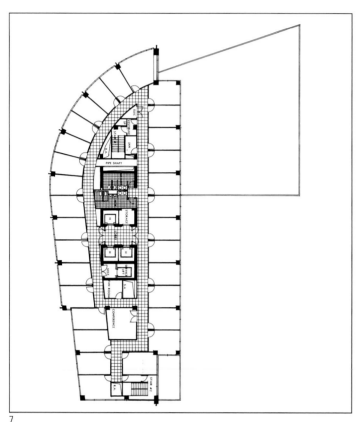

7

8

9

10

11

Headquarters Branch Bank and Building Lobby
R.M.Kliment & Frances Halsband Architects

Completion: June 1996

Location: Brooklyn, New York, USA

Client: Independence Savings Bank

Area: 930 square metres; 10,010 square feet

Structure: Stainless steel; glass; granite

Materials: Stone with tile and carpet inlay; wood; metal

The Branch Bank accommodates a full service branch that includes automatic teller area, safe deposit vault, teller counter and customer service platform. The building lobby links the street with the new Independence Savings Bank headquarters above.

These facilities are strategically located in downtown Brooklyn with many other retail banks, just west of historic Borough Hall and the adjacent transportation hub.

The building lobby vestibule, the automatic teller area and the Branch Bank are spaces defined under a shared high ceiling. Each of these functions is further defined by a perforated metal, half-vaulted ceiling. The lobby includes an information desk and building directory. The Branch entrance includes the automatic teller machines, and functions as the vestibule to the main banking hall, which accommodates customer service desks, teller counters and waiting areas.

The new exterior wall is made of stainless steel, glass and granite. There is a new radiant-slab sidewalk. The interior renovation has floors made of stone with tile and carpet inlay; walls are painted plaster, with stone and wood panelling; ceilings are metal panels set between plaster bands.

The lighting provides generous task and ambient illumination; a row of large custom designed pendant fixtures are visible from the street and give a special character to the space.

1

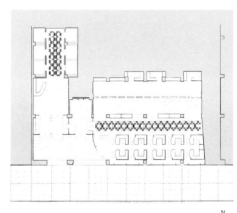

3

4

2

1   Exterior, Bank from Montague Street
2   Interior, teller area
3   Floor plan
4   Interior, customer service area
5   Section through elevator and building lobbies
6   Exterior, entry doors and view into Bank toward customer service area
Photography: Cervin Robinson

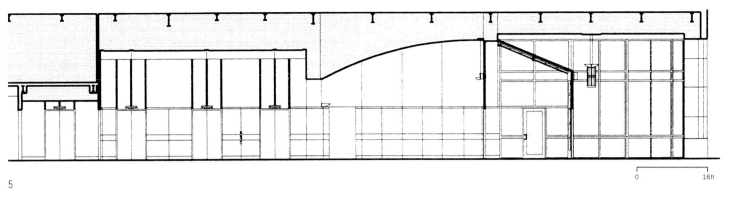

5

6

Hochhaus RWE AG Konzernzentrale Essen

Ingenhoven Overdiek Kahlen und Partner

Completion: December 1996

Location: Essen, Germany

Client: Hochtief AG

Gross Floor Area: 35,000 square metres; 376,750 square feet

Structure: Climaplus white glass

Materials: White glass; aluminium lamella

Awards: 1991 International Competition - RWE AG/ RAG Dienstleistungszentrum Essen, First Prize

The first pro-ecological high-rise in the world, RWE AG building in the PASSAREA development area of Essen, has already caught the eye of Greenpeace.

The striking feature of this building is its 'second skin', a 120 metre (393 foot) high glass cylinder which allows natural air flow and roof gardens even at such heights. This marks a turning point in the construction of high-rise buildings and a move away from the dominant American principle of a strict separation of inside and outside environments using air conditioning systems. It was wind tunnel tested and does not shut out what nature has to offer. On the contrary, thanks to its energy and synergy efficiency, it incorporates nature in both its architectural and technical features. The individual needs of the users were met with regard to daylight, natural ventilation, climatisation, workplace and living space quality using a simple, logical building concept and intelligent technical solutions.

The building has 30 floors and the top of the antenna reaches 162 metres (525 feet) up into the sky, making it the highest building in the German state of North Rhine-Westphalia.

1

2

1   Aerial view
2   Main entrance
3   Overall view
4   Garden view
5   Section
6   Ground floor restaurant

3

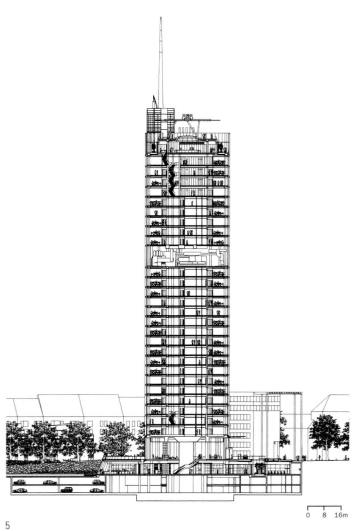

4

5

0　8　16m

6

7

8

7 Entrance
8 Conference room
9 Part of entrance hall
10 Section
11 Lobby
Photography: Holger Knauf

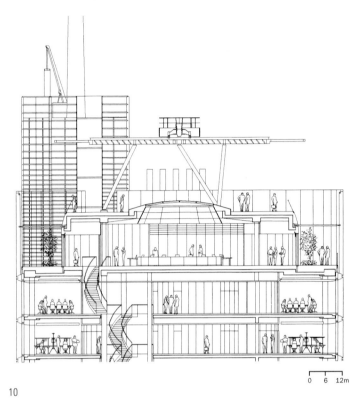

0 6 12m

9

10

11

International Finance Corporation

Michael Graves, Architect PA

Completion: January 1997

Location: Washington, DC, USA

Client: The International Finance Corporation

Area: 92,900 square metres; 1 million square feet

Structure: French limestone; precast, block and cast-in-place

Materials: Burlington slate; curly maple wood

This 92,900 square metre (one million square foot), office building was originally designed as a speculative office building for another client and has been redesigned to suit the office space needs of the site's new owner, the International Finance Corporation, a member of the World Bank Group. The triangular site is bounded by Pennsylvania Avenue, K Street, 21st Street and Washington Circle.

In addition to general office space, the program includes a training/conference centre, a multi-purpose auditorium, a library, and a cafeteria, among other amenities and support facilities.

The 12-storey building reflects the traditional architecture of historic Washington, and yet provides a fresh approach to classical organisation. Following the cornice height typical of the surrounding blocks, the major facades are subdivided and articulated with a variety of window types to offer relief along their 600-foot length. A series of pavilions pulled forward from the body of the building help break down the scale of the long facades along Pennsylvania Avenue and K Street and provide increased opportunities to plan corner offices in the building. A cylindrical belvedere turns the corner at Washington Circle, allowing views in all directions.

1 Transverse section
2 View toward building across Washington Circle
3 Pennsylvania Avenue facade viewed from Washington Circle
4 View of atrium from second floor promenade

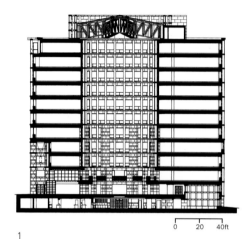

1

2

3

66

4

CORPORATE International Finance Corporation

67

5

6

5   View toward atrium from entry lobby
6   Auditorium
7   Lobby waiting area
8   Conference/private dining room
9   Private dining room
Photography: Andrew D. Lautman

7

8

9

International Financial Park, Federal Territory of Labuan

Arkitek MAA Sdn Bhd

Completion: December 1996

Location: Labuan Federal Territory, Malaysia

Client: Financial Park (Labuan) Sdn Bhd

Area: 232,250 square metres; 2.5 million square feet

Structure: Reinforced concrete; prestressed and waffle slabs

Materials: Marble; granite; ceramic tiles; aluminium composite panels

Cost: RM400 million

The International Financial Park in Federal Territory of Labuan is designed as a self-contained development for working, living, shopping and leisure. Comprised of a podium block which houses all the retail activities, two condominium blocks, three office blocks and a multi-purpose hall, the project is set to become a catalyst to the economic growth of the island.

The 11-acre site is prominently located within walking distance to the seafront and harbour.

The three office blocks which are the nucleus of the development are arranged to respond to the unique site frontage. The inter-relationship with the various components of the development led to the evolution of the convex and concave shaped forms with the major curved facade facing north and south. Deeply recessed balconies on the condominiums, reduce the amount of direct sunlight against the glazing area.

The main office block (16 storeys high) is situated in the centre of the development and is flanked by two secondary office blocks (13 storeys high). The two condominium blocks (15 storeys high) flank the main office block, with each condominium having private entrances and recreational facilities such as swimming pool, playground and gymnasium. The terraced area is heavily landscaped creating a pleasant ambience to the surrounding area.

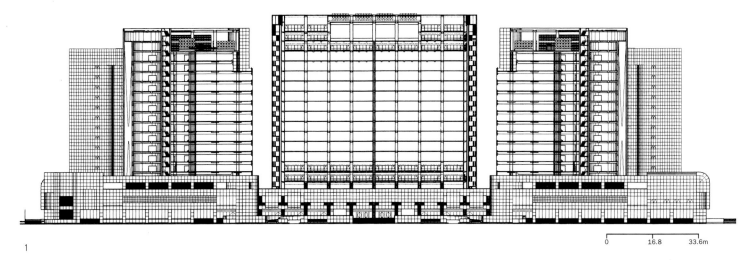

1

0   16.8   33.6m

2

3

4

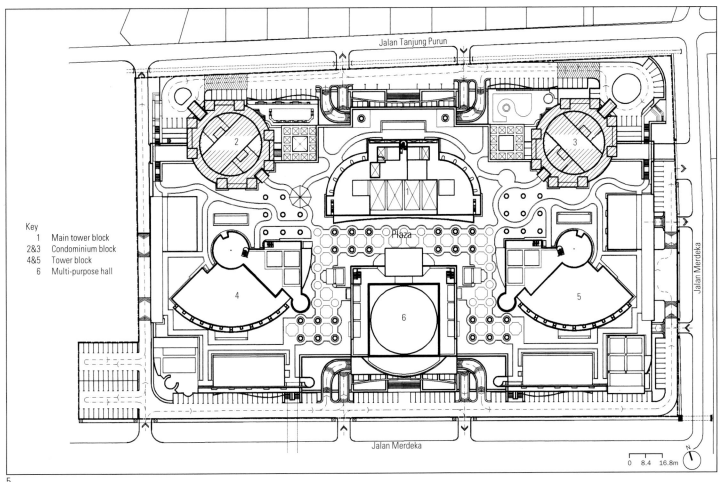

Key
1   Main tower block
2&3 Condominium block
4&5 Tower block
6   Multi-purpose hall

5

6

7

8

1   Section
2   Overall view of condominiums from northeast
3   Overall view of development from southwest
4   Interplay of curvilinear forms at office blocks
5   Site Plan
6   Entrance at multi-purpose hall
7   Entrance lobby of multi-purpose hall
8   Main entrance to the complex
Photography: courtesy Arkitek MAA Sdn Bhd

K.J. McNitt Construction Company

Elliott + Associates Architects

Completion: December 1996

Location: Oklahoma City, Oklahoma, USA

Client: Mr Kelly McNitt

Area: 725 square metres; 7,800 square feet

Structure: Concrete

Materials: Concrete; steel; glass

Cost: US$400,000

The architectural concept was 'to build a living illustration of the concrete panel construction process and express the honesty of concrete panel construction shown by various expressions'.

A: Precast concrete panel reception desk illustrates material beauty, mass (round pipe panel supports) and structural cantilevers (desk tops);

B: Panel slits continued through interior gives building transparency and architectural continuity; and

C: Vertically freestanding cantilevered panel wall illustrates thickness ('thinness').

Concrete finish includes: light sandblasting (exterior/interior), smooth finish (reception desk), stained concrete (floor slabs), poured-in-place plywood formed concrete (west retaining wall), unfinished concrete (west wall west face).

Metal studs, drywall panels with glass slits, define interior spaces.

Lighting is designed to enhance material, textures and volume. Central skylights, pendant mounted metal halide fixtures provide lighting for central space. Suspended, inverted bat wing two-lamp strip fluorescent provide office lighting. Cable lighting provides additional fill light and accent for central work spaces.

Owner tours clients and demonstrates special expertise in concrete construction; building illustrates simple materials used to yield memorable results.

The architecture celebrates the construction process.

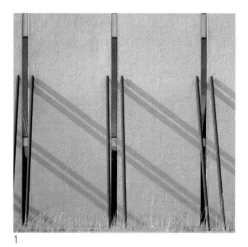

1

2

3

4

1 Precast panels with steel pipe bracing
2 Exterior view looking southwest
3 Southwest corner
4 Exterior view looking south showing 'free-standing' west wall panels
5 East elevation sketch
6 Second floor view
7 Conference room

Photography: Bob Shimer/Hedrich-Blessing

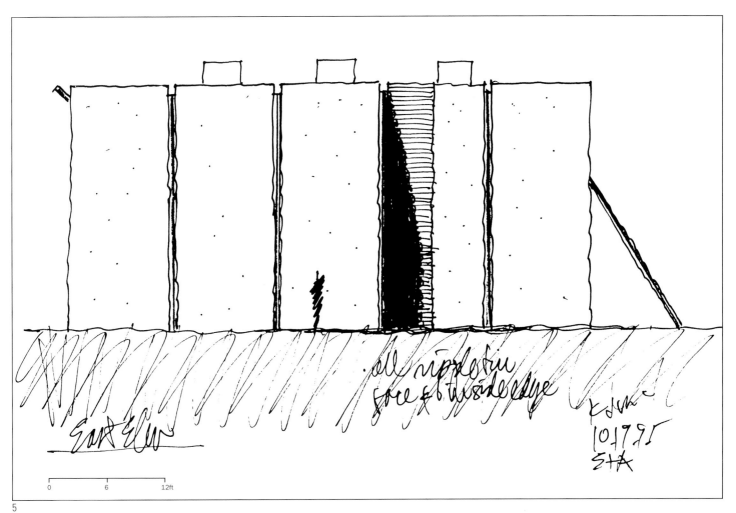

East Elev

all riprotu
face @ inside edge

K dwc
10.19.95
S+A

0   6   12ft

5

6

7

Library Square, Vancouver, B.C.

Moshe Safdie and Associates, Inc.
in joint venture with Downs Archambault & Partners

Completion: May 1996
Location: Vancouver, B.C., Canada
Client: City of Vancouver
Area: 60,400 square metres; 650,161 square feet
Structure: Cast-in-place concrete
Materials: Sandstone colour precast concrete; glass
Cost: C$125 million

Library Square, Vancouver, B.C., occupies a city block in an expanding section of downtown Vancouver. It consists of a seven-storey rectangular core containing open book stacks, library services, circulation and the latest data technology. This core is wrapped by an ellipse, a freestanding, precast concrete double shell that holds study alcoves, reading arcades and public walkways with views of the city. At the northeast corner of the site, this curving exterior facade rises into the 21-storey federal office tower.

From either end of the library complex, a public promenade flows from the street around the library's interior core. Enclosed by one glass face of the library block and the inside face of the arcaded shell holding small cafes and stores, this glazed urban room is flooded with sunlight.

Within the library, visitors rise through the centre to collect books and study materials, and traverse light steel bridges to a long curving reading arcade with tables, carrels, and interior and exterior views. Mechanical sub-floors carry all the building services, computer data and air circulation systems, providing continuous, uninterrupted shallow barrel-vaulted ceilings. The rectangular library core is roofed with a garden overlooked by two storeys of provincial government offices.

1

2

74

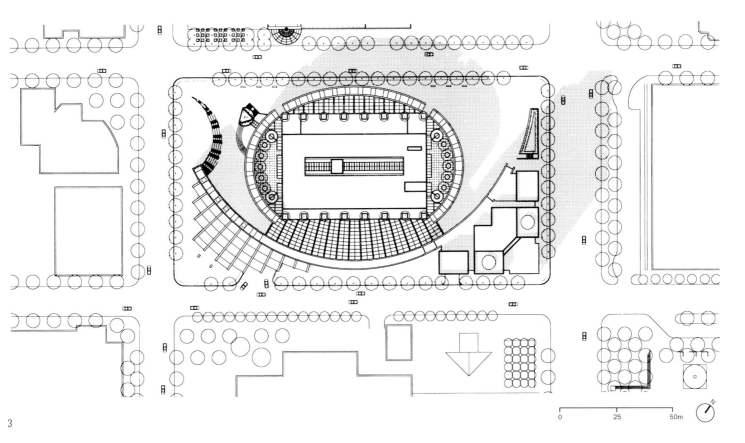

3

5

4

1   Library at night
2   View of library and federal office tower
3   Site Plan
4   View of entrance to concourse
5   Concourse

6

7

8

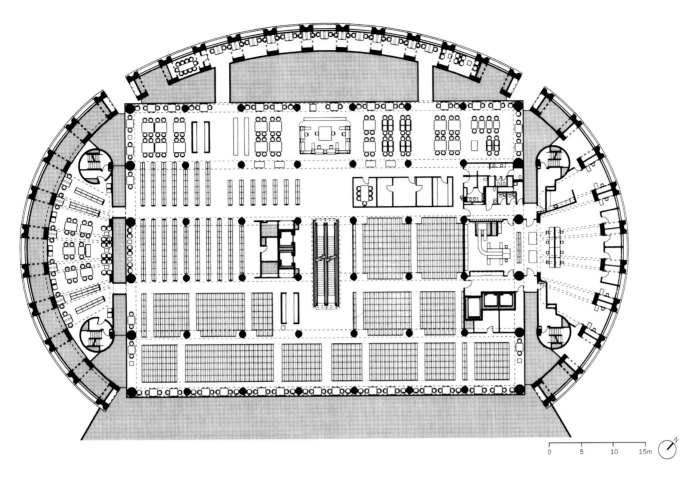

9

10

11

6   Detail of reading areas in arcade
7   Detail of access flooring at several library levels
8   Library levels and reading galleries
9   Library, level 5 plan
10   Library looking across to arcade
11   Detail of interstitial spaces for mechanical systems
Photography: Timothy Hursley

Malietoren, The Hague

Benthem Crouwel Architekten BV bna

Completion: December 1996

Location: Bezuidenhoutseweg 10/12, The Hague

Client: Multi Vastgoed bv Gouda

Area: 25,000 square metres; 269,106 square feet

Structure: Prefabricated concrete; in situ concrete; steel

Materials: Glass; steel; stainless steel; aluminium

Cost: 50,000,000 DFL

The tower on the Utrechtsebaan marks the transition from the central urban area to the green zone which is Malieveld and the Haagse Bos (Hague Forest).

The building acts as a gate to the city for the traffic on the Utrechtsebaan, while diagonally at ground level, the partitioning of the city is countered by the Utrechtsebaan's lower location.

The structure's location at this striking point in the city and the unique technical conditions of the site are reflected in the design with both the progression of impetus and the mechanics of the construction being visible at a single glance. The edifice is constructed largely on air; only narrow strips on both sides of the gallery base are suitable for the foundation of the building. The building's entire weight is concentrated upon these two strips.

The longitudinal facades are in the form of a rigid concrete bearing framework with horizontal window chasings, connected at both heads by steel stabilising structures. The fact that the stability is established in the external skin means that heavy structures can be avoided inside the building, resulting in savings in weight.

Concrete triangular segments span the Utrechtsebaan, supporting the upper floors and allowing the office floors to be used as flexibly as possible with the parking garage located on levels 1–5, easily integrated into the overall structure.

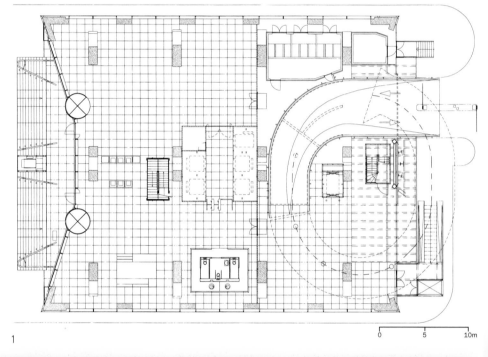

1   Ground floor plan
2   Entrance
Opposite:
    South facade

1

2

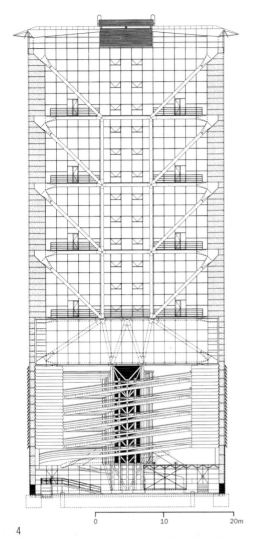

4   North facade
5   View from southeast
6   South facade entrance
Opposite:
    South facade detail
Photography: Jannes Linders (2,6)

0   10   20m

4

5

6

Megan Corporate Park

T.R. Hamzah & Yeang Sdn Bhd

Completion: May 1997
Location: Desa Petaling, Kuala Lumpur
Client: Salak Park Development Sdn Bhd
Area: 43,000 square metres; 462,863 square feet
Structure: R.C. frame
Materials: Brick; cement sheeting; aluminium

The development consists of two blocks situated within a new business park in Salak Park, near Kuala Lumpur. Orientated parallel to the nearby north–south Kuala Lumpur-Seremban highway, Megan Corporate Park's location minimises the solar heat gain to its rectangular configuration and maximises views towards the Kuala Lumpur-Seremban highway below.

Careful analysis of the natural topography resulted in stepping the buildings across the site. This reduced the impact of the development and in turn, moderated the earthwork cut.

A full-height elliptical-shaped internal atrium space was introduced to provide natural lighting to the interior corridor spaces while providing an internal focus to the office spaces upon entry to the building. At roof level, the detached canopy over the atrium allows hot air to escape, thus enabling natural ventilation to cool upper floor lobbies.

A reinforced concrete frame supports a mixture of rendered brickwork and yellow compressed-cement sheet-cladding panels that articulate the facades.

1

2

3

4

1 Main entrance facade
2 Canopy over entrance
3 Naturally ventilated internal atrium
4 Main elevation from the highway
Photography: K.L. Ng

National City Bank Corporate Headquarters
Boarman Kroos Pfister Vogel & Associates

Completion: March 1996

Location: Minneapolis, Minnesota, USA

Client: National City Bank

Area: 8,732 square metres; 94,000 square feet

Structure: Elliptical gypsum; glass

Materials: Maple wood; stainless steel; perforated metal

Cost: US$10 million

Until March of 1996, National City Bank's mid-sized bank headquarters were located in a building that formerly housed the local branch of the Federal Reserve. After 20 years in this space, the building no longer served the client's organisational needs. A move was in order.

The project mission was to recreate the headquarters of a mid-sized, conservative bank into a contemporary, value-added financial centre. The design team's challenge was to architecturally realise, through the use of materials, technology and furnishings, the client's vision of banking as 'conversations focused on satisfying the customer'.

The design team conducted a series of workshops with bank leadership. The workshops evaluated the client's operations, departmental relationships, space utilisation and standards. From this dialogue, the client's stated 'visioning' words—integrity, flexibility, warm, inviting, connectedness, equity and human scale—were identified and became the foundation of the design solution.

1 First floor plan
2 Second floor plan
3 Third floor plan
4 Atrium view of bank operations
5 Third level, bank transaction area
Opposite:
    Third level, bank entrance
Photography: George Heinrich

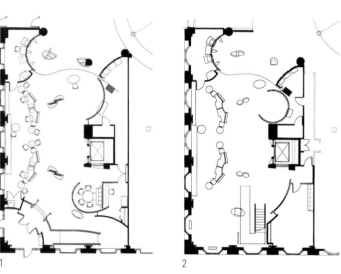

1

2

4

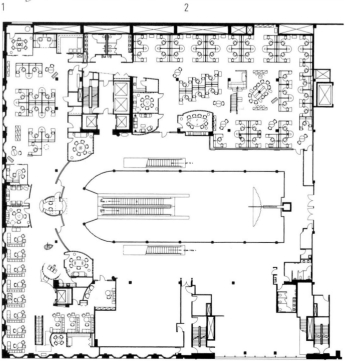

3

5

Principal Mutual Life Insurance Company Corporate Expansion
Murphy/Jahn

Completion: March 1996

Location: Des Moines, Iowa, USA

Client: Principal Mutual Life Insurance Company

Area: 48,122 square metres; 518,000 square feet

Structure: Steel frame; composite deck

Materials: Clear patterned/spandrel glass; fluoropolymer coated aluminium; limestone cladding

An eight-storey building located in Des Moines, Iowa, is situated on the north side of Principal's downtown 'campus'.

Development of the site responds to the planned northerly expansion of Principal's campus and to the future growth of downtown Des Moines. The design develops an appropriate response to building requirements, creates a 'public' plaza, a visual and physical connection between the 'downtown' on the south and the area to the north, maintains visual continuity of existing street spaces, and exhibits sensitivity to the scale of the local context.

Large floor plates allow the mass of the building to be reduced to a height of eight storeys and conform to the scale of the surrounding buildings and open space. In plan, the building may be interpreted as a long linear element folded into the shape of an 'N'. Levels six, seven and eight of the building are contiguous floor plans. Levels one through five are interrupted at approximately mid-building creating a Gateway 90 feet (27.5 metres) wide and five storeys high through the building. A transparent glass bridge connects the east and west sides of the building at Level three without visually obstructing the Gateway. Viewed from the plaza, the building becomes a 'wall' defining the north edge of the plaza with the roof height trellis creating a 'forecourt' which provides a transition between the plaza and the building's entrances in the Gateway.

1

1 Gateway front glass facade with civic plaza and garden
2 Limestone facades providing visual and historic
  continuity with existing buildings
3 Roof height trellis creating a 'forecourt'

2

3

4

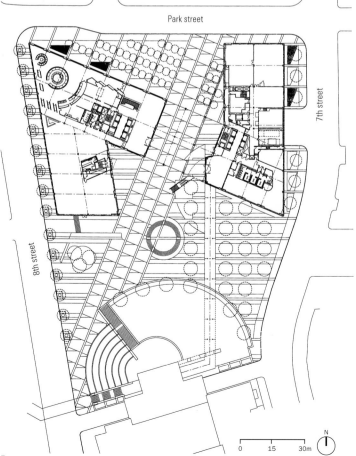

Park street

7th street

8th street

0   15   30m   N

5

6

4   Pedestrian bridge walkway
5   Site plan
6   Gateway becomes a pedestrian 'street'
7&8 Ground floor cafeteria
Photography: Dean Tanner/Primary Image

7

Queensferry House, Carnegie Campus
Jestico + Whiles

Completion: July 1996
Location: Dunfermline, Scotland
Client: Miller Developments
Area: 20,000 square metres; 215,285 square feet
Structure: Steel frame
Materials: Aluminium; steel; in situ concrete
Cost: £1.5 million

In 1994, Miller Developments, a local developer, invited Jestico + Whiles' Glasgow office to join a competition to design a speculative office building on a new business park development, Carnegie Campus. The resulting winning design, Queensferry House, is a two-storey, steel frame building with a low pitched roof. Two wings of accommodation are located either side of a double-height glazed reception.

The project was Jestico + Whiles' first to be designed and run exclusively using CAD. This computerisation led to an accuracy of as-built drawings impossible to achieve with a roll of marked-up dyelines. Furthermore, the ease with which information on ideas and details can be retrieved has created a 'lineage' of buildings. In architecture's cultural terms, the idea of one building informing the next is a well-established principle.

1

2

3

1   Detail, glass
2   Staircase detail
3   Reception
4   Front elevation
5   Emergency stair
Photography: David Churchill

4

5

RCID Administration Building
Murphy/Jahn

Completion: January 1997

Location: Buena Vista, Florida, USA

Client: Walt Disney Imagineering (Management)
Reedy Creek Improvement District (User)

Area: 2,322 square metres; 25,000 square feet

Structure: Glass; aluminium curtainwall

Materials: Concrete frame

The Reedy Creek Improvement District Administration Building (RCID), demonstrates the integration of formal sculptural qualities and symbolism in a building of modern vocabulary and unique image. As the headquarters of the RCID, the building centralises the agency functions and projects the independent identity of the organisation. The floor-to-ceiling glass wall and the inviting cut-away entrance indicate the ideal of civic openness.

The project exemplifies the boldness of simplicity and the qualities of minimalism extended by circumstance. A simple square plan is chamfered at the corners to create on two sides upward slopes and on two sides a sloped overhang. A heavy steel trellis structure retains the outline of the original cubic composition, creating a dramatic asymmetry within a static frame.

The site design recognises the intrusion of a development project on the landscape and explores the juxtaposition of the two. The building sits on a hardscape plinth of parking in the manner of a European urban plaza, but this parking area is striped with bright colours, reinforcing the constructed nature of the ground plane. The trellis constructions are read as 'trees' which project from the directly adjacent naturalistic site, embracing the building. Thus, the constructed ground plane extends under the existing trees and the existing canopy extends over the constructed building.

The RCID project provides a fresh, bold, civic presence of high quality and character, befitting work done under the Disney corporate umbrella. It achieves this without resorting to theatrical mannerism, but through the exploration and presentation of the essential components of modern architectural design: space and the nature of materials.

1 South elevation
2 Floor-to-ceiling glass walls
3 Cut-away entrance
4 Entrance lobby
5 Offices
6 Stair core
Photography: Peter Aaron/Esto

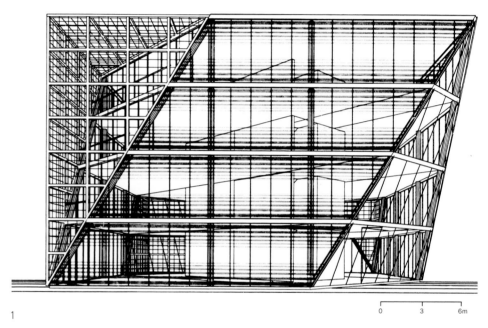

1

0   3   6m

2

92

3

4

5

6

The Executive Studio
Studio Downie

Completion: May 1997

Location: Hounslow, West London, UK

Client: Dr Phil Blackburn, West London Training and Enterprise Council (WLTEC)

Area: 372 square metres; 4,000 square feet

Structure: Concrete; brickwork

Materials: Aluminium; glass; polycarbonate

Cost: £200,000

The vision for The Executive Studio, came from research in 1992 by the WLTEC into how Information Technology (IT), is used in business. The findings showed that there were large gaps in people's understanding of how best to use IT and how to maximise its use to make their business successful.

There was also a need to have a location available to businesses where they could experience IT in a best practice environment, so The Studio was created, its mission to help organisations manage information to transform business performance and enhance competitive edge.

The brief was to create an environment that challenged the perception of corporate spaces placed within a traditional floor plate. Three bold interrelated spaces each with a changing coloured feature wall were created.

The Demonstration Suite is the heart of The Studio; a long rectangle extruded from the existing fabric.

Visitors enter the departure lounge to log-in, relax, use games, internet links and news sources. From here they step into the flexible Demonstration Suite where software and applications are tested. This provides a platform for change; software demonstrations, exhibitions, seminars, lectures and receptions. The Office of the Future and Learning Centre are located to each end respectively which can be opened up to the main space.

The Boardroom is an interactive software inspired 20-place glass circular table with concealed computers below, designed by Studio Downie Architects.

The ambience of the spaces is one of calm and simplicity with a constantly changing spectrum of lighting colour to the feature walls.

1   Entrance to Demonstration Suite
2   Demonstration Suite
3   Sectional perspective
4   Approach to Boardroom
5   Boardroom of 21st Century
Photography: Chris Gascoigne/ VIEW

1

2

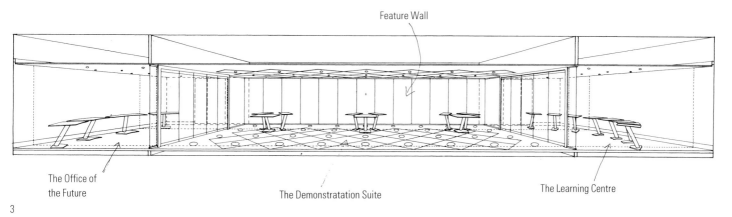

Feature Wall

The Office of
the Future

The Demonstratation Suite

The Learning Centre

3

4

5

Tokyo Gas Earth Port

Nikken Sekkei

Completion: March 1996

Location: Yokohama, Japan

Client: Tokyo Gas Urban Development Co., Ltd.

Area: 1,652 square metres; 17,782 square feet

Structure: Steel reinforced concrete; reinforced concrete; steel; wood

Materials: Recycled insulation glass panels; ceramic tiles

Awards: Good Design Award, Japan Structural Consultants Association Prize

To what extent can a congenial energy conserving environment be achieved through maximum use of natural energy? Tokyo Gas Earth Port addresses this question from the viewpoint of life cycle energy consumption of small- to medium-sized offices that take up a majority of urban office buildings.

In this architecture, the support space is opened up to constitute an 'ecological core' that serves as a vertical passage for light and wind. The building makes maximum use of natural energy through natural ventilation and intake of light from both sides. The ecological core brings the added benefit of providing a new communication space for offices that had been isolated floor by floor. Using the most adequate heat insulating materials in different parts of the building, making active use of lumber, and recycling rainwater are some of the measures adopted to ensure the efficient use of energy and resources.

1 Northwest facade
2 Approach
3 Section
4 Ecological core stair
Photography: Shinkenchiku-Sha; SS Tokyo (4)

1

2

4

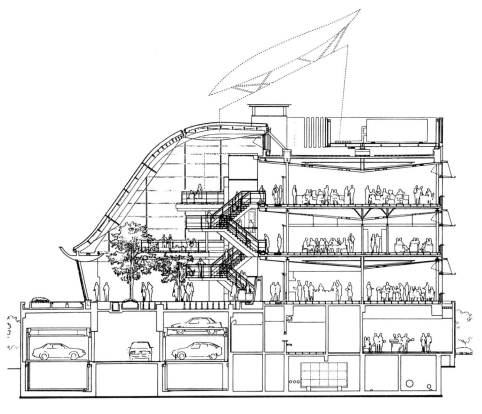

3

Total Administrative Services Corporation

Flad & Associates

Completion: October 1996

Location: Madison, Wisconsin, USA

Client: Total Administrative Services Corporation

Area: 2,136 square metres; 23,000 square feet

Structure: Steel

Materials: Tongue and groove fir; low 'E' glass; aluminium

Cost: US$2.2 million

Small businesses tend to express the personalities of their founders. That is true for the Total Administrative Services Corporation (TASC), a Madison-based company that administers employee-benefits plans for small businesses nationwide. The founder of TASC, of Scandinavian descent, called on Flad & Associates to design an appropriate home for his growing company—a distinctly modern building with crisp, clean detail.

Situated on a high clearing with a wooded backdrop, the TASC building is distinct along the approach to the Dane County Regional Airport. The 2,136 square metre (23,000 square foot) facility, clad in a natural finish of vertical tongue-and-groove fir, expresses a tactile quality for high visual impact.

Within prominent view of the airport approach is the building's primary feature, a curved glass curtain wall enclosing the reception area, an expressive form offering elevated, panoramic views of the surrounding landscape. Floor-to-ceiling windows on the north wall of the 3.9 metre (13 foot) high office space combine with indirect lighting for quality illumination and openness while eliminating glare and shadows cast on work stations. Rolling files in custom-designed work stations enable an effortless flow of paperwork among employees.

A reflection of the vision of the client, the TASC headquarters provides an ideal setting for this small business to realise its potential.

1 Floor plan
2 Detail of curved reception area glass
3 Building viewed on pedestal approach
4 Office reception desk
5 View into light-filled office area
Photography: Steve Hall/Hedrich-Blessing

1

2

3

4

5

WH Smith Office Headquarters Extension

Ahrends Burton and Koralek

Completion: May 1996

Location: Swindon, Wiltshire, UK

Client: WH Smith and Son Ltd

Area: 2,465 square metres; 26,533 square feet

Structure: Concrete; steel

Materials: VE steel cladding panels; aluminium roofing; double-glazed screens

Cost: £3.92 million

1 Site plan
2 Meeting room suite
3 Aerial view of extension
4 East elevation
5 Section through meeting room suite
6 Southwest elevation
7 Northwest elevation
8 Meeting room suite waiting area

Photography: Dennis Gilbert

In 1985 Ahrends Burton and Koralek (ABK), completed a new office building for WH Smith beside their existing distribution centre in Swindon. The building plan takes the form of a two-storey matrix providing a grid of flexible office accommodation and landscaped courtyards. This matrix is served by a diagonal route leading to the reception drum, the main entrance and a bridge link to the existing WH Smith premises. Energy conservation considerations led to a naturally ventilated building; automatic external roller blinds control solar heat gain. The scheme anticipated the future extension of the office matrix and provision for this was made in the structure at future connection points.

The client returned to ABK in 1994 with a wish to extend. The original building had proved to be a success and the need was identified for a suite of meeting rooms to have a different character relating more to the public world of the diagonal route than the more private world of the office matrix. This would help to prevent them from being used as private office spaces or storage.

The plan incorporates 11 additional bays of office matrix accommodation on two floors and a meeting room suite in circular form terminating the diagonal route linking in to the matrix and enclosing a new landscaped courtyard. The meeting room suite comprises 28 six-person meeting rooms, a 20-person conference room, a waiting area and ancillary accommodation.

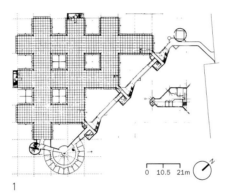

0 10.5 21m

1

2

3

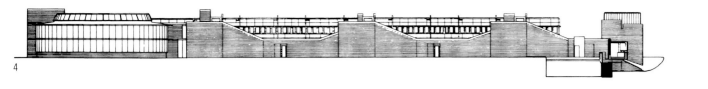

4

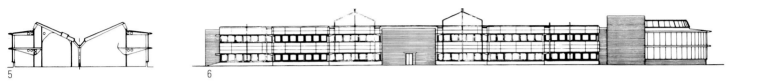

5　6

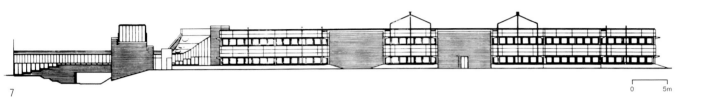

7

0　5m

8

Central Tower
P&T Group

Completion: October 1996

Location: Central, Hong Kong

Client: Central Development Ltd Group

Area: 23,500 square metres; 252,960 square feet

Structure: Steel

Materials: Aluminium; granite; glass

Cost: HK$340 million

1 First floor plan
2 Typical floor plan
3 Exterior view
4 Main lobby
5 Lift lobby
6 Atrium

Photography: Bobby KC Shum

The redevelopment of the former Shell House and Hartlane House site in Central, now renamed Central Tower, adds a major new prestigious development to the heart of Hong Kong's Central Business District.

Located at the corner of Wyndham Street and Queen's Road Central with a strong visual axis to Pedder Street, the development consists basically of an office tower above a commercial podium and a basement.

Provision for footbridge access to Central Building and the Landmark across Queen's Road Central, and to Entertainment Building across Wyndham Street, adds accessibility and convenience to both visitors and members of the public.

Exclusive retail outlets form the lower levels of the podium, at basement, ground and first floor with the main office lobby located on the second floor away from the busy and congested noisy streets, easily accessible with direct escalator links from both Queen's Road Central and Wyndham Street.

The spacious main entrance hall with an area of 1,300 square metres (13,994 square feet), and a clear height of 9 metres (96 feet) is the focal point of the overall development. Bamboo, artwork and water features combined with rich stonework create an unprecedented elegant space in the heart of Central.

The overall elevation expresses the crisp and bold architectural solution with the use of silver natural anodised aluminium panels and dark grey tinted glass; the reflectivity of the aluminium panels in combination with the distinct architectural articulation provides an elegant and distinct addition to core Central.

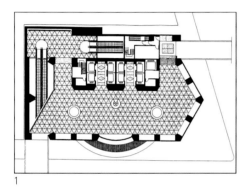

1

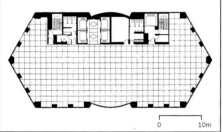

0   10m

2

3

4

5

6

Eastern Central Plaza

Liang Peddle Thorp Architects & Planners Ltd

Completion: October 1996
Location: Shaukeiwan, Hong Kong
Client: Tai Cheung Properties
Area: 25,200 square metres; 271,259 square feet
Structure: Concrete
Materials: Glass; aluminium; stone
Cost: US$19.2 million

The building occupies a site in Shaukeiwan facing the mountain side. The perimeter wall of the building is fitted to the site boundary to maximise the number of tenancies and view for those tenancies.

The plan form is therefore an 'L' shape with a deep courtyard at the rear of the scheme. The height restriction for this site necessitates a flat-topped building with 23 floors and 3 basement levels of car parking.
The requirement to maximise the perimeter restricts opportunities for volumetric and encasing composition. The design therefore focuses on colour, texture, pattern and overlapped planes. An illusion of depth and transparency is created through the use of these planes. The planes themselves are identified through variation of glass colour, curtain wall gridding, spandrel treatment and depth.

A gently curving green outer plane to the front of the building peels away to reveal the blue flat wall behind. The blue flat wall is further eroded at the entrance to the tower.

Four overlapped planes make up the side elevation. These are further developed through the introduction of a vestigial curtain wall frame at the top of the building where the innermost plane is revealed as a solid element with portable windows. This element becomes a blade sliding through the building and marking out the entrance.

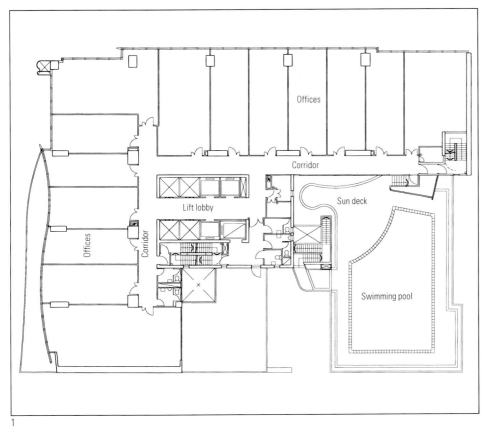

1   Typical floor plan
2   Building exterior
3&4 Lobby
Photography: John Nye

Horreya Mall

Dr Farouk Elgohary Architectural Consultants

Completion: February 1996

Location: Heliopolis, Cairo, Egypt

Client: Egyptian Engineers Group

Area: 1,200 square metres; 12,917 square feet

Structure: Composite concrete; steel and space truss

Materials: Concrete; steel; burnt bricks; ceramic and porcelain tiles; marble and corian

Cost: US$7 Million

The design revolves around the use of new materials yet utilises traditional design patterns in a modern mannerism. The result is a sophisticated juxtaposition of both horizontal and vertical corbelling system. It's a formalistic complexity within the use of simple pure forms, producing a universal atrium space with robust social and commercial activities. The use of colour is an integral part of the design that mixes well with the use of shadows.

The site is surrounded by three streets, one being a main street with site dimensions of 54 x 22 metres (177 x 72 feet).

The project consists of a basement, a ground floor and eight upper floors. The height reaches 36 metres (118 feet) and consists of 80 shops, two cinemas seating almost 600

each, two restaurants, a billiard room, fast-food cafes, four lifts, two escalators, and one main staircase and two fire exits on each floor.

The entire building is centrally air-conditioned and equipped with a complete fire alarm system.

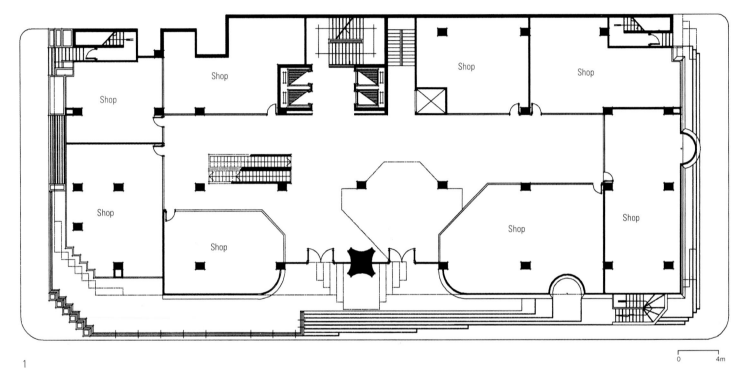

1

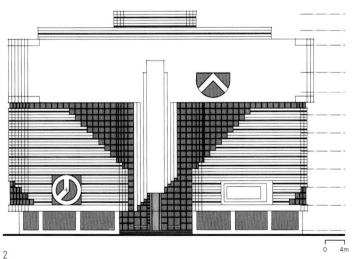

2

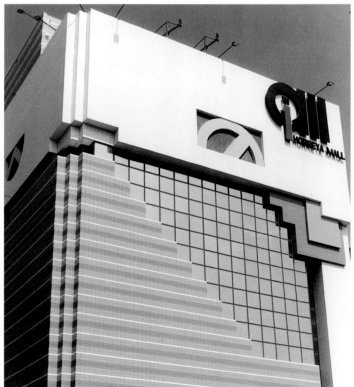

3

1   Ground floor plan
2   Entrance elevation
3   Main facade, High Street
Photography: courtesy Dr Farouk Elgohary
Architectural Consultant

Nationale-Nederlanden Building

Frank O. Gehry & Associates, Inc.

Completion: June 1996
Location: Prague, Czech Republic
Client: Nationale-Nederlanden/International Netherlands Group
Area: 5,842 square metres; 62,885 square feet
Structure: Flat-slab concrete
Materials: Concrete; glass; steel; Douglas fir; stainless steel; stone
Cost: 12.9 million DM

1　Longitudinal section
2　View of tapering glass tower
3　View of river front facade and solid tower
4　View from across Vltava River
Photography: Marc Salette

Located along the Vltava River, the site for the Nationale-Nederlanden Building is one of only three in the historic district of central Prague on which new construction has been permitted. The site is located at the corner of two streets, adjacent to an unusually shaped public square. In response to the site, the design employs a twin tower scheme at the corner, creating a smooth transition from street to street, while at the same time creating a strong visual focal point. This massing strategy also establishes a sculptural dialogue appropriate to the context of the immediate urban environment.

The twin towers, one developed as a cylindrical solid volume, the other as a tapering glass tower, are supported by a number of sculptural columns, creating a small covered entrance plaza at the ground level of the building. The glass tower is comprised of a double-layer steel-supported glass curtain wall. The main exterior facade, overlooking the river bank, responds to the rich textures and scales of the adjacent row houses. Its staggered windows and horizontal striations gradually break into a wave pattern that relates to the undulating cornice lines of the lively neighbouring river front facades.

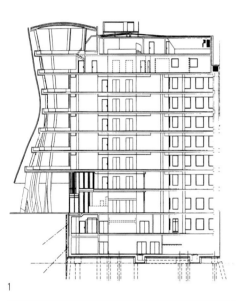

1

2

3

4

Palais Equitable—Vienna 1, Stock im Eisen Platz 3

Architect Rüdiger Lainer
in association with Architect Werner Silbermayr

Completion: February 1997

Location: Vienna, Austria

Client: Auricon Holding Group

Area: 760 square metres; 8,181 square feet

Structure: Steel; concrete; brick

Materials: Steel, concrete; glass; wood

Cost: 8,360.000 Mio A$

The architectural measures have by large, been restricted to exposing the basic spatial structure.

Along the three external walls this consists of a series of spaces roofed with brick vaults carried on steel beams. The area between the central wall and the light-wells or staircase was filled with residual rooms which have been removed to create a very generous, continuous circulation area.

The flooring is Doussier wood parquet throughout without door saddles. On the courtyard or staircase side, there is a piece of furniture at a slight angle, which is in fact, a service space incorporating cloakrooms, a kitchen, a small wine store and the washrooms with mirrored ornamental glass and a particularly attractive detail: a 'light wall' by the artist Michael Kienzer.

On the other side along the central wall, you gain access to the various offices and the large meeting area. The door elements here are partly of glass, partly of wood roughly painted in places like a crude priming coat and in places smoothly finished in a noble stucco lustro. All new measures are in white or various shades of; this fact is also a slight source of irritation—it does not disturb the design but prevents the development of an unpleasant glib or smooth feeling.

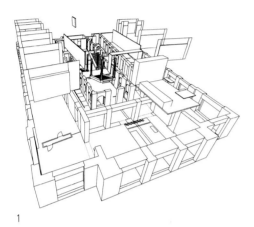

1

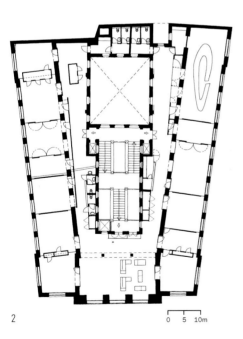

2

3

4

0 5 10m

5

1   Axonometric
2   Floor plan mezzanine
3   Night time view from Haas Haus
4   View along middle wall
5   Conference table, steel
Photography: Margherita Spiluttini (3,4)

Shinhan Building
Kyu Sung Woo Architect, Inc.

Completion: February 1997

Location: Boon Dahng, Korea

Client: Shinhan Engineering and Construction Co, Ltd.

Area: 23,830 square metres; 256,512 square feet

Structure: Reinforced concrete; aluminium panels; glazing

Materials: Wood; granite; aluminium

Cost: US$24 million

This project is located in a new town of 280,000 people, south of Seoul. Urban design guidelines determined the massing and siting of the building. The design accepts traditional notions of shell and core, developing the texture of the skin to give the building presence and respond to the differing character of adjacent streets and their respective entries.

1 Front elevation
2 Lobby entry
3 Main facade
4 Rear facade
Photography: Timothy Hursley

1

2

3

4

Tenneco

Fox & Fowle Architects

Completion: June 1996

Location: Greenwich, Connecticut, USA

Client: Tenneco Inc.

Area: 9,290 square metres; 100,000 square feet

Structure: Steel

Materials: Wood; stone panels; amarilla/quartered North American cherry veneer

This project enabled the relocation of the executive offices of Tenneco—one of the forty largest industrial companies in the U.S.—from Houston, Texas to Greenwich, Connecticut.

In mid-1995, Tenneco purchased the former Claire Booth Luce estate—an 8,361 square metre (90,000 square foot), structure on a picturesque, 16-acre site. Over the years, this once stately home had not fared well through a series of renovations and additions that had served to convert the structure into a commercial office facility. Fox & Fowle renovated the building's core and shell and designed its interiors to create an appropriate home for Tenneco's top executives and its Board of Directors. The facility includes executive offices and support spaces for approximately 100 persons, a conference facility with cutting-edge audiovisual and telecommunications capabilities, and a grand stair designed in the spirit of the estate's 1920s-era architecture.

As a further challenge, Tenneco needed to achieve occupancy of its new offices by the end of the first quarter of 1996, while incorporating design standards commensurate with the executive nature of the facility and the Board of Directors' meetings that will be held in its conference facility. To reach these goals, Tenneco elected to organise the project in 'design-build' fashion, and teamed Fox & Fowle with the construction management firm of WWB Inc. Construction. The project was completed on schedule.

1

2

3

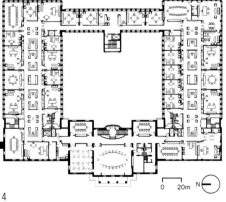

4

0   20m   N

5

1 New courtyard facade and stairway
2 Grand staircase
3 Executive waiting area
4 2nd floor plan
5 Boardroom
Photography: Jeff Goldberg/Esto

Washington Tower
G&W Architects, Engineers, Project Development Consultants

Completion: September 1996

Location: Metro Manila, Philippines

Client: Marina Properties Corporation

Area: 52,000 square metres; 559,742 square feet

Structure: Reinforced concrete

Materials: Rigid vinyl windows; curtain walls; reflective glass

1   Exterior parameter detail
2   Worm's eye view
3   Reception lobby
Photography: RRL Photography, Inc.

Located on a reclamation area along Manila Bay, Washington Tower is part of a mixed-use total community development along the Coastal Road.

A luxury condominium designed to suit the elite culture, the imperial-like structure features many distinct amenities for entertainment and recreation; function rooms, swimming pools, health spas, a children's centre and a coffee shop. The interior of every unit showcases a mix of form and function; complementing the finest marble floors are large glass windows that mingle with natural tropical light.

This 30-storey structure has 10-typical units per floor; each room has a touch of majestic individuality with premier features such as spacious rooms, high ceilings for better ventilation, and practical kitchens with views of the bay.

A very functional Filipiniana motif of bricast planes graces the facade in lieu of the utility portion in residential space.

1

2

3

Educational

Casa Italiana Restoration

Buttrick White & Burtis
in association with Italo Rota, Associate Architect

Completion: May 1996

Location: New York, New York, USA

Client: Columbia University

Area: 2,600 square metres; 28,000 square feet

Structure: Steel; concrete; brick

Materials: Brick; limestone

Cost: US$7.5 million

Awards: 1997 New York Landmarks Conservancy
Lucy G. Moses Preservation Award
1996 Preservation League of New York State Award

The Casa Italiana is a 1926 neo-Renaissance palazzo designed by McKim, Mead & White for Columbia University. It was sold to the Italian Government in 1991 to establish the Italian Academy for Advanced Studies in America, a new institution created to foster creative discourse between scholars of all disciplines and sponsoring activities ranging from private study and informal collaborations to exhibitions and public presentations.

The design process included the restoration of the exterior envelope as well as completion of the unfinished elevations in accordance with the 1926 drawings. The scope of the exterior restoration included new windows and window repair, stone cleaning and repointing, composite patching of decorative terra cotta, rechinking

the clay tile roof, and relining the gutters. Materials for the unfinished elevations included new brick, limestone and windows to match the originals.

The building's original interiors, a mix of elaborate period rooms and utilitarian academic spaces, required total renovation. After being scrupulously restored, the historic rooms were equipped with modern services. The balance of the building was gutted and refitted with new interiors. The new scheme opens the building in plan and section to overcome the isolation of small offices and separate floors and to enhance communication at all levels.

1

2

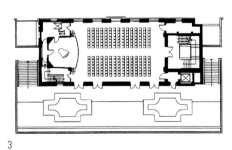

3

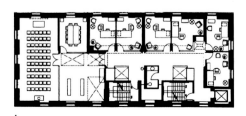

4

5

1 Section
2 First floor plan
3 Second floor plan
4 Fifth floor plan
5 Front facade (Amsterdam Avenue) after restoration
6 Sixth floor open office space
7 Sixth floor administrative and support areas
8 Two-storey space between fifth and sixth floors

6

7

8

9   The library
10   Sixth floor Loggia with view of Columbia University to west
11   The Teatro restored to its original splendour

Photography: Eduard Hueber (5–7, 9–11); Michael Moran (8)

9

10

11

Centenary Building
Hodder Associates

Completion: January 1996

Location: University of Salford

Client: University of Salford

Area: 3,623 square metres; 38,999 square feet

Structure: Glazed freeform element of crosswall construction

Materials: Rendered blockwork panels; Uginox G3 stainless steel rainscreen system; glazing and steel curtain walling

Cost: £3.5 million

Awards: 1996 Royal Institute of British Architects Award
1996 Royal Institute of British Architects Education Category Award
1996 The Stirling Prize for Architecture

1   First floor plan
2   Front elevation
3   South elevation
4   Entrance
5   Internal street
6   Studio
Photography: Dennis Gilbert

When setting the brief, the client described the function of this building as a 'fusion of design and technology' and asked that the building reflect this. It houses the Departments of Spatial, Graphic and Industrial Design.

The form of the building is generated from the desire to articulate a clear expression of the brief, the internal programme and a response to the building's context astride the threshold between the city and the academic campus. Diagrammatically the building defines a collegiate courtyard to an existing university building.

Flexible studio and seminar space, and three service towers, are contained within a four-storey orthogonal 'bar' of accommodation which defines the edge of the city block. Prescribed tutorial accommodation and technology suites arranged in a free form three-storey element address the newly defined courtyard thus establishing a dialogue between the collegiate and city 'sides'. The primary organisational device between the two types of

accommodation is a linear atrium or 'street' within which all horizontal circulation via galleries is contained. In this way street life becomes an aspect of the life of the building; common areas and adjoining offices and studios engage with the street to animate the building and render it with a sense of fusion and purpose.

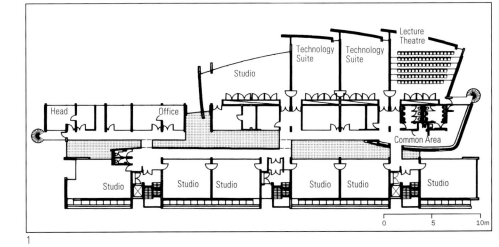

1

2

116

3

4

5

6

Compton Drew Investigative Learning Center

The Wischmeyer Architects, Inc.
in association with Louis Saur & Associates

Completion: July 1996

Location: St. Louis, Missouri, USA

Client: St. Louis Public School

Area: 8,361 square metres; 90,000 square feet

Structure: Reinforced concrete; steel frame

Materials: Brick veneer; limestone; metal panels

Cost: US$9 million

Awards: 1997 St. Louis Construction News & Review
Readers' Choice Award

The City of St. Louis enjoys a rich variety of school architecture ranging from turn-of-the-century masonry masterpieces to new state-of-the-art facilities. None of these schools are more important and more visible than the Investigative Learning Center Middle School just west of the St. Louis Science Center.

A specific challenge of the design team headed by The Wischmeyer Architects, Inc. with Louis Saur & Associates was to respond to the school's prominent location along Highway 40 and across from Forest Park. This opportunity established a design objective to create a school that would serve as an image building for the revitalised St. Louis Public School System. Additionally, the school's science-oriented curriculum is intended to create a functional relationship with the adjacent St. Louis Science Center. This led the designers to create an exterior that was in aesthetic harmony with the Science Center Complex.

The exterior for the 510-student centre consists primarily of a warm grey utility sized brick articulated by projecting band courses and a limestone coping. Two stair towers and two bays on the three-storey classroom tower are clad with metal panels. The blue-green panels, metal window frames and green tinted glass match the colours of the Science Center.

The interiors have been designed to provide a stimulating learning environment. An atrium, a spacious open stair tower and an inviting food court facilitate social interaction and allow for a variety of educational exhibits.

The primary goal was to create an urban design that was compatible with its neighbours while making its own unique statement as a special learning place for the young people.

1   Main entrance
2   Cafeteria and public entrance
3   Specialised instruction floor plan
4   Main stairwell
5   Library
Photography: courtesy The Wischmeyer Architects, Inc.

1

2

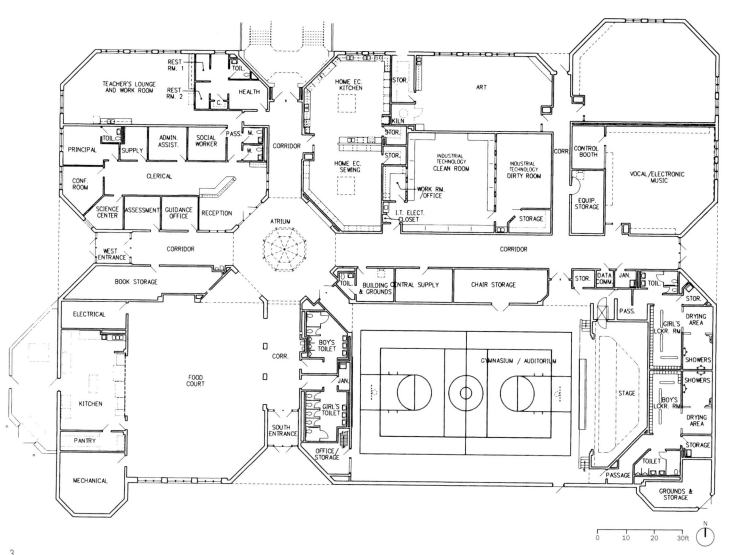

3

4

5

Davis High School Library and Classroom Building
The Steinberg Group

Completion: August 1996
Location: Davis, California, USA
Client: Davis Joint Unified School District
Area: 3,065 square metres; 33,000 square feet
Structure: Steel
Materials: Cement plaster; steel
Cost: US$4 million

Located in a university town focused on education and environmental responsibility.

Goal 1: Develop knowledge, skills, character and values of discipline, responsibility, honesty, fairness and desire for lifelong learning in safe, nurturing environment while creating a main entry and defining student quad area. Building is a composition of three interlocking components. Library space embraced by L-shaped classroom wing; provides protection from southwest solar exposure. The small 'technology square' penetrates northeast corner. Its geometry enhances acoustics and reinforces link between entry and quad. Solar study and desire to maximise natural light in the Library inspired forms of interior space and helped create individual character of exterior facades.

Goal 2: Provide functionality, flexibility: classrooms dedicated for expansion, non-load bearing walls reconfigurable, computer network in floor for easy access to expand or upgrade. Large space easily supervised, can be subdivided for themed approach and intimate study areas.

Goal 3: Address environmental concerns: space quality and character directly related to goal of utilising natural light and conserving energy. Curved white ceiling rises over glass wall permitting flow of diffused light, protects from direct exposure to south. Translucent glass allows no direct sunlight. Shape and treatment of ceiling minimises noise levels.

1 East side of library, classroom entry plaza
2 Library forms and lighting at night
3 Classroom/library sketch from north quad
4 Site plan
5 View of library from north
6 Library and classroom wing, north elevation

1

2

3

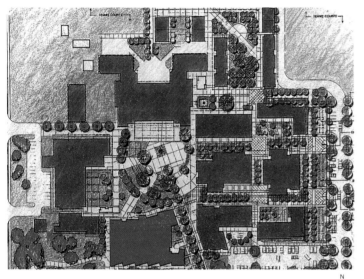

4

5

6

7 First floor plan
8 Main library entry, circulation desk
9 Main library space
10 Main reading area
Photography: Timothy Hursley

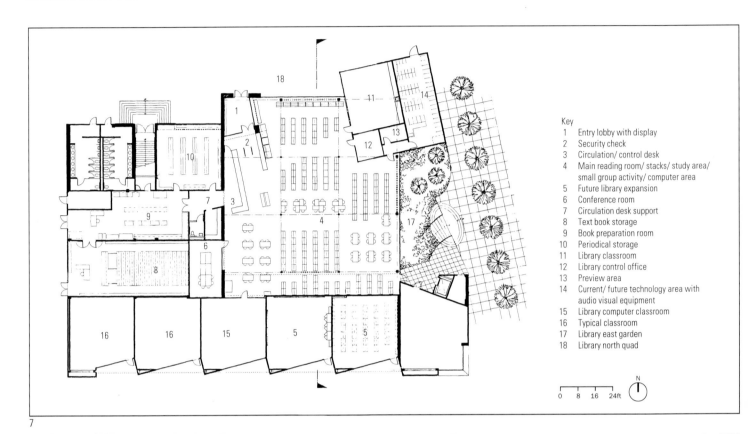

Key
1   Entry lobby with display
2   Security check
3   Circulation/ control desk
4   Main reading room/ stacks/ study area/
    small group activity/ computer area
5   Future library expansion
6   Conference room
7   Circulation desk support
8   Text book storage
9   Book preparation room
10 Periodical storage
11 Library classroom
12 Library control office
13 Preview area
14 Current/ future technology area with
    audio visual equipment
15 Library computer classroom
16 Typical classroom
17 Library east garden
18 Library north quad

7

8

9

10

Housatonic Community-Technical College
The S/L/A/M Collaborative

Completion: December 1996

Location: Bridgeport, Connecticut, USA

Client: State of Connecticut, Department of Public Works

Area: 16,722 square metres; 180,000 square feet

Structure: Steel

Materials: Brick; precast with metal panels

Cost: US$27.3 million

The additions and renovations to an abandoned 36,510 square metre (393,000 square foot) shopping mall, located in the heart of an inner city, created a new home for the Housatonic Community-Technical College. The new building enhances the learning atmosphere through a variety of spaces that range from public galleries to private study areas. Art is displayed throughout the building including the galleria—the main entrance to the college. The college also houses two museums; one for its own collection of art, which includes sculpture and original artist paintings; the other for rotating exhibits from different local artists. These museums are separated by movable panels and can be combined for use as one large museum.

In addition, the college includes a 1,546 square metre (16,640 square foot) library with a capacity to house 44,000 volumes in the main stack area; laboratory facilities for biology, microbiology, chemistry, and physics; eight computer science classrooms; seminar spaces; museum; cafeteria, and theatre. There is also a nationally accredited early childhood centre which has room for 40 children and an enclosed exterior play area. Site improvements such as the creation of public plazas and private courtyards transformed the surrounding area into a campus environment.

1

1 Main entrance to college and adjacent parking garage
2 State Street entrance
3 Rotunda, main entrance to college

4

5

6

4 Library overlooks interior courtyard
5 Science lab
6 Galleria and reception area
7 Art classroom
8 First floor plan
Photography: Nick Wheeler/Wheeler Photographics

7

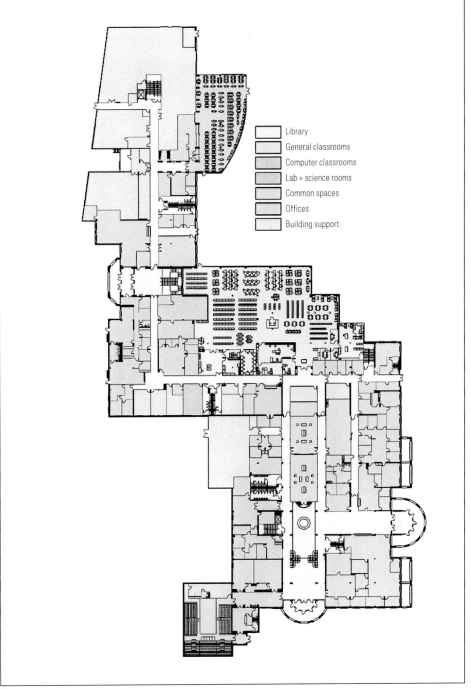

Library
General classrooms
Computer classrooms
Lab + science rooms
Common spaces
Offices
Building support

8

Humanities and Social Sciences Building, University of California, Santa Barbara

Zimmer Gunsul Frasca Partnership

Completion: April 1996

Location: Santa Barbara, California, USA

Client: The Regents of the University of California

Area: 14,295 square metres; 153,875 square feet

Structure: Cast-in-place slab; concrete shear walls

Materials: Rusticated precast concrete; sandstone; slate; limestone; stainless steel; seam copper

Cost: US$26 million

Awards: 1992 AIA Honorable Mention, Orange County Chapter

The new Humanities and Social Sciences Building is designed to play a dual role in the community life of the campus. The site was a parking lot in a precinct of the campus which lacked clear definition and a sense of place.

The building houses a diverse set of university programs in the departments of anthropology, Asian American studies, classics, drama and dance, history, philosophy, and religious studies and is organised into four connected academic elements; a one-storey wing for drama and dance, two four-storey elements for classroom space and academic offices; and at the prominent northeast corner

of the site, a six-storey academic and administrative office block.

Three front doors address the surroundings and the two edges of the complex define major campus bikeways. The arcades and porches both direct pedestrian flow and punctuate activity centres at several points at the edges of the complex. The varied series of roof forms explain the diversity of the interrelated disciplines housed within.

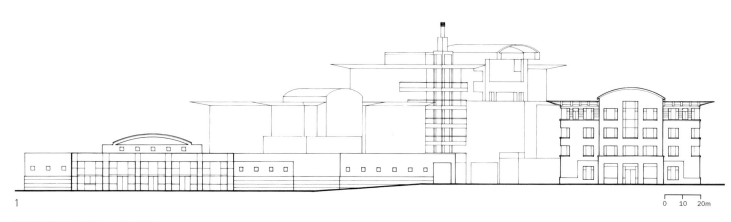

1

0   10   20m

2

3

1   South elevation
2   Arcades outside of classrooms face the quadrangle
3   Four-storey classroom and academic office component
4   Building wings form quadrangle
5   Curved east boundary of site along Arts Lane
6   Ground floor plan
7   Colloquium room at the top of the building
8   Dance and drama facilities
Photography: Hedrich-Blessing

4

5

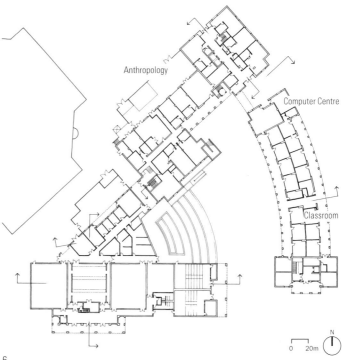

6

Anthropology

Computer Centre

Classroom

0   20m   N

7

8

Iwadeyama Junior High School
Riken Yamamoto & Field Shop

Completion: March 1996
Location: Tamatsukuri-gun, Miyagi Prefecture, Japan
Client: Iwadeyama-machi (town of Iwadeyama)
Area: 201,811 square metres; 2.2 million square feet
Structure: Reinforced concrete; steel
Materials: Glass

Iwadeyama Junior High School was built in a de-populating town in the countryside of northern Japan with a new scheme for classifying laboratories, classrooms and media galleries within the five different systems: language, natural science, domestic science, art and physical education.

The school is arranged in a system of layers for classrooms, student lounges and media galleries placed north to south. The student forum, enclosed by an atrium, has the central traffic line running through it which,

together with the student lounge situated above, becomes the hub of the school life. It also accommodates meetings, exhibitions, or other activities and allows views into the student lounge above, the media galleries below and the surrounding classrooms.

The layers interlock both horizontally and vertically allowing views from each layer through to other layers and levels. Multi-directional access and the communication generated in between the access, create a new environment for learning.

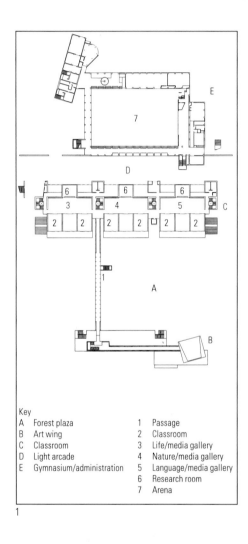

Key
A   Forest plaza
B   Art wing
C   Classroom
D   Light arcade
E   Gymnasium/administration
1   Passage
2   Classroom
3   Life/media gallery
4   Nature/media gallery
5   Language/media gallery
6   Research room
7   Arena

1

2

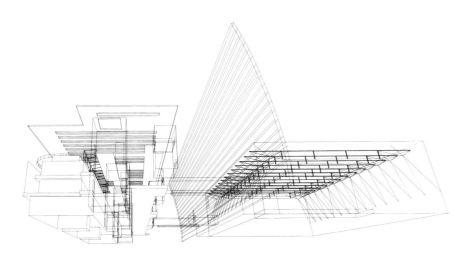

3

4

5

1 Site Plan
2 View of media gallery situated between research room and classroom
3 Axonometric
4 View from upper student lounge situated over student forum
5 View of louvre-screened terrace situated along south side of classroom wing
Photography: Fujituka Mitsumasa

Jean Parker Elementary School

Kwan Henmi architecture/planning, inc

Completion: January 1996

Location: San Francisco, California, USA

Client: San Francisco Unified School District

Area: 3,456 square metres; 37,201 square feet

Structure: Steel; reinforced concrete

Materials: Brick; limestone; precast concrete

Cost: US$8.8 million

Awards: 1997 Award of Excellence, Coalition for Adequate School Housing (in conjunction with the American Institute of Architects California Council) 1997 Exhibition of School Architecture Special Jury Citation, National School Boards Association

This elementary school replaces an unreinforced masonry structure severely damaged in the 1989 Loma Prieta earthquake. Designed to maximise usable playground area on the restricted 0.6-acre Chinatown site, this 550-student school is centred around a south-facing courtyard, providing protection from the winds that sweep the site year round. The school is organised into three parts in order to reduce the mass of the building and relate to the surrounding, densely-populated neighbourhood.

The main entry is adjacent to the administrative areas for visual control and incorporates a terracotta entry portal salvaged from the demolished school. The north-facing classrooms are organised efficiently into a three-storey block and have bay windows, keeping with Bay Area tradition.

The 465 square metre (5,005 square foot), multi-purpose room, with its own entry for public events, contains a full stage/music room and a community kitchen. Additional playground spaces are provided by two rooftop play terraces.

1 Facade of building
2 Site plan
3 Street elevation
4 Ground level play area
5 Typical classroom

1

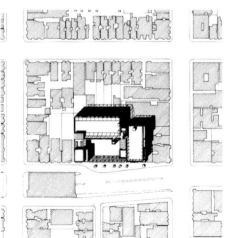

2

3

4

5

6

7

8

6 Interior view of multi-purpose room
7 Stage end of multi-purpose room
8 Interior view of library
9 First floor plan
10 Typical classroom
Photography: courtesy Kwan Henmi architecture/planning, inc.

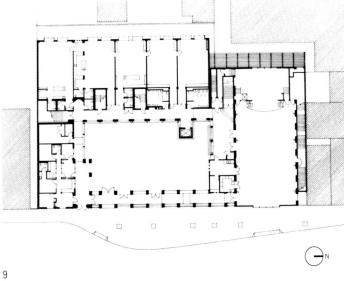

9

10

Lynn University Library
Herbert S. Newman and Partners P.C.

Completion: July 1996

Location: Boca Raton, Florida, USA

Client: Lynn University

Area: 5,388 square metres; 58,000 square feet

Structure: Reinforced concrete

Materials: Concrete; plaster stucco

Cost: US$6 million

At Lynn University it was attempted to design a library that would unequivocally convey its central role on campus and its importance to the pursuit of learning. The Lynn University Library is classical in form and monumental in scale, but the materials are regional. The columns and walls are unadorned stucco in the manner of contemporary Florida construction. In response to the heat and sun, windows are set deep into the walls and are shaded with metal screens. Screened, shaded porches at the front and rear also reflect the climate and local patterns of building use.

The role of the library is changing and flexibility of space is a prominent theme of state-of-the-art library technology. The Lynn University Library has been designed to accommodate the 200,000 volume collection that is projected by the year 2010 and is fully networked for computer and telecommunications access.

The major information hub is placed at the entrance to the Library so that users can easily find their way to reference librarians, reading rooms, meeting rooms and support staff. A dramatic, circular stairway marks this major point of confluence and is illuminated with a skylight. Rather than one main reading room, smaller reading and study areas are interwoven among the open stacks. They are positioned near windows to provide readers with natural light. Computer areas and book collections are located in the interior of the library to minimise harmful glare.

1   South facade
2   Entrance
3   Porch, second floor
4   Site plan
5   Screened porch, third floor
6   Central staircase with skylight
Photography: Thomas Delbeck

1

2

3

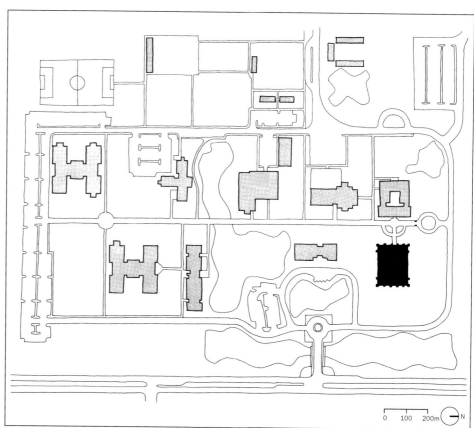

4

5

6

Miller Performing Arts Center

Kallmann McKinnell & Wood Architects, Inc.

Completion: February 1996

Location: Alfred, New York, USA

Client: Alfred University

Area: 2,975 square metres; 32,023 square feet

Structure: Brick; precast concrete

Materials: Aluminium; English slate

Cost: US$8 million

Located at the focal end of the main campus cross street, the Miller Performing Arts Center establishes an order for campus academic building expansion. In organisation and expression, the building addresses the small scale of the campus street to the south and the large scale of the valley and landscape to the north and has become the most prominent campus building at the entrance to the town of Alfred.

Programmatically, the building is organised vertically, with faculty offices on the lowest level, a 250-seat theatre and support on the middle two levels, and two-storey music and dance rooms at the top which offer commanding views of the valley beyond.

The building has two entrances from the campus street: the student entrance to the west, and the theatre entrance to the east, which is linked to the lower level theatre lobby by a grand staircase.

1

1   View from northwest
Opposite:
    East elevation

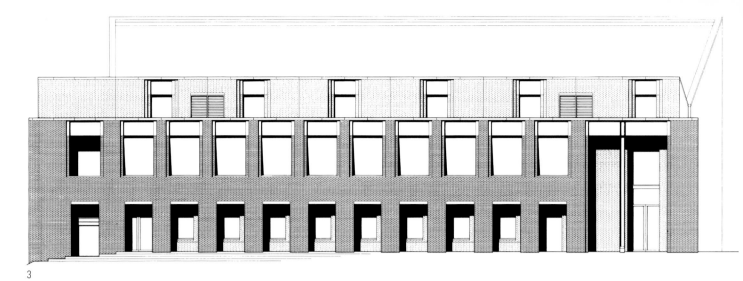

3

4

5

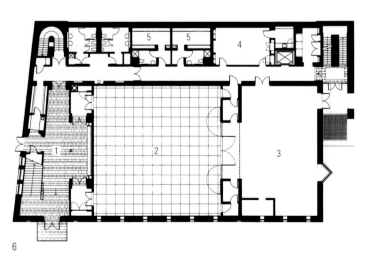

6

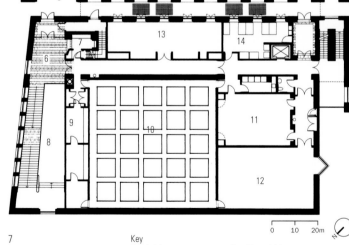

7

3   Elevation
4   Detail of South Arcade at student entrance
5   Night view from northwest
6   First floor plan
7   Second floor plan
Opposite:
    C.D. Smith Flexible Theater, view from catwalk
Photography: Peter Vanderwarker

Key
1   Lobby   8   Upper lobby
2   Flexible theatre   9   Control room
3   Scene shop   10   Theatre catwalk
4   Green room   11   Classroom
5   Dressing room   12   Acting/directing/rehersal studio
6   Foyer   13   Costume shop
7   Box office   14   Design studio

PS 88, The Seneca School

Mitchell/Giurgola Architects

Completion: September 1996

Location: Queens, New York, USA

Client: New York School Construction Authority

Area: 10,049 square metres; 108,169 square feet

Structure: Steel

Materials: Red brick; terracotta, aluminium; glazed block; terrazzo floor

Cost: US$16.4 million

Originally built in 1907, this five-storey neo-classical structure is the chief landmark in a residential neighbourhood of two- and three-storey row houses.

Two-storey additions have been added to the ends of the existing building to nearly double the area of the school and at the same time, to reduce its apparent size. New stair and elevator towers replace outmoded and non-complying stairs. The west wing houses a new boiler plant and gym; the east wing houses 19 classrooms. Modernisation of the existing building includes a 400-seat lunchroom, a kitchen and upgrading of mechanical, electrical and data systems.

On the exterior, the two new wings form a welcoming entry court and reinforce the symmetry of the original neo-classical building. Brick, terracotta and stone details and projecting bays have been introduced to integrate with the historical qualities of the original structure.

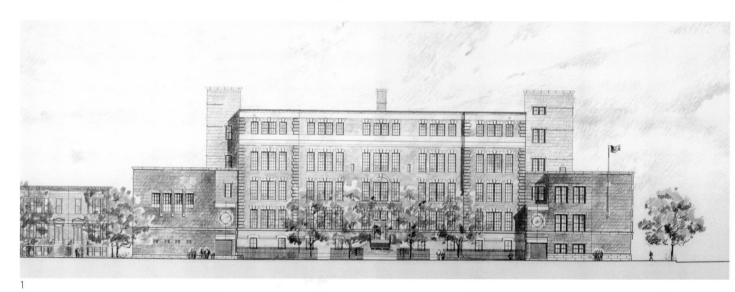

1

2

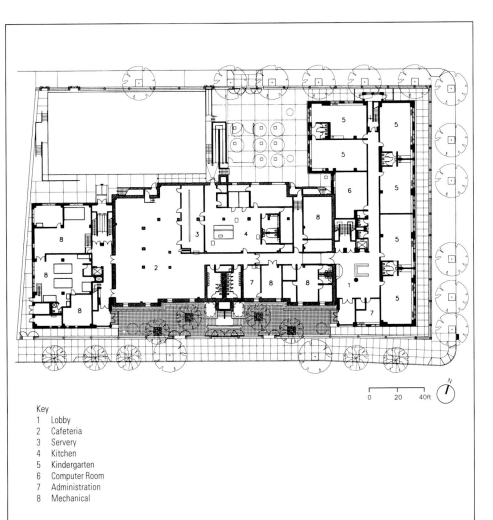

1   South elevation, including additions
2   Southeast corner
3   First floor plan
4   Gymnasium interior
5   Lobby view with tile mural
6   Kindergarten classroom
Photography: Jeff Goldberg/Esto

Key
1   Lobby
2   Cafeteria
3   Servery
4   Kitchen
5   Kindergarten
6   Computer Room
7   Administration
8   Mechanical

0   20   40ft

3

4

5

6

Royalston Community School

TAMS Consultants, Inc. Architects, Engineers & Planners

Completion: October 1996

Location: Royalston, Massachusetts, USA

Client: Athol/Royalston Regional School District

Area: 3,000 square metres; 32,293 square feet

Structure: Steel

Materials: Ground and split-face CMU; aluminium windows; asphalt roof tiles

Cost: US$3.6 million

The Royalston Community School is designed to accommodate 250 K-6 students with provisions to support continuing education and recreational activities for adults. Located on 21 acres of forest land, the site is laced with wetlands and covered with mature tree growth which delimit the final position of the building.

The school is sited along the western edge of the property, forming a semi-courtyard and preserving the natural features to the east for outdoor activities. The 12-classroom school is divided into two parts: an academic wing of individualised towers holding classrooms/support spaces and a community and school use 'barn' containing cafeteria, library and gymnasium.

The rural character of Royalston is reflected in the individualised masonry classroom towers, a reference to Royalston's original nine, one-room school houses of the 18th and 19th centuries. A special octagonal tower for art and kindergarten classes occupies the end of the classroom wing, offering a 270° panoramic view.

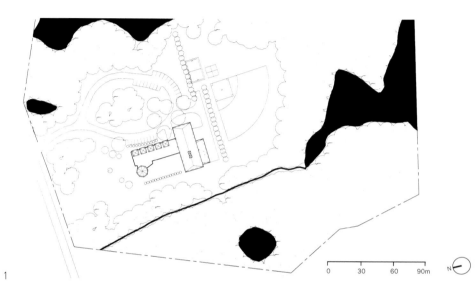

1

2

3

4

5

1   Site plan
2   View of gymnasium, entry and
    classroom wing
3   Approach to school
4   View of school entrance
5   Classroom wing north elevation

6   Detail of corridor exterior wall
7   School entry
8   First floor plan
9   Classroom wing corridor
10   Entry lobby
Photography: Chuck Choi (2,3,4,6,8); Chris Iwerks (5,7,9,10)

6

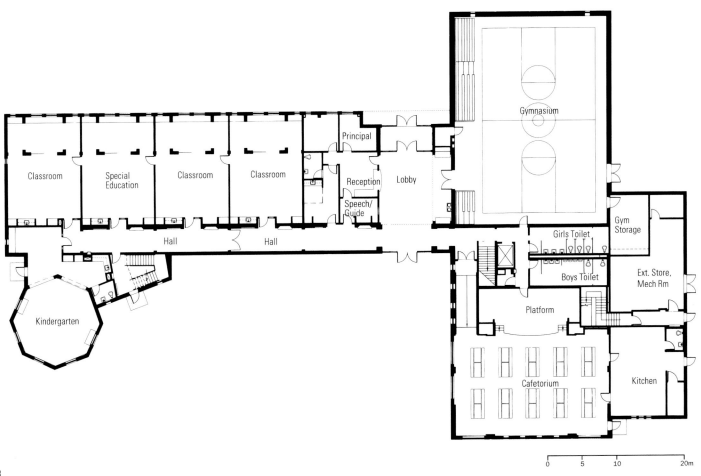

Principal

Classroom

Special Education

Classroom

Classroom

Reception

Speech/ Guide

Lobby

Hall

Hall

Kindergarten

Gymnasium

Gym Storage

Girls Toilet

Boys Toilet

Ext. Store, Mech Rm

Platform

Cafetorium

Kitchen

0 5 10 20m

8

9

10

St Mary's Infant School

Allford Hall Monaghan Morris

Completion: March 1996

Location: Kilburn, London, UK

Client: The Roman Catholic Diocese of Westminster

Area: 140 square metres; 1,507 square feet

Structure: Steel; reinforced concrete

Materials: Untreated western red cedar; rendered blockwork; steel

Cost: £165,000

The nursery, built in the grounds of an existing school, provides a special protected realm for the very young children. The play area, conceived as a 'secret garden', is elevated above the surrounding roads and shielded by green walls of Virginia creeper.

The plan is ordered by the interplay of the two main walls—a U-shaped external wall clad in cedar, and a masonry wall which divides the main space before emerging through the cedar to form the curved entrance.

The building is scaled to control views out on to a tough environment. Four systems of windows are employed: the clerestory framing the sky; the low-level windows scaled to the children's viewpoint; the wall of sliding glass letting in southerly light and opening to the outside; and the rooflights which march playfully down the spine of the building.

The building section is ordered by the clerestory glazing which is set forward providing complete reflection of the sky from outside and allowing the roof to float.

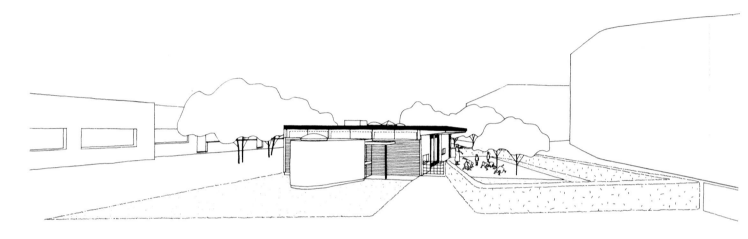

1

2

148

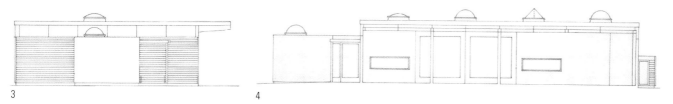

3

4

5

7

6

1   Perspective drawing
2   View of approach
3&4 Elevations
5   New nursery with existing school behind
6   Building in its surroundings
7   View along spine from entrance
Photography: Dennis Gilbert

Sussex Innovation Centre

Eric Parry Architects

Completion: May 1996

Location: University of Sussex, Brighton,
United Kingdom

Client: Sussex Innovation Centre Development Co.

Area: 1,790 square metres; 19,268 square feet

Structure: Masonry with concrete and steel frames

Materials: Brickwork; curtain walling; zinc roof

Cost: £1.7 million

The Sussex Innovation Centre is an incubator for the development and application of good ideas, and a catalyst to bridge the divide between theory and practice, academia and business.

The building developed as a result of three principal influences:

The Site: to the west, the plan of the Centre is defined by and defines a new public space overlooking the university buildings designed by Basil Spence. To the south, the carpark lies screened below. To the east, the brick wall and roof mark the boundary of the campus.

The Building Form: a deceptively simple two-storey rectangle 60m x 17.5m (197ft x 57ft). The building is naturally ventilated and passively controlled and therefore the width is critical for cross ventilation. The developed solution increases the normal dimension by the triple use of the central spine for circulation, light and ventilation.

The Community: there is a deliberate openness of the common areas and in the way interior passages open onto the rest of the building. In a year of use, the building is fully occupied and many opportunities have emerged through the interaction of the tenants.

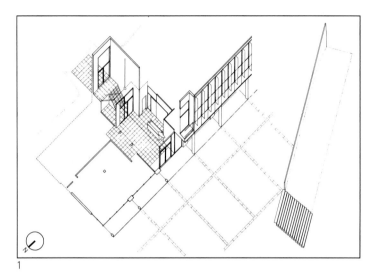

1

2

3

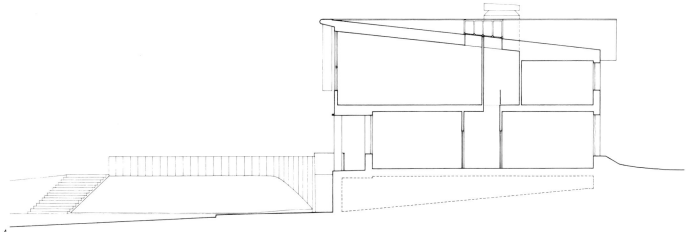

4

6

5

1   Axonometric of entrance and terrace
2   East elevation
3   Terrace overlooking campus
4   Cross section, tenant area and carpark
5   Corridors lit from above and
    ventilating interior
6   West facing colonnade
Photography: Peter Cook/VIEW

Temasek Polytechnic, Singapore

James Stirling Michael Wilford and Associates

Completion: January 1997

Location: Tampines Avenue One, Singapore

Client: Temasek Polytechnic

Area: 215,000 square metres; 2.3 million square feet

Structure: Reinforced concrete frame with painted brick infill

Cost: S$380 million

Temasek Polytechnic is a 'city of learning' for 11,500 students with 1,500 staff, encompassing Schools of Applied Science, Technology, Business, and Design, in a 30-hectare landscaped park between Tampines New Town and Bedok Reservoir at the eastern end of the island of Singapore.

The four schools are organised along spacious pedestrian concourses radiating from the promenade and sheltered by upper levels of accommodation. The spatial organisation optimises vertical and horizontal movement, with the most densely used spaces such as lecture theatres situated on, or below, concourse level. Each school has its own student canteen overlooking the park.

A raised entrance plaza, enclosed by the horseshoe-shaped administration building and opening towards Tampines Avenue, is the focus of the campus and a public forum representing the Polytechnic's open relationship with the community. A large 'window' through the horseshoe frames panoramic views across a triangular garden to the Reservoir.

The highest building on campus is the library tower which is connected to the administration and announces the presence of the Polytechnic on the Singapore skyline.

Contrasting landscapes of the Plaza Parterre, triangular garden and open park land surrounding the school and recreational facilities, ensure a variety of experiences, sense of orientation and unify the campus.

1   Site plan
2   View of entrance plaza
3   'Window' through administration building
    and view of city skyline
4   Axonometric view of administration building
    and central garden
5   Library and central garden
6   View of Technology School promenade
Photography: Richard Bryant/ Arcaid

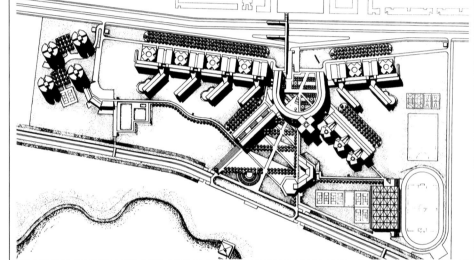

1

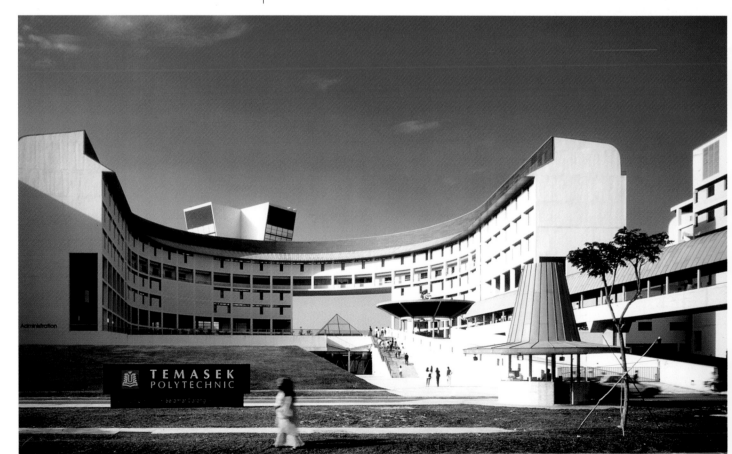

2

3

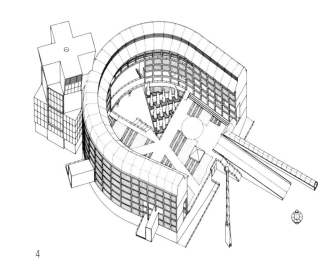

4

5

6

Totoro Kindergarten
Katsuhiro Kobayashi + Design Studio Architects

Completion: January 1997

Location: Yokohama, Kanagawa Prefecture, Japan

Client: Totoro Kindergarten

Area: 258 square metres; 2,777 square feet

Structure: Wood

Materials: Galvanised steel; shingle roofing; corrugated steel

Cost: ¥45,000,000

Totoro Kindergarten is managed by the chief director Masaaki Shimane, a former explorer, with an educational motto to grow up cheerful children by means of outdoor activities. In response to this motto, we attempted to design such a unique kindergarten that its interior spaces themselves are a kind of playfields. It is composed of two main rooms, a nursing room and a playing/gathering room. The former room open to a play ground, is like a huge jungle gym with trussed wooden beams. Beside this space are added an alcove and stepped slit, spaces which are painted in green and good for children to play 'hide-and-seek'. The playing/

gathering room constructed by post and grid beams of parallel strand lumber, has a half-oval plan and embraces children softly and gently. Also here, large stairs, a low and narrow space below them and a cantilevered catwalk provide nice interior playfields for children.

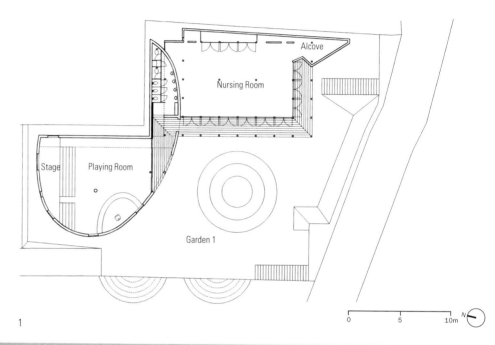

1

2

3

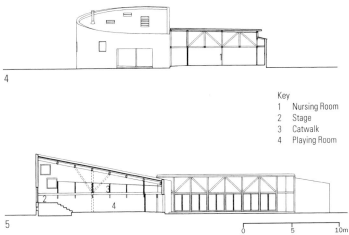

4

5

Key
1 Nursing Room
2 Stage
3 Catwalk
4 Playing Room

0   5   10m

6

1 Site plan
2 Overall view from south
3 Interior view of playing/gathering room
4 East–west section
5 North–south section
6 View of nursing room at night
7 Exterior view from west, curved wall leads
   to entrance

Photography: Design Studio Architects

7

University of New England, Center for the Health Sciences

Ellenzweig Associates, Inc.

Completion: October 1996

Location: Biddeford, Maine, USA

Client: University of New England

Area: 7,339 square metres; 79,000 square feet

Structure: Steel

Materials: Brick; granite; glass; metal

Cost: US$14.8 million

This major new teaching facility establishes a new image for the only osteopathic medical school in New England, providing expanded facilities for increased enrolment and making a significant contribution to the overall campus plan. The three-storey building is sited to capture the predominant view from the main road and other campus buildings. Splayed wings define two edges of a large green, creating a major open space designed to be used for academic ceremonies as well as informal gatherings.

The design of the facility supports the University's commitment to interaction among the medical and scientific disciplines housed in the building. The innovative curriculum is evidenced by the third-floor osteopathic procedures and practice laboratory, offering 60 tables, a stage for demonstrations, and strategically placed video monitors to enhance demonstrations.

A major architectural challenge was to respond to the sloped site, while accommodating the complex program of laboratories and classrooms for the College of Osteopathic Medicine as well as the Life Sciences disciplines of the College of Arts and Sciences. Reflecting its dual occupants, the building is designed as two rectilinear wings flanking a central, semi-circular form that houses lecture halls for the University. The articulation of multiple volumes, through the use of brick, granite, and glass, expresses various program elements and reduces the building's apparent mass.

1

1 View from campus green
2 South elevation
3 Site plan
4 View of upper entry and plaza

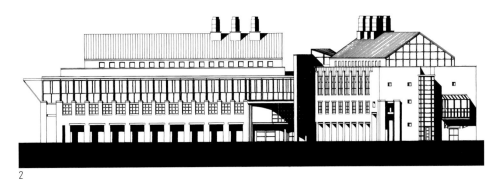

2

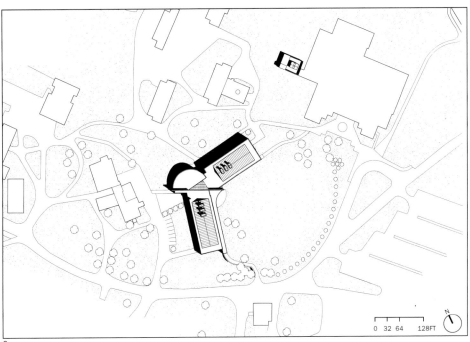

3

0 32 64   128FT

4

5

6

7

8

5 West gallery
6 Laboratory
7 Staircase
8 Tiered lecture hall
9 Osteopathic procedures and practice laboratory
Photography: Steve Rosenthal

9

The Lingnan College

P&T Group

Completion: June 1996

Location: Tuen Mun, Hong Kong

Client: Lingnan College

Area: 34,000 square metres; 365,985 square feet

Structure: Reinforced concrete

Materials: Ceramic tile; spray aggregate coating; steel

Cost: HK$388 million

Awards: 1996 Hong Kong Institute of Architects Certificate of Merit

In Lingnan College Tuen Mun's new campus, references are made to the long historical link with the old Canton Campus, and the realisation of the Lingnan spirit inspiring the architecture and landscape design.

A landscape spine running north–south lies between the central facilities and the faculty buildings, stretching from the knoll on the south, through the Chinese garden, central plaza, and contemporary garden, ending at the swimming pool.

The various functions are carefully programmed to integrate with the existing landscape. The preserved landscape and added features of the central landscape spine, mingling with the ample spaces provided at ground level outside the mass teaching facilities, serve as a place for students and teachers to interact.

Orientation of building mass was carefully considered; central facilities such as lecture theatres and the indoor sports' hall which require minimal windows, flank on the west as effective shading to the western sun, noise and dust generated from Castle Peak Road.

Faculty buildings lying east–west maximise the natural cross-ventilation from southerly winds while at the same time, minimising the elevation area facing the undesirable western sun.

The site profile has preserved much of the original landscape including the southern knoll; existing trees and landform help to create a green and shady environment with the natural wind breeze through the central landscape spine creating a comfortable micro-climate.

Detailing is done with contemporary regional characteristics embodied, trying to deliver a special touch to add to the identity and image of the College.

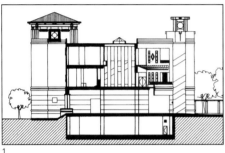

1

2

3

4

1   Section
2   Faculty buildings
3   Main entrance
4   Contemporary garden
Photography: Bobby KC Shum

UCSB Materials Research Lab

Koning Eizenberg Architecture
in association with Reid & Tarics Associates

Completion: December 1996

Location: University of California, Santa Barbara, USA

Client: University of California

Area: 2,323 square metres; 25,000 square feet

Structure: Steel frame

Materials: Plaster; aluminium; steel; elastomeric decking; corrugated metal; ceramic tile

Cost: US$5.6 million

The Materials Research Laboratory at UC Santa Barbara (designed in association with Reid & Tarics Associates) represents an innovative effort in the sciences to facilitate interdisciplinary research. Program requirements included flexible laboratory space (NMR, chemistry, etc.), faculty and student offices, conference rooms and meeting spaces. The program was configured to enhance opportunity for collegiality and reinforce campus urban design objectives through the outward-reaching gestures of courtyards and the definition of pedestrian-friendly streets.

1

2

3

4

1 View from west
2 Entry
3 Third floor patio
4 Second floor patio
Photography: Benny Chan

161

Institutional

ACTEW Redevelopment, Fyshwick

Bligh Voller Nield Pty Ltd

Completion: June 1997

Location: Fyshwick, ACT, Australia

Client: ACTEW Corporation Ltd/Project Coordination (Aust) Pty Ltd

Area: 4,500 square metres; 48,439 square feet

Structure: In situ concrete; steel

Materials: Steel; zinc; aluminium

Cost: $12 million

The master plan for the Australian Capital Territory and Water (ACTEW) authorities redevelopment provides new accommodation for a number of business units currently located throughout the Australian Capital Territory (ACT). They include: a fully certified laboratory and related administrative functions; a control centre for their regional grid and a related computing centre located on different levels within the same building; hydrology/hydrography department containing office/admin areas and workshop/storage areas. External space combines a security enclosure to the computer control building, staff amenities and extensive xeroscape landscaping fully maintained by stormwater runoff retained on site through tanks and constructed water courses.

The design provided a comprehensive response to ACTEW's brief, taking into account the existing on-site building and landscaping, public exposure to shopfront areas and street frontage, provision for future modular expansion of the laboratory, provision of natural light to all areas by way of skylighting and sun screen glazing, and low maintenance materials combined with a sophisticated aesthetic to further ACTEW's corporate image.

1

2

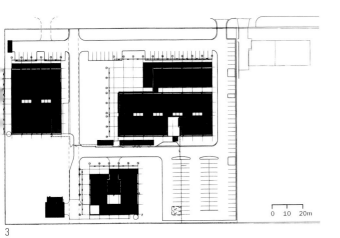

1. ACTEW laboratories and computer control campus
2. Laboratory forecourt and northern entrance
3. Site plan
4. Computer control northern elevation
5. Computer control room and service floor
6. Typical laboratory

Photography: Leigh Atkinson/Image Makers

3

0 10 20m

4

5

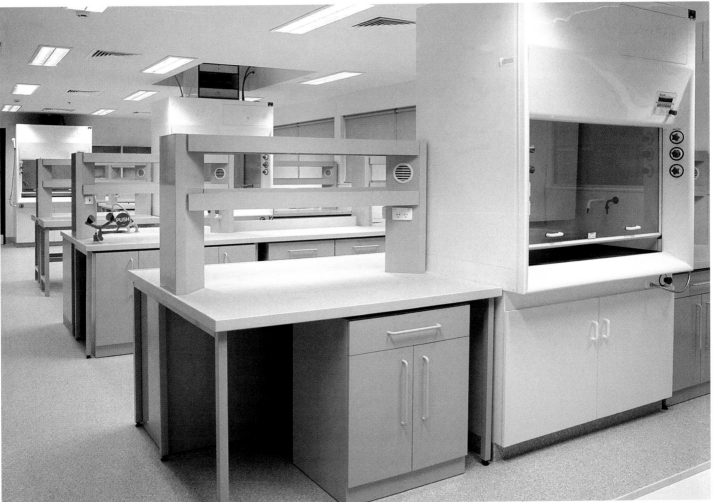

6

Center for Integrated Systems Extension

Antoine Predock Architect

Completion: March 1996

Location: Stanford University, Palo Alto, California, USA

Client: Stanford University

Area: 4,923 square metres; 53,000 square feet

Structure: Cast-in-place concrete and steel braced frame

Materials: Sand-stone and cast-in-place concrete; copper roof

Cost: US$14 million

Sited on a prominent pedestrian axis, the Center for Integrated Systems acts as a mediator for the diverse academic and architectural conditions of the campus.

Reinterpreting the architectural qualities of the Stanford campus, the Center has an identifiably academic presence that reflects the contemporary character of the advanced computer chip technology research occurring within the building.

An internal courtyard, and office spaces for faculty and students off a centralised lobby are designed for informal interaction to create a community of scientific inquiry that will result in cooperative advancement in the field of computer technology.

1   Main entry at dusk northeast corner
2   Section
3   Flanking stair/ramp to loggia
4   Copper entry vault looking east
5   Glass enclosed stair to lower level
Photography: Timothy Hursley

1

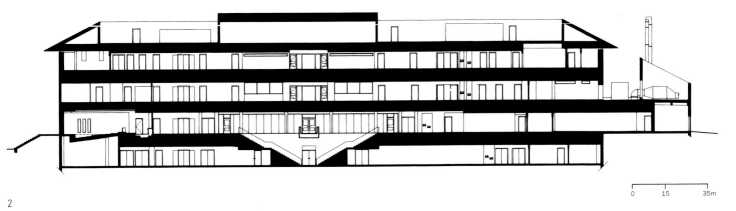

2

0   15   35m

3

4

5

Cheek—Powell Heart & Vascular Pavilion

TRO/The Ritchie Organization

Completion: August 1996

Location: Clearwater, Florida, USA

Client: Morton Plant Mease Health Care

Area: 9,476 square metres; 102,000 square feet

Structure: Flat slab cast-in-place; auger cast concrete

Materials: Precast concrete; aluminium; steel

Cost: US$11.5 million

Reaching out to serve the needs of its customers in an integrated system approach, the 9,476 square metre (102,000 square foot), four-storey Heart & Vascular Pavilion houses programs designed to provide a continuum of care that develops a 'heart healthy' community.

The program, all under the roof of the Heart & Vascular Pavilion, includes the following: Wellness Center, Cardiac Rehabilitation, Invasive Diagnostics, Community Education Center, 'Heart Smart' cafe and a Resource Library in the lobby. A new multi-level parking facility directly across from the Pavilion offers participants convenient parking.

Abundant windows on three sides of the first floor street facade create high visibility for the activities of the 2,136 square metre (23,000 square foot) Wellness Center, which

occupies 23% of the building. The clearly announced entrance of the pavilion, its spacious two-storey atrium with trees, water sculpture, artwork, ample glass and natural light, serves to communicate a sense of entry into a special environment—one which is tranquil, uplifting and open.

Emulating an interior garden where life is attended and nurtured, the two-storey atrium space is the organising element for the building, designed by TRO to reflect its integrated functional program. It serves as an orientation point inviting access and visibility to the Pavilion's services.

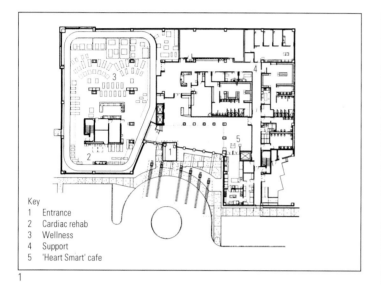

Key
1   Entrance
2   Cardiac rehab
3   Wellness
4   Support
5   'Heart Smart' cafe

1

2

3

1   Floor plan
2   Northeast corner and entry to Morton Plant Hospital Campus
3   Drop-off and entry to Heart & Vascular Pavilion
4   First floor dining at the 'Heart Smart' cafe
5   Nurses' station and recovery suites for Outpatient Invasive Cardiology Services
6   Wellness and Cardiac Rehabilitation Center
Photography: George Cott

4

5

6

Drake and Curtis Halls, Colgate University

Herbert S. Newman and Partners P.C.

Completion: January 1996

Location: Hamilton, New York, USA

Client: Colgate University

Area: 11,461 square metres; 123,375 square feet

Structure: (Curtis Hall) precast panels; cast-in-place roof and floor slabs; steel

Structure: (Drake Hall) cast-in-place concrete

Materials: (Curtis Hall) brick; precast concrete trim; slate roof; metal panels

Materials: (Drake Hall) brick; precast concrete trim; slate roof

Cost: US$12 million

Awards: National Honor Award, American Concrete Institute

A new campus quadrangle was created next to the main campus dining hall by carefully siting a new dormitory to bridge an important pedestrian path and by designing a new entry tower for an existing 1950s dormitory. This project created a new campus centre, an 'outdoor living room'.

The new dormitory, Drake Hall, has rooms for 188 students, as well as lounges, study areas, offices, and a radio station. A dark russet brick and matching precast concrete trim was used to harmonise with other campus buildings. Precast concrete panels form a rusticated base and giant precast voussoirs frame the semicircular arch which bridges the pedestrian path. This arch both defines and encloses the quadrangle and also entices the viewer through it to the campus beyond.

Curtis Hall, the existing four-storey dormitory, was renovated and expanded. A new entry tower was added that has common rooms and study areas. A partial fifth floor with more bedrooms was also added. Bathrooms and stairs were relocated and all windows and doors were replaced as were the HVAC and MEP systems.

The additions to Curtis Hall were clad in the same dark russet brick with matching precast concrete trim and slate roofs that were used at Drake Hall. Aluminium panels and fins were integrated into the window system to provide a sense of scale and sun protection. The original yellow brick cladding was stained to match the new brick, thus completing the transformation.

1

2

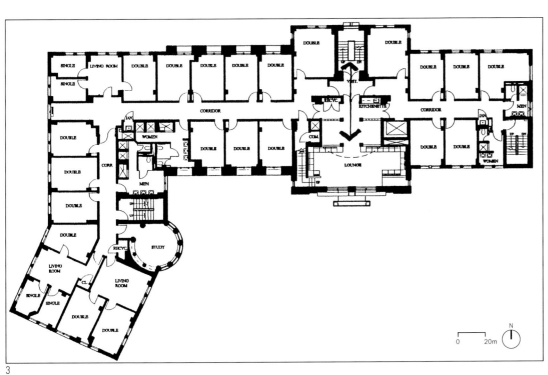

3

1   Curtis Hall
2   Drake Hall
3   Second floor, Drake Hall
4   Entrance Detail, Curtis Hall
5   Stair detail, Drake Hall
6   Second floor lounge, Drake Hall
Photography: Peter Aaron/Esto

4

5

6

Hale Medical Pavilion, Day Kimball Hospital
The S/L/A/M Collaborative

Completion: September 1997

Location: Putnam, Connecticut, USA

Name of Client: Day Kimball Hospital

Area: 4,366 square metres; 47,000 square feet
(new construction and renovations)

Structure: Steel frame, precast base; precast accents

Materials: Brick veneer, copper roof

Cost: US$9.3 million

Day Kimball Hospital, a 104-bed community hospital, was losing patients to area healthcare facilities, because of its undersized and outdated maternity and surgical departments. The facility hadn't had any major building renovations since the 1960s.

The construction and renovations began with the demolition of several sections of the building. Because the facility had to remain open at all times and every department had to remain functional, construction noises and vibration to the existing building were of primary concern. Consequently, the project was developed in two phases. The addition was constructed as a separate building and then tied into the existing facility.

The new addition, which wraps around the original building, includes a state-of-the-art surgical suite of approximately 1,579 square metres (17,000 square feet) and four new operating rooms. The suite replaces the existing four ORs, which were approximately 557 square metres (6,000 square feet) and built in the 1930s. These older ORs have been renovated and included in the new Maternal and Child Care Unit. This unit incorporates seven Labour Delivery Recovery Postpartum rooms (LDRP) and includes two nurseries, one for well babies and one for sick babies.

1

2

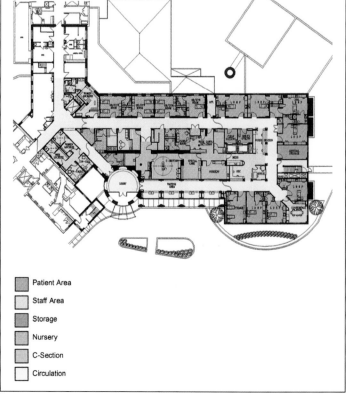

1 Entrance
2 Surgery conferee room
3 First floor plan
4 Surgery recovery room
5 Central sterile supply
6 Operating room with window for natural light
Photography: Nick Wheeler/Wheeler Photographics

Patient Area
Staff Area
Storage
Nursery
C-Section
Circulation

3

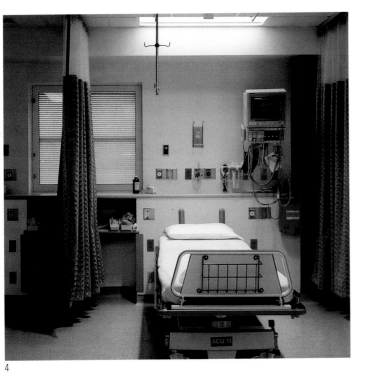

4

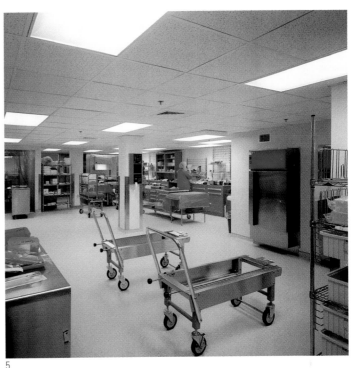

5

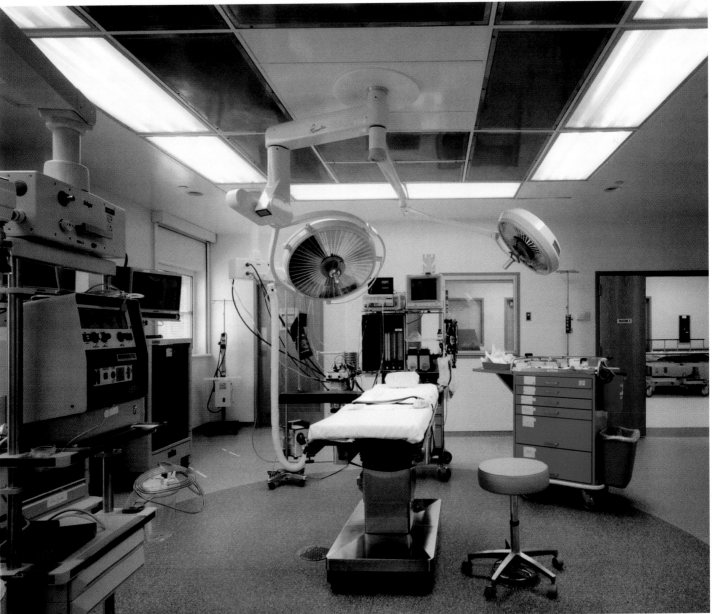

6

Haven of Hope Hospital Redevelopment

Kwan & Associates Architects Ltd

Completion: April 1997

Location: Tseung Kwan O, Hong Kong

Client: Haven of Hope Christian Service

Area: 26,000 square metres; 279,871 square feet

Structure: Reinforced concrete column and beam

Materials: Ceramic mosaic tiles

The redevelopment works included the demolition of the existing family quarters and administration buildings as well as the construction of a low-rise non-acute hospital with 316 beds. In-house support services include occupational therapy, physiotherapy, clinical pathology and linguistic therapy. There is also a low-rise annexe housing a nursing school, pupil nursing, various staff accommodation and staff kitchen/canteen.

A major influence on the design was the need for the hospital to conform to the profile of the naturally landscaped 70,000 square metre (763,498 square foot) site. The hospital itself is subject to horizontal planning based on a 'hospital street' concept with 'plug-in' departments organised in a cruciform for maximum flexibility.

Four green-roofed, landscaped courtyards form the basis of the plan, recalling a traditional Chinese village. These courtyards introduce natural light and fresh air to the complex. Vertical and horizontal elements on the elevation break down the scale and shade the rooms within. The hospital climbs from three to six stories, and this stepping parodies the natural contours of the site. Verdant roof gardens are also included to complement the 'village' look.

The hospital buildings stand on a two-storey podium with a manifestly different identity, suggesting a medieval castle and moat. The podium houses the workshops, storage facilities and carpark.

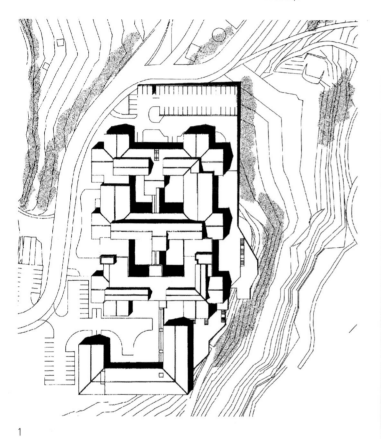

1

2

3

1 Site plan
2 Aerial vista
3 The building sits impressively in its heavily wooded site
4 Staircase detail
5 Nurses' station
6 Main entrance detail
Photography: courtesy Kwan & Associates Architects Ltd

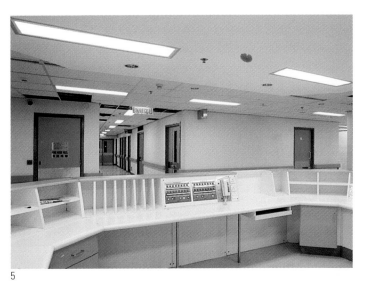

4

5

6

LG Research & Development Park

Tai Soo Kim Partners
in association with Chang Jo Corporation

Completion: October 1996
Location: Daeduk, Korea
Client: LG Group
Area: 71,569 square metres; 770,387 square feet
Structure: Steel; concrete
Materials: Concrete; blue-grey glass
Cost: $120 million

The LG Group required a first-class research facility to meet universal standards, which would draw and inspire world class staff. The architect designed an environment which honours the staff, by featuring the natural environment. The design provides numerous amenities and opportunities for informal interaction, reflection, reading and conferencing overlooking reflecting pools, landscaped courtyards and rooftop gardens.

The first two phases of this 162,000 square metre (1.7 million square foot), facility are aesthetically and functionally complete. The first 71,570 square metre (770,387 square foot), of construction provide a research

and pilot plant wing, and a head building consisting of a 500-seat auditorium, 800-seat dining hall, health club, library, conference areas, administrative and executive offices.

The rectangular site is tight due to the mountainous terrain at the western end. The building plan is composed of four repeatable research and pilot plant wings and a head building arranged in a horseshoe. A monumental glass atrium spine connects all five elements.

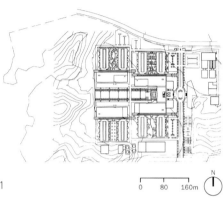

1

2

1   Site plan
2   Main entrance and head building look onto a reflecting pool
3   Towering, four-storey atrium/spine
4   Each wing features a uniquely landscaped courtyard
5   Enclosed bamboo court

176

3

4

5

6

7

8

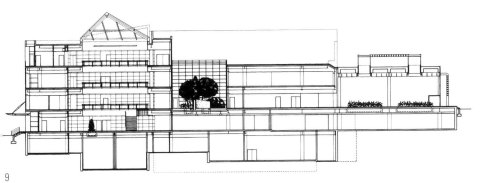

6   Ground floor of atrium/spine
7   Skylit atrium
8   Atrium/spine allows natural light into more secure areas
9   Elevation
10 Research laboratory
11 Glass and steel enclose dining hall
Photography: Timothy Hursley

9

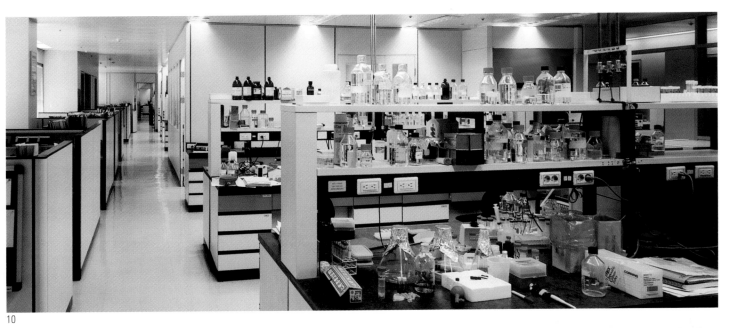

10

11

New Patient Care Tower—Saint Francis Hospital and Medical Center

TRO/The Ritchie Organisation

Completion: August 1996

Location: Hartford, Connecticut, USA

Client: Saint Francis Hospital and Medical Center

Area: 33,258 square metres; 358,000 square feet

Structure: Steel; concrete

Materials: Precast concrete; pre-patina copper

Cost: US$81 million

Awards: 1997 Boston Society of Architects/New England Healthcare Assembly Healthcare Design Awards, Honorable Mention
1994 Modern Healthcare magazine/American Institute of Architects Design Awards Citation
1993 Boston Society of Architects Unbuilt Architecture Design Awards, First Citation

1   Detail of main entry canopy
2   Site plan
3   New Patient Care Tower creates focal point on campus
4   Main entry features rotunda with artwork

Faced with the spiralling costs of operating two hospital campuses three miles apart, Saint Francis Hospital and Medical Center (SFHMC), embarked on a bold strategic plan to consolidate ambulatory care services and update outmoded inpatient facilities.

The Patient Care Tower became the catalyst for change by satisfying four major planning objectives.

Campus Unification: by creating a central focal point on campus, unifying disparate elements and linking all clinical and support structures on campus as a 'main street' of circulation;

Vertical Integration of Ambulatory Services: by grouping ambulatory services around a three-level atrium, enhancing accessibility and patient convenience, while upper floors house inpatient services;

Flexible Planning: by designing a regular structural grid, adaptable facade and 'universal' room dimensioning and detailing that readily accommodates physical change; and

Patient Orientation-Wayfinding: by clearly establishing vertical and horizontal paths of travel.

Inside, interiors feature warm neutral colours with vibrant accents appearing throughout on individual walls, reception desks, nurses' stations and furniture. The use of natural light and nature as a healing tool is a central theme; daylight floods the rotunda and patient rooms while indoor planters add touches of greenery.

The fast-tracked project was successfully completed within 36 months at a cost approximately 10-15% below national norms.

1

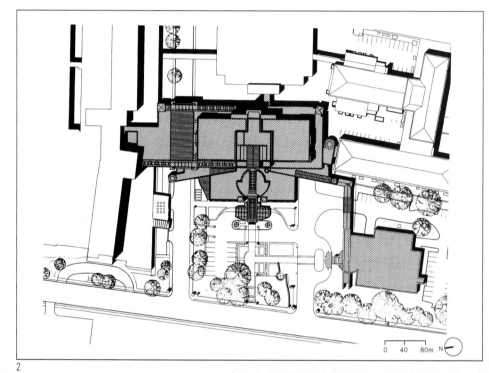

2

3

5

5 Large atrium windows provide daylight to rotunda and waiting areas
6 The auditorium provides meeting space for medical lectures and community events
7 The Critical Care Unit affords good visibility from nurses' station
8 LDRP rooms are cosy and home-like
Photography: Scott McDonald/Hedrich-Blessing

6

7

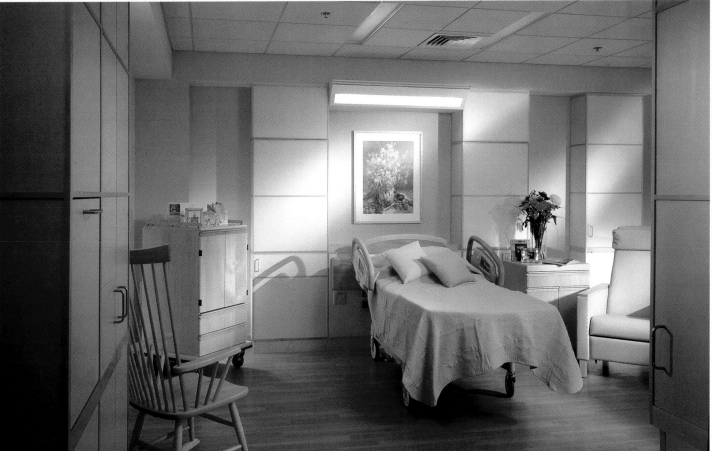

8

RESOWI Centre Graz, Faculty of Law and Social Economic Sciences and Extension of University

Architects Domenig—Eisenköck

Completion: September 1996

Location: Graz, Austria

Client: BIG (Federal Estate Company)

Area: 21,100 square metres; 226,050 square feet

Structure: Steel; concrete; aluminium

Materials: Steel; concrete; composite steel

Cost: ATS 1,111 million

The RESOWI Centre Graz is equipped for over 14,000 students with 32 institutes, a faculty library, 11 lecture theatres and an EDP centre. The 21,100 square metre (226,050 square feet) site is bordered on three sides by streets. The south side faces on to the university property and the building is accessible on all sides. A system of corridors runs through the centre, linking the main paths and roads of the university with the surrounding streets. The entire organisational programme was incorporated in a long body, subdivided into individual architectural elements.

The university library was extended eastwards, connected underground with the faculty library. The books are stored on the two underground floors; the ground floor and first floor contain the reading rooms and library administration

is on the second and third floors.

The choice of skeletal structure was made in view of economic production costs and time constraints, utilising a conventional steel-concrete structure on the lower floors and a composite steel on the two upper floors.

There are a total of 242 parking space; 32 of the spaces plus a large number of allocations for bicycles are located in the basement.

The remaining space has been transformed into gardens and flowerbeds with a pond beside the south entrance serving as a retention basin for rainfall.

1

1 Piazza with cafeteria
2 View from south, in front of main entrance
3 University library extension
4 Lecture theatres 6–11
5 View from south, access zone
Photography: courtesy Domenig—Eisenköck

Tai Po Hospital

Kwan & Associates Architects Ltd

Completion: March 1997
Location: Tai Po, Hong Kong
Client: Architectural Services Department
Area: 39,000 square metres; 419,806 square feet
Structure: Reinforced concrete; post and beam
Materials: Ceramic mosaic tiles

Set in landscaped grounds, this six-storey complex is home to 1,020 convalescent and infirmary beds as well as occupational therapy, physiotherapy, pharmacy, radiology, general administration units and centralised kitchen facilities.

Functional planning is vital; the hospital comprises four wings grouped around a central core in a cruciform arrangement reflecting the need for efficiency. Wards are generally located on upper floor levels with views onto the landscaped exterior. This 'nucleus' scheme adopts a streamlined vertical circulation system in both the core and the tips of the wings.

The treatment of light entering the wards is central to the elevational design. White-tiled concrete fins have been angled so that diffused sunlight is reflected inside. These sun-shading devices also articulate the simple facade.

For further embellishment, the core, interpreted as the trunk of the building, is dressed up with a glass block feature and capped roof. In a move to break down the scale, the tips of the four wings are recessed, and semi-circular holes punched through the capped roofs.

Outside, a tinted, transparent covered walkway leads through geometrically landscaped grounds to the entrance courtyard where a multi-grid skylit canopy echoes the curvilinear movement of the landscape.

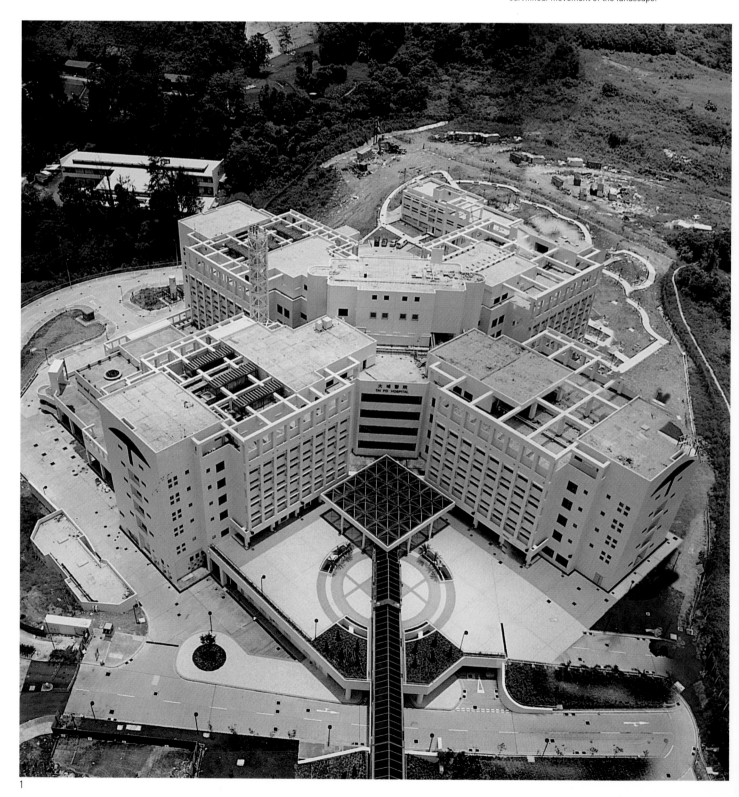

1

1 Aerial vista
2 Facade detail
3 Lift lobby
4 External view
Photography: courtesy Kwan & Associates Architects Ltd

2

3

4

The Music Facility

Antoine Predock Architect

Completion: January 1997

Location: University of California, Santa Cruz, California, USA

Client: University of California, Santa Cruz

Area: 3,530 square metres; 38,000 square feet

Structure: Cast-in-place concrete; solid grout CMU; steel roof

Materials: Sand-blasted concrete; CMU; veneer plaster; precast gypsum; fabric-faced acoustic panels

Cost: US$12 million

Awards: 1997 AIA Western Mountain Region Merit Award

The poetic topographic elements of the UCSC: ravine, meadow and rocky outcropping, have been organised in a choreographed sequence to form a music village where the great meadow meets the edge of the redwood forest. Composed about the existing solitary oak tree and the sweeping vistas of the Monterey Bay, the programmatic components of the Music Center have been stretched and moulded to create a series of professional discoveries, courtyards and framed views. Built from concrete, masonry block and steel, the Music Center is designed to achieve and integrate the highest standards in acoustic and audio visual technologies, within the matrices of durability, economy and delight. The interiors of the building have been sculpted for acoustic performance and aesthetics. The Music Center represents an alchemical transformation of the architectural elements into a music analogy.

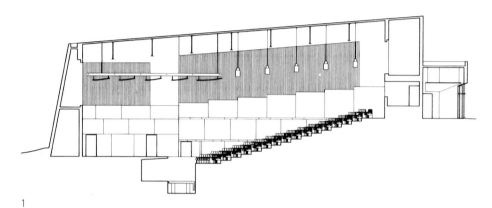

1

2

3

4

5

1 Section
2 View of percussion and performance wing from great meadow
3 Ravine
4&5 Recital hall
Photography: Timothy Hursley

Science Facility Three—Math, Technology and Science Education, Western Washington University

Zimmer Gunsul Frasca Partnership

Completion: September 1996

Location: Bellingham, Washington, USA

Client: Western Washington University

Area: 3,729 square metres; 40,144 square feet

Structure: Concrete; steel

Materials: Cast-in-place concrete; brick; glass curtainwall

Cost: US$16 million

This 3,729 square metre (40,144 square foot), building provides classroom and laboratory space for the Department of Science Education; five lecture halls for university-wide use; and a state-of-the-art learning resource centre for the training of science teachers. The building is set back on its site at the entrance to the Science Quad to create a large plaza, which serves as the forecourt to the building.

A primary goal of the facility in the training of prospective science teachers is an emphasis on learning through investigation and experimentation, instead of textbooks and lectures only. Toward that end, a variety of technological features are incorporated into the classrooms and lecture halls.

The two-level building is designed in response to its programmatic components, as well as to accommodate a 5.5 metre (18 foot) slope of the site. The plan is organised

horizontally into a series of three zones: the public zone located on the plaza side of the building, contains a glass-enclosed two-storey arcade/gallery, building lobby and primary waiting area outside the lecture halls; the second zone is the teaching zone, including five lecture halls at the first level, the Learning Resource Center and teaching labs on the second floor; and the third zone accommodates support areas including the prep and storage areas, the building's mechanical and electrical rooms, and faculty offices.

Science Facility Three mediates between the brick architecture of the north campus and the concrete architecture of the south campus by weaving together these materials.

1–4 Science Facility Three
Photography: Strode Eckert Photographic

1

2

3

4

Summerlin Medical Center and Facilities Site Master Planning
RTKL International Ltd.

Completion: February 1996

Location: Las Vegas, Nevada, USA

Client: Universal Health Services Inc.

Area: 37,810 square metres; 407,000 square feet

Structure: Exterior insulating finish system

Materials: Exterior insulating finish system; red sandstone; glass; metal

RTKL International Ltd. was commissioned to design this 37,810 square metre (407,000 square foot), progressive medical facility in four phases, to allow for the rapid growth of the Las Vegas community of Summerlin. The master plan ensures that the Center's final overall impression will be greater than the sum of each phase. In turn, each component of the Center is unique, yet aptly refers to the whole through unified planning, forms and materials.

The hospital's initial phase includes a medical office building, a diagnostic and surgical centre and a cancer treatment centre. Subsequent phases include an acute-care hospital, sub-acute (skilled nursing) facility, and additional medical offices and outpatient facilities.

The mass of the medical office building is broken into three precast concrete forms which are held apart by glass and metal panel planes. The masses rest on a base of red sandstone retaining walls and free-standing columns. The diagnostic and surgical centre and the cancer treatment centre repeat the same vocabulary. A sloping profiled metal screen wall separates the Facility's public and private functions and rises to meet the site of future hospital functions.

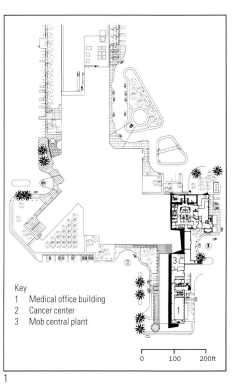

Key
1 Medical office building
2 Cancer center
3 Mob central plant

0   100   200ft

1

2

3

4

1 Site plan
2&3 Exterior
4 Interior seating area
Photography: Hedrich-Blessing; RTKL Associates Inc. (4)

Public

Arizona Science Center

Antoine Predock Architect
in association with Cornoyer Hedrick Architects, Phoenix

Completion: April 1997

Location: Phoenix, Arizona, USA

Client: City of Phoenix

Area: 11,789 square metres; 126,900 square feet

Structure: Concrete; masonry; steel

Materials: Cast-in-place concrete; stucco; aluminium panels; steel

Cost: US$16 million

Awards: 1997 AIA Arizona Merit Award
1997 AIA Western Mountain Region Merit Award

Located at the edge of historic Heritage Park Square along a major vehicular arterial to downtown Phoenix, the Arizona Science Center provides a pedestrian crossover into Heritage Park Square from the south, while establishing itself as a destination for occupation and exploration.

The Center includes 2,787 square metres (30,000 square feet), of exhibit galleries, a demonstration theatre, a special format film theatre and a planetarium along with educational and support facilities. The building blends, in an abstract manner, influences from regional and local history, geological events, site specific concerns and urban opportunities. Silhouette and horizon, combine with light, water, reflection, and mirage creating a processional and

participatory architecture: beginning with a descent into the coolness of the earth at the entry courtyard, and culminating in a celebration of the sky at the peak gallery with its celestial viewing terrace. While urban, it possesses a post-cataclysmic science fiction ambience. The building is intended to stimulate a multitude of responses: at times powerful visceral connections to this desert place, while at other times seem as ephemeral as a mirage.

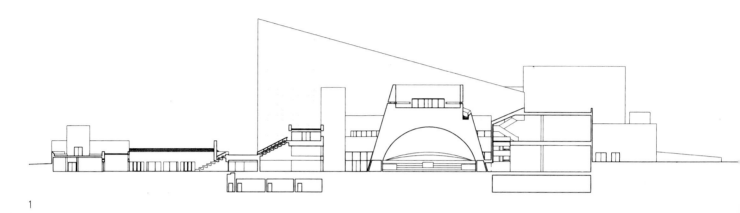

1

2

1 Longitudinal building section
2 Evening view from north
3 Looking west over entry court at dawn
4 Star mountain terrace
5 Exhibit terrace from west
Photography: courtesy Antoine Predock Architect

3

4

5

Cube (Shiroishi City Cultural and Athletic Activity Center)

Hideto Horiike + Urtopia

Completion: May 1997
Location: Miyagi, Japan
Client: Shiroishi City
Area: 30,756 square metres; 331,065 square feet
Structure: Steel trusses
Materials: Aluminium; glass; concrete

This is a complex facility focusing on the function of 'Messe' planned in the newly developed area where the urban context of the once existed land form and history has been discontinued. The clear aerial division in this city is to be called the 'Civitas Parallelus'.

Having the site next to the Shinkansen (Bullet train) station, the concern was how to respond to the super-scaled sense of 'velocity' brought by the Shinkansen.

Groping for a powerful form to vanquish the sensation of velocity, they reached the simple geometric form which easily responds to the linear form of the Shinkansen and the linear compositional axes found in the urban structure, which also relates to the sense of simplicity and conscientiousness of the 'Bushido' (Samurai spirit).

The transparently glazed concert hall, which will be the first trial in the world, will be devised to face the exterior environment as an amphitheatre through the transparent wall in the 'piano nobile' level.

It is expected that this transparent skin will manifest to the internal festiveness beside the reflecting urban situation in the outside of its observical plane ie the 'doublage' effect of glazing screens to deliver the visual information.

Cube, which is expected to be the leading project of the city planning in Shiroishi, causes an image of a factory or manufacturing plant, because it is planned as the concept of a sphere as a receptor and an incubator of productions in the information, ray and electronic semiology.

1 South section
2 West elevation
3 Night view of entrance
4 Exterior view of south elevation

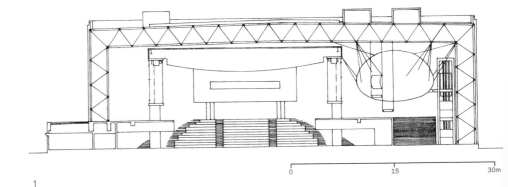

1

2

3

4

5

6

5 Main lobby ('piano nobile')
6 Concert hall
7 Lavatory
8 Dressing room
Photography: Hiroaki Tanaka

7

8

Fukui City Museum of Art

Kisho Kurokawa architect & associates

Completion: September 1996
Location: Fukui, Japan
Client: Fukui City
Area: 34,000 square metres; 365,985 square feet
Structure: Steel; reinforced concrete
Materials: Glass; aluminium panels
Cost ¥2,600,000,000

The Fukui City Museum of Art was designed to provide the people of Fukui City a place to appreciate art and an opportunity to engage in creative activity. Located on the outskirts of the city, the architecture of the Museum blends effortlessly into the greenery of the adjacent 4-hectare park; the view of the centre from the park is a priority.

The cultural centre is a combined fine-art exhibition and performance-art facility including a public atelier, library and an auditorium with seating for up to 1,000. The fine-art exhibition permanently houses the works of the late sculptor Hiroatsu Takada and the library contains extensive material on the life of the actor Shigeyoshi Uno, who was born in Fukui. A three-storey common entrance hall, cafeteria and lecture auditorium is situated between these two facilities.

The entire structure is sheathed with a glass curtain wall and all of the gallery passageways are connected to exterior exhibition spaces and the park, creating an intermediate space between nature and the building.

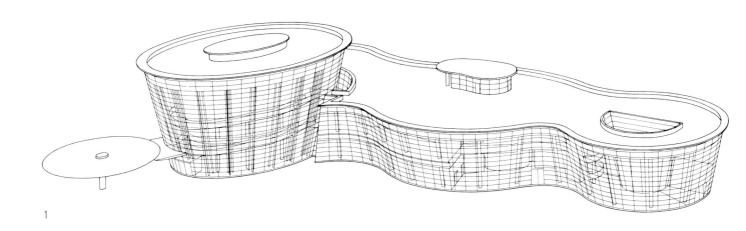

1

2

3

4

1   Axonometric
2&3   General view
4   Eaves of entrance

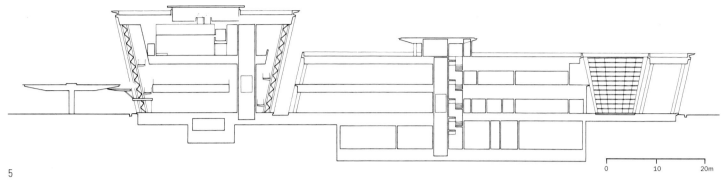

5

6

5   Section
6   Children's atelier
7   See-through elevator, spiral stairs
8   Looking up slope of entrance wing
9   Atelier 1
Photography: Tomio Ohashi

7

8

9

Jordan Hall at the New England Conservatory of Music

Ann Beha Associates, Inc.

Completion: January 1996

Location: Boston, Massachusetts, USA

Client: The New England Conservatory of Music

Area: 4,645 square metres; 50,000 square feet

Structure: Steel; concrete

Materials: Wood; metal

Cost: US$8.2 million

Awards: 1996 Preservation Award,
The Massachusetts Historical Commission
1996 Preservation Commendation, Victorian Society
in America
1996 Preservation Award, Boston Preservation
Alliance

Jordan Hall at the New England Conservatory of Music is a national historic landmark renowned for its beauty, intimacy and outstanding acoustics. The concert hall serves as a major centre for musical performances and as Boston's teaching and rehearsal hall for America's oldest Conservatory of Music. After nearly a century of constant use, the concert hall was aged and inefficient with outdated systems, worn finishes and few patron services. In January 1996, a US$8.2 million restoration was completed, providing the amenities of a modern concert hall while retaining both acoustic and architectural brilliance. Key project features include: researching and restoring the original design and integration of modern

technology, including lighting systems and code compliance features; access for the disabled; and new patron services which serve the entire community.

The project has been widely acclaimed for its stunning results and technical innovations. With new climate control, the concert hall's season has expanded from nine to 12 months, creating additional revenue and outreach. This season, coupled with new audio/visual equipment, allows for new types of presentations and new audiences. This restoration has moved the concert hall into the 21st century by preserving the past, and welcoming the future.

1

1   Expanded entry, with accesible entrance
2   Renovated foyer, incorporating new accessible
    entrance
3   View towards stage after renovation
4   View of audience seating after restoration
Photography: Nick Wheeler/Wheeler Photographics

2

3

4

Kum Ho Art Gallery
Tai Soo Kim Partners

Completion: April 1997
Location: Seoul, Korea
Client: Kum Ho Foundation
Area: 2,248 square metres; 24,198 square feet
Structure: Steel
Materials: Granite; lead coated copper
Cost: $5.3 million

The new art gallery is on a small site across from the old Imperial Palace in Seoul. Its mission is to exhibit the work of talented unknown artists. Zoning regulations in the historic palace district prohibit building heights which exceed that of the adjacent palace. In order to fit the program within the 14 metre (46 foot) height, three of the seven levels of the building are underground, including parking, which is accessed through a portal in the street elevation.

Client and architect desired a building that would complement the old Imperial Palace. The architect achieved a respectful dialogue with the old palace wall and with its more modern neighbours. The long continuous palace wall of stone is capped by a darker tiled roof. The gallery's exterior is composed of a similar sized stone and is capped by a darker band, consisting of windows for the administrative floor.

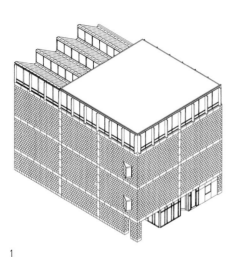

1

2

3

4

5

6

1   Axonometric
2   New gallery
3   Facade
4&6   Galleries
5   Central open stair
Photography: Timothy Hursley

Lake Biwa Museum

Nikken Sekkei
in association with Shiga Prefectural Government

Completion: July 1996

Location: Shiga, Japan

Client: Shiga Prefectural Government

Area: 13,208 square metres; 142,174 square feet

Structure: Steel reinforced concrete; reinforced concrete; steel

Materials: Ceramic and porcelain tiles on reinforced concrete structure

Lake Biwa Museum, which was conceived as a facility for 'ideal coexistence between lakes and human beings' with environmental conservation as its main theme, has an adjacent aquarium which boasts the largest range of fresh water fish in Japan. The site is in Kusatsu, on the Karasuma Peninsula near the banks of Lake Biwa, where the dynamic beauty of the lake stands out against the backdrop of the surrounding mountains. Various natural features of the lake are echoed in the building design in an attempt to merge with Mother Nature.

The Museum shares a front garden with UNEP International Environmental Technology Center, Shiga which stands to the south of the Museum. The two buildings directly face each other, and their sense of massiveness is thereby alleviated. On the lake side, the public space accommodates a lobby and a restaurant, which looks out onto the outdoor exhibition area and is topped with a huge, 120 metre (393 foot) wide crescent-shaped flat roof inspired by the bilge of a 'Maruko-bune', a log ship with a unique shape that traditionally cruised Lake Biwa. The roof symbolises the wide expanse of the lake.

1   Elevation
2   North elevation from Lake Biwa
3   West elevation seen from lawn square
Opposite:
    Large-sized wooden roof and north elevation

1

0   25   50m

2

3

Opposite:

Spacious restaurant

6   Old *Japanese-style* private house is displayed in cylindrical exhibition room

7   Atrium lobby commanding view of Lake Biwa and surrounding mountains

8   Atrium lobby

Photography: Kiyohiko Higashide

6

7

8

Okazaki Art and Historical Museum

Akira Kuryu and Associates Co., Ltd

Completion: July 1996

Location: Okazaki City, Aichi Prefecture, Japan

Client: Okazaki City

Area: 6,444 square metres; 69,364 square feet

Structure: Reinforced concrete; steel

Materials: Concrete; granite

Cost: US$43 million

Awards: Aichi Architectural Award
Okazaki Townscape Award

The Museum site which inclines to the edge of a pond is surrounded by a lush natural environment with rich greenery and the museum is loved by the citizens as a place of recreation and relaxation. Visible above the ground surface are an atrium which also serves as the entrance hall to the Museum and a restaurant with light-weight roofing. The restaurant provides a delightful view of the surface of the pond with the surrounding greenery on the hill as well as an unobstructed view of Okazaki city.

The exhibition at the Okazaki Art and Historical Museum is not confined to the facilities inside the building. On the contrary, the Museum presents objects for exhibition in the natural environment around it, too. A total design of the site including the landscape was advocated, aiming at realising a 'museum in the form of a park' or a 'park in the form of a museum'.

The Okazaki Art and Historical Museum is sufficiently equipped for the general public, with relaxing facilities such as a museum shop and a restaurant , as well as the relaxing harmony which exists between the Museum facilities and the greenery-rich environment. The total atmosphere of this Museum introduces a 'new type of museum integrated with the environment', representing its policy of defining a museum newly as a 'place to enjoy' or a 'museum garden' generously open to all.

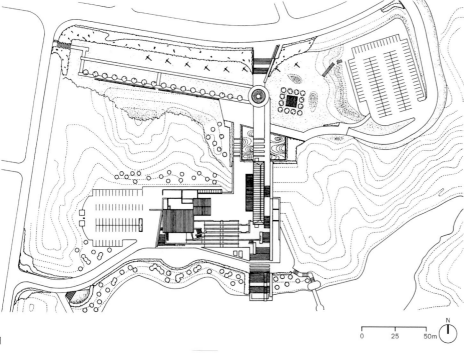

0   25   50m   N

1

1 Site plan
2 Birds-eye view
3 Building view

2   3

4

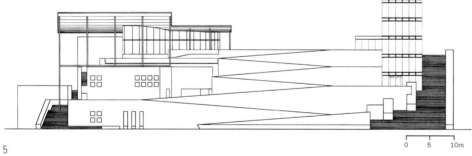

5

0 5 10m

4 Atrium
5 South elevation
Opposite:
    Roof and slope
Photography: SS Nagoya Co., Ltd (1); Nakasaka & Partners Inc

Portland Art Museum

Ann Beha Associates, Inc.

Completion: January 1996
Location: Portland, Oregon, USA
Client: Portland Art Museum
Area: 6,750 square metres; 72,658 square feet
Structure: Reinforced concrete
Materials: Brick; travertine cladding; steel
Cost: US$3 million

The Portland Art Museum, comprised of three buildings originally designed by Pietro Belluschi, is the heart of Oregon's cultural resources. Ann Beha Associates has completed the first phase of renovations at the Museum, including the renovation of the 1930s Belluschi buildings and the adjacent 9,290 square metre (100,000 square foot) landmark Masonic Temple building. The project introduced new visitor services, gallery improvements, climate control and features which support building preservation and the care and exhibition of collections. Ann Beha Associates was Architect for the Museum's recent record-breaking 'Imperial Tombs of China' exhibit. The firm is currently engaged in planning for the Museum expansion into its third Belluschi building, and further renovations to the adjacent Masonic Temple to serve as a centre for museum operations and other Portland arts' organisations.

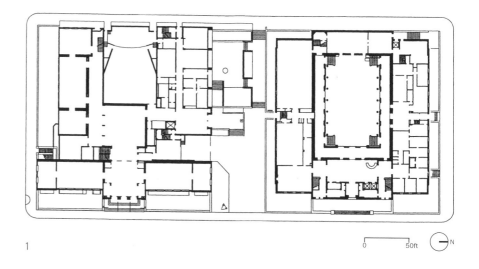

1

0   50ft   N

2

3

4

5

1   Floor plan
2   Exterior of original Portland Art Museum
3   Renovated entry foyer
4   New skylights above restored sculpture court
5   View of renovated exhibit gallery
Photography: Hewitt-Garrison Architectural Photography

Queensland Conservatorium of Music

Bligh Voller Nield Pty Ltd

Completion: June 1996

Location: South Bank, Queensland, Australia

Client: Queensland Government on behalf of Griffith University

Area: 17,500 square metres; 188,375 square feet

Structure: Brick; metal cladding

Materials: Rendered brick; corrugated metal; timber parquetry

Cost: $26.8 million

Awards: 1997 Royal Australian Institute of Architects, Queensland Chapter Education Award 1997 Metal Building Awards, Certificate of Merit 1997 Dulux Colour Awards, Commendation for Commercial Exterior

This new and highly complex facility situated at Brisbane's Cultural Precinct houses the Queensland Conservatorium of Music, Griffith University and is also the new home of Opera Queensland. Although predominantly an educational building it is also an important public venue. A range of teaching studios, lecture theatres, performance spaces, rehearsal and practice rooms, recording facilities, offices and a large library are provided and the special needs of the Conservatorium's piano, orchestral, voice, percussion, jazz and electronics departments have all been incorporated.

The centrepiece of the building is a 600-seat auditorium which was required to meet world-class acoustic performance standards. It features a movable soundshell, which can vary acoustic performance to suit the normally incompatible requirements of opera and concert performances, and a fully operational fly-tower.

A dramatic foyer space separates the performance and rehearsal facilities from the three-storey teaching wing which is arranged around an internal courtyard.

The design solution relies on bold massing, both to reduce the apparent bulk of the building and to create a provocative, striking and bold external form.

1 Site plan
2 East elevation
3 North elevation facing Performing Arts Centre
4 East elevation, parklands entrance
5 Main foyer
6 Main auditorium in concert mode
Photography: David Sandison

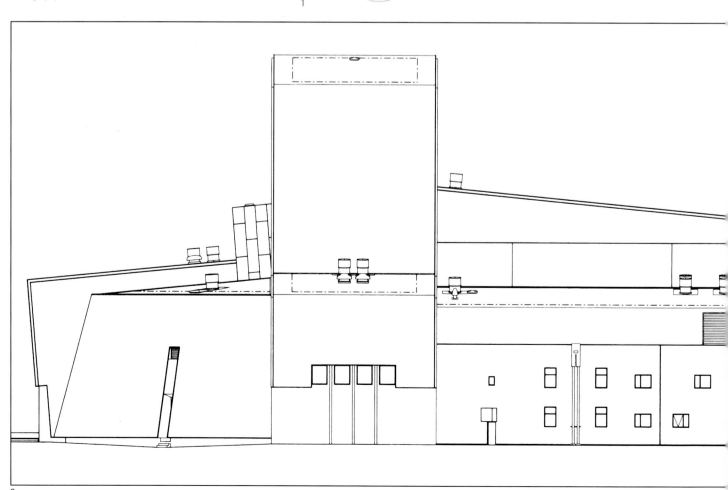

1

2

3

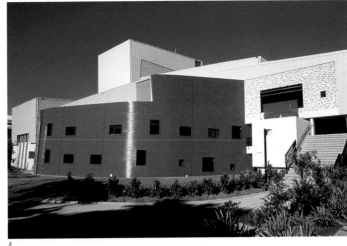

4

5

6

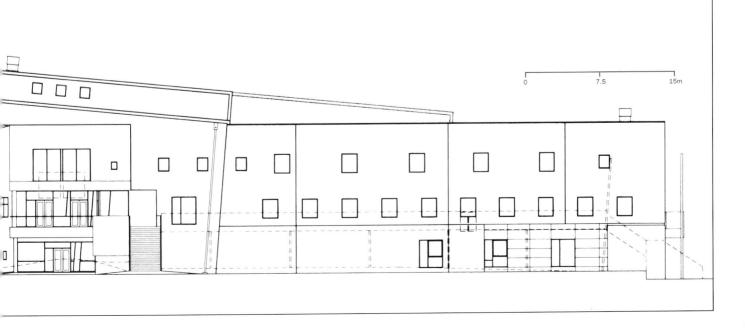

0   7.5   15m

Shiga Kogen Roman Art Museum

Kisho Kurokawa architect & associates

Completion: March 1996
Location: Nagano, Japan
Client: Yamanouchi Town
Area: 2,984 square metres; 32,121 square feet
Structure: Reinforced concrete; wood
Materials: Glass curtain wall; exposed concrete
Cost: ¥1,090,000,000

The Art Museum is situated at the base of Kanabayashi Ski Run in Shiga Kogen Ski Resort, which is host to the Nagano Olympics. A small brook flows by the site which is blessed with abundant nature. The town of Yamanouchi gave birth to Chinese-style painting and this museum will house some 70 pieces created by Katei Kodama and his school. In addition, a donation of Edo-, Meiji-, and Taisho-era artificats, collected by the eminent artist Nobutaka Oka and his forefathers will be exhibited together with a collection of Roman and antique iridescent glass. Part of the Roman glass collection is placed in specially designed conical glass cases.

The fragmented elliptical shape of the structure introduces elements of light, shadow, wind and landscape into the spatial composition. A stream winds its way around the building which has been designed with a gently sloping roof to prevent the accumulation of snow. The museum shop and cafe are housed in a transparent, cone-shaped structure.

Although sponsored by the town, the Art Museum will also be assisted by the cooperation of local citizens' groups.

1   Museum entrance facade
2   Night view
3   Looking up roof light of exhibition gallery
4   Axonometric
5   View of Museum entrance

1

2

3

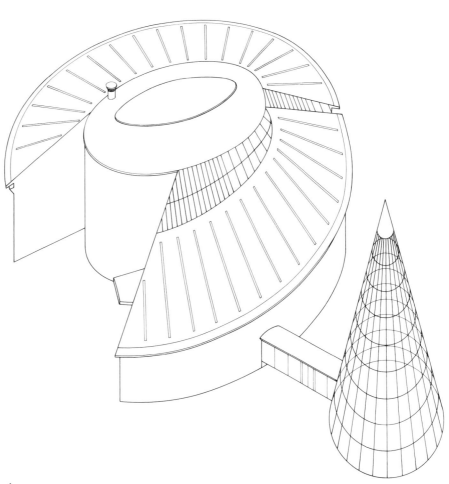

4

5

221

6

6   Conical exhibition cases, exhibition gallery
7   Service counter of Museum shop
8   First floor plan
9   First floor lobby
Photography: Tomio Ohashi

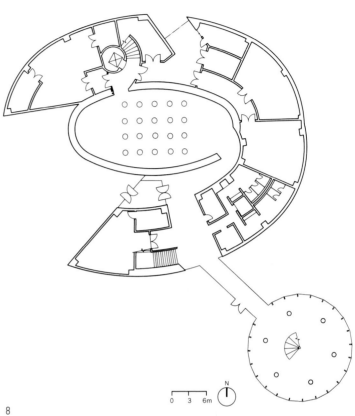

0   3   6m

N

7   8

9

223

Skirball Cultural Center

Moshe Safdie and Associates Inc.

Completion: April 1996
Location: Los Angeles, California, USA
Client: Hebrew Union College
Area: 11,600 square metres; 125,000 square feet
Structure: Cast-in-place concrete
Materials: Granite; stainless steel; aluminium; slate
Cost: US$34 million

The Skirball Museum and Cultural Center stands at the base of the Santa Monica Mountains off the 405 freeway, a midpoint between the Los Angeles basin and the San Fernando Valley. The 11,600 square metre (125,000 square foot), building houses a museum of the Jewish-American experience, a conference centre, an educational centre, classrooms and meeting rooms, a resource centre, and a 350-seat auditorium. The 2,500 square metre (27,000 square foot), communications centre and event hall is scheduled to begin construction in 1997.

Responding to the site's dramatic topography, the building forms a series of longitudinal wings tucked against the steep natural slope. An amphitheatre and the back wall of the communications centre buttress an unstable area of the mountain against mud slides. Courtyards are

oriented towards views of the hills and canyon beyond. The main outdoor gathering space, a shaded water court for conferences, events and receptions, is defined by a double-height, trellised arcade. From the courtyard, a stair leads to a sculpture garden and a footpath that curves around the hill. A lookout and meditation pavilion, as yet unbuilt, will serve as a beacon for the complex with a panoramic view.

The building's exposed concrete frame supports stainless steel infill panels that contrast with and reflect the alternating pink granite and warm-coloured concrete bands of the base. Precast concrete trellises, covered in wisteria, extend over outdoor walkways and courtyards. At sunset, the stainless steel vaulted roofs of the building glow against the darkening Santa Monica hills.

1

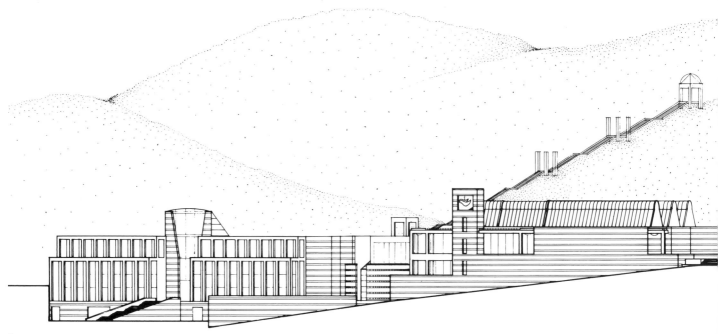

2

5

1 Exterior of complex, night
2 Site elevation
3 Exterior detail of entrance
4 Exterior of courtyard
5 Exterior detail

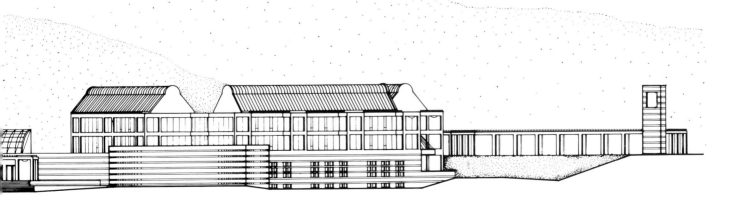

0   20   40m

6 Exterior of courtyard
7 Exterior showing trellises
8 Courtyard at night
9 Exterior building detail
Photography: Timothy Hursley

6

7

8

Sterling and Francine Clark Art Institute

Ann Beha Associates, Inc.

Completion: August 1996
Location: Williamstown, Massachusetts, USA
Client: Sterling and Francine Clark Art Institute
Area: 9,500 square metres; 102,260 square feet
Structure: Reinforced concrete; steel
Materials: Red granite; wood; bluestone;
birch wood
Cost: US$4.8 million

Set within a 122-acre campus in the Berkshire Hills, the Clark Art Institute houses one of the nation's premier collections of 19th century European and American art. With Ann Beha Associates' 1996 renovations and additions to the Clark's main building, designed in 1973 by Pietro Belluschi in association with The Architects Collaborative (TAC), the Institute has entered a new era of scholarship, exhibitions, and public outreach.

The design challenge called for finding additional space within the footprint of Belluschi's granite-clad structure. The solution carefully fitted three additions into the building, within, above and below existing exterior courtyards. They provide a new special exhibitions gallery,

a new multi-purpose dining and gathering space, new compact library storage, and new classroom and office space for the Williams College graduate program in the History of Art and the Getty Information Institute. Finish materials selected by Ann Beha Associates respond to the building's strong modernist vocabulary, while still establishing a distinct identity for the new work.

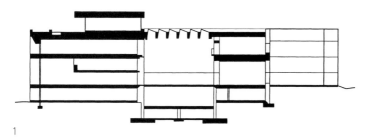

1

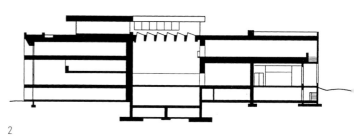

2

3

1 Building section, before additions
2 Building section, after additions
3 New offices, multi-purpose room and expanded special exhibition gallery
4 New special exhibition gallery and stairway
5 New special exhibition gallery
6 New multi-purpose room
Photography: courtesy Ann Beha Associates, Inc.

5

Teylers Museum, Haarlem, The Netherlands

Hubert-Jan Henket bna architecten

Completion: February 1996

Location: Teylers Museum, Haarlem,
The Netherlands

Client: Teylers Foundation

Area: 7,000 square metres; 75,350 square feet

Structure: Steel columns; laminated timber beams

Materials: Glass; steel; timber

Cost: US$5 million

The Teylers Museum (1780) is the oldest in The Netherlands and a clear example of the ideals of the Enlightenment, being both archive and laboratory of scientific objects and works of art. Until the recent extensions, the museum was untouched since the 1870s, resulting in a beautiful time machine where atmospheres of the various periods are still in tact.

To strengthen this unique quality, the old is visually kept untouched. For example, the new exhibition hall is kept separate to guarantee the original daylight quality in the fossils and instruments' room. Perpendicular to the existing axis, a new one is introduced to connect the new offices in the refurbished building 'Zegelwaarde' with the 'Oval Room'. Although the new extensions have their own character, new details, materials and colours are related to the intentions of the old.

1

2

1   Cross section
2   Link between new building and old museum
3   Glazed passage between old museum and new
    exhibition hall
Opposite:
    'Oval Room' in main museum
Photography: Sybolt Voeten; Martin Zegel (opposite)

3

Two Rivers Landing

Schwartz/Silver Architects Inc

Completion: July 1996

Location: Easton, Pennsylvania, USA

Area: 22,000 square metres; 236,813 square feet

Structure: Brick; steel

Materials: Brick; steel

Cost: US$6 million

Awards: Boston Society of Architects Honor Award for Design Excellence

Two Rivers Landing is the core of the revitalisation of downtown Easton. Located in two former department store buildings, the Landing houses a new visitors' and activities centre for Binney & Smith, makers of Crayola Crayons and other art products; The National Canal Museum; and a visitors' centre that introduces the attractions and resources of the Delaware and Lehigh Canal National Heritage Corridor.

Museum design and urban planning specialists Schwartz/Silver Architects recognised that Two Rivers Landing had a dual role to play if it was to be a catalyst for revitalising Easton's downtown: the museums had to attract people and the architecture of the complex had to energise the area.

In response, the architects created new brick and glass facades that strengthen the character of the downtown and create a strong focal point for Center Square.

Two entrances are lined by a lobby which forms an internal street providing convenient access from the parking garage to downtown shops and offices to passers-by and business people.

Circulation in the complex is placed along the perimeter of the building so that the activity within the building can be seen and appreciated from the street. Stairs are revealed by large windows, a glass enclosed bridge flies over the entry court, and a glass elevator ferries visitors between floors.

Visitation has exceeded all expectations and the project has proved a critical and popular success.

1

2

1   View from Center Square to inner court
2   View from Center Square
3   View to Pine Street entry and admissions desk at lobby

3

4

4 Entry to Crayola factory
5 View of bridge within inner court
Photography: courtesy Schwartz/Silver Architects Inc

5

Broadway Mongkok

Tonkin Design Limited

Completion: April 1996

Location: Mongkok, Kowloon, Hong Kong

Client: Edko Films Ltd

Area: 279 square metres; 3,000 square feet

Structure: Steel

Materials: Red fabric

Cost: HK$1.1 million

Awards: 1996 Chartered Society of Designers Display and Exhibition Category

Mongkok Broadway Cinema needed a powerful idea to compete with the chaos of the street and to put Broadway cinemas on the map. The designer's answer was 'red'. This simple move turned up the volume on the cinema's neon neighbours and became a walk-in sign. The extreme but simple move of making a glowing red walk-in billboard complements and competes successfully against the background of Mongkok's neon clamour.

Having employed the traditional red colour of theatre the designer further explored the iconography of cinema in a journey that began with the idea of light. The whole foyer glows through backlit red glass and fireproof red fabric. Behind the glass is a film strip of cinema information and billboards under a tickertape banner of "now, next, soon". Behind the fabric are large steel numbers (taken from the final countdown seconds of a film reel) backlit to project shadows on to the fabric. As the city breeze moves the fabric back and forth the numbers fall in and out of focus while the scale numbers relates to the grand order of the big screen; it also relates to city scale.

Black/grey tiles on the floor effectively continue the street into the lobby space. The red taxi queue in front of the foyer further blends the space with the city from which its inspiration comes.

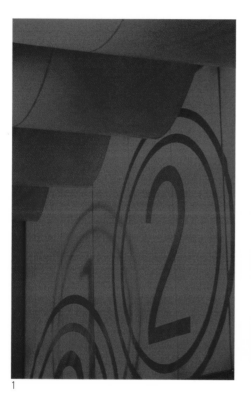

1

2

3

4

1   Red fabric
2   Billboards
3   Entrance
4   Poster wall
Photography: courtesy Tonkin Design Limited

236

Broadway Yuen Long

Tonkin Design Limited

Completion: August 1996
Location: Yuen Long, New Territories, Hong Kong
Client: Edko Films Ltd
Area: 1,115 square metres; 12,000 square feet
Structure: Reinforced concrete
Materials: Red spray wall; stainless steel
Cost: HK$3.3 million

The act of going to the cinema is turned into drama in itself at Yuen Long Broadway Cinema. Glowing red walls of images and glass draw customers into the red triple volume space of the cinema lounge. The ceiling undulates, compressing and expanding the visitors view towards a 10 metre (33 foot) tall James Bond.

Scale, colour and light are the key components in the designers play of image and experience. Huge countdown numbers taken from early film reels are projected obliquely across the space emphasising the three dimensional nature of the big red room while blurring the distinction between floor, wall and ceiling.

All pre-theatre spaces are in 'hot red', important elements are highlighted in white and the auditorium is all black. The designer imagined sitting in the auditorium was like being inside a pin hole camera; the only addition to the blackened space being the sharks' gill lights that heighten the nervy pre-movie anticipation of the darkened room.

Lighting in the foyer lounge comes in the form of blob lamps and glowing chairs which, along with the projected numbers and flood-lit James Bond, complete the spectacle.

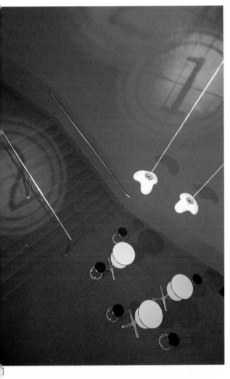

1&2   Cinema lobby
3   Route to upper level
Photography: Jonathan Pile/Mike Tonkin

Michael Hue Williams Gallery

John Pawson

Completion: June 1996
Location: London, UK
Client: Michael Hue Williams
Area: 120 square metres; 1,292 square feet

The gallery, located on the upper level of a shared commercial building, is the product of a tightly organised plan that accommodates all the elements specified in the brief: storage, and office space, as well as the necessary gallery area in which to display work to clients and visitors, without any sense of crowding, or compromise. There are windows in the front and back walls, which form the main organisational element.

Visitors are admitted from a communal staircase and reach the gallery after encountering the reception area, turning through 90 degrees, and passing the library and secondary office space on one side, and the window wall on the other. The route provides a suitable decompression chamber, a buffer between the outside world, and the art displayed here. The gallery is inserted as a cube within a cube, which opens in turn into the main storage area, and then the daylit principal office which serves as a second gallery space. The result is an interior which provides the maximum of quiet, well-lit gallery space in which art can be viewed in a sympathetic setting, whilst also accommodating work and storage space.

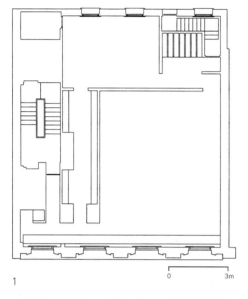

1

0   3m

2

3

1   Floor plan
2   View of entrance from gallery
3   Gallery office
4   Gallery library
Photography: Richard Glover

4

Noh Stage in the Forest—Toyama Center for Traditional Performing Arts

Kengo Kuma & Associates

Completion: May 1996

Location: Toyoma, Miyagi Prefecture, Japan

Client: Toyoma-Cho Miyagi Prefecture

Area: 1,700 square metres; 18,299 square feet

Structure: Steel; wood; reinforced concrete

Materials: Slate; cryptmerika japonica; tatami flooring

Cost: ¥195,000,000

Awards:1997 Grand Prize of AIJ (Architectural Institute of Japan) for Design

The plan was to create a stage that would open onto the beautiful natural surrounding of the forest rather than create a closed public space after the style of the Noh Theater.

The seating in front of the stage (called the *shomenkensho*) is designed as a transparent space with tatami flooring. When a play is performed, the glass partitions are all removed and a completely transparent space emerges, set off by the horizontal elements of the thin roof and the floor.

This space functions not only as a frame through which to view the forest and the Noh, but is also used on a daily basis by local residents to practice the tea ceremony and Japanese dancing. Thus every space is open to the forest and to the town as well. In order to emphasise this openness, a light wooden latticework was employed rather than more substantial material for the wall between the stage and the town. This latticework functions as an 'interface' between the 'Stage in the Forest' and the town.

1   Site plan
2   View from the 'shirasu' (stepped sitting space)
3   Detail of facade
4   View from east
Photography: courtesy Kengo Kuma & Associates

1

3

4

Recreational

Evercrest White Cove Resort

G&W Architects, Engineers, Project Development Consultants

Completion: December 1996

Location: Nasugbu, Batangas, Philippines

Client: Gotesco Properties, Inc.

Area: 4,152 square metres; 44,693 square feet

Structure: Precast concrete

Materials: Stone cladding; tile

Spread across prime beachfront, this resort is part of a worldwide chain of resort hotels catering to the international market for businessmen and vacationists.

Evercrest White Cove Resort consists of an array of recreational and sports' facilities, a hotel, exclusively furnished cabana units and a dancing water display feature.

Its 21 maisonettes, 17 apartment blocks, five villas and a five-storey hotel with 250 rooms were inspired by the Philippines' 'Bahay na Bato' architecture. Elements are simple, functional and accessible. The resort units were placed along the land's contour to flow with the natural terrain, thus achieving organic unity with the environment.

Other structures and facilities include a casino, water sports' facilities, tennis courts, basketball courts, a swimming pool, gym-spa, restaurant, a business centre and a helipad.

1&2   Apartment facade

3&5   Living room

4   Interior seen from dining area leading to bedroom

Photography: RRL Photography, Inc

2

3

4

5

Ford Centre for the Performing Arts

Moshe Safdie and Associates Inc.

Completion: January 1996

Location: Vancouver, B.C., Canada

Client: Live Entertainment of Canada, Inc.

Area: 5,575 square metres; 60,020 square feet

Structure: Steel

Materials: Stone; metal shingles; glass

Cost: C$18 million

Conceived in the tradition of the great Broadway theatres, this 1,800-seat theatre occupies a compact site located in the middle of a city block. On the street facade, the stone base of the building cuts away to reveal the gently arching volume of the auditorium within. Small metal shingles reflect the changing skies and the urban evening's neon glow.

At the south end of the facade, a five-storey glass cone forms the theatre entrance, parting the opaque street wall and breaking the cornice line of the facade. A glowing pinnacle by night and a vertical window by day, the transparent cone both lights and exposes the sequence of curving, layered lobby spaces within. During the day, the glass cone and a continuous south-facing, vertical window introduce light and views of the surrounding city to

matinee crowds. In the evening, the interior drama of theatre-goers radiates over the street. To the north end of the elevation, an arch framing the stage becomes a live electronic marquee in the skyline.

The public sequence through the theatre begins at the street level entrance lobby and proceeds up a series of dramatic stairs that fill a grand oval atrium. A faceted four-storey mirrored wall rises with the curving stair, fragmenting and reflecting the activity of three upper lobbies served by bars and lounges for the orchestra and balconies. Within the performance hall, the intimate scale of the balcony and dress circle is achieved by a maximum distance from seat to stage of only 27 meters (90 feet).

1   Exterior view, day
2   Exterior view, night
3   Interior view of cone and staircase
4   Interior view of cone and staircase looking up

1

2

244

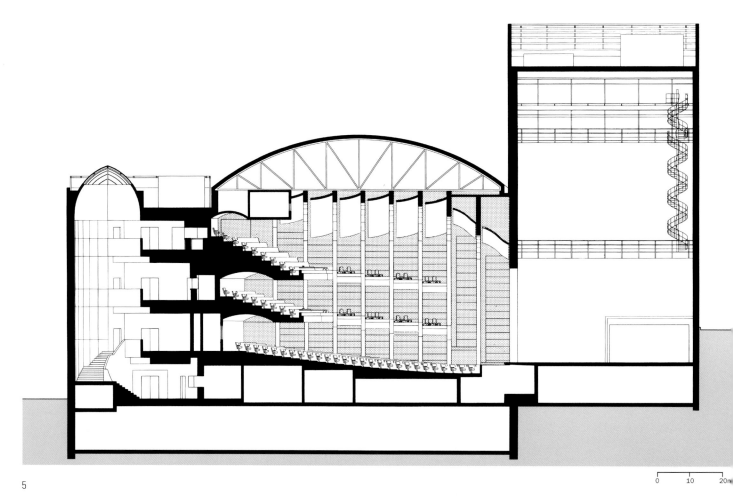

5

6

7

5   Building section
6–8   Interior view of entry staircase
9   Orchestral level
10   Interior of auditorium
Photography: Timothy Hursley

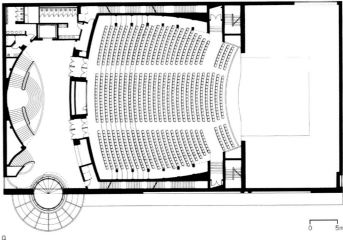

8

9

0   5m

10

247

Fujinomiya Golf Club Clubhouse

Kisho Kurokawa architect & associates

Completion: February 1997

Location: Shizuoka, Japan

Client: Fujinomiya Kanko Kaihatsu

Area: 446,660 square metres; 4.8 million square feet

Structure: Steel; reinforced concrete

Materials: Glass curtain wall; exposed concrete

Cost: ¥1,070,000,000

Fujinomiya Golf Club Clubhouse is located on a hill with breathtaking views of Mt Fuji.

To match the undulating site, the building is situated making a fractal curve; the glass exterior is frameless, emphasising the building's pellucidity.

The corner of each room has a movable glass louvre, taking advantage of the natural ventilation during the periods when the air conditioning is not being utilised. The glass exterior is slanted inward, efficiently creating shade.

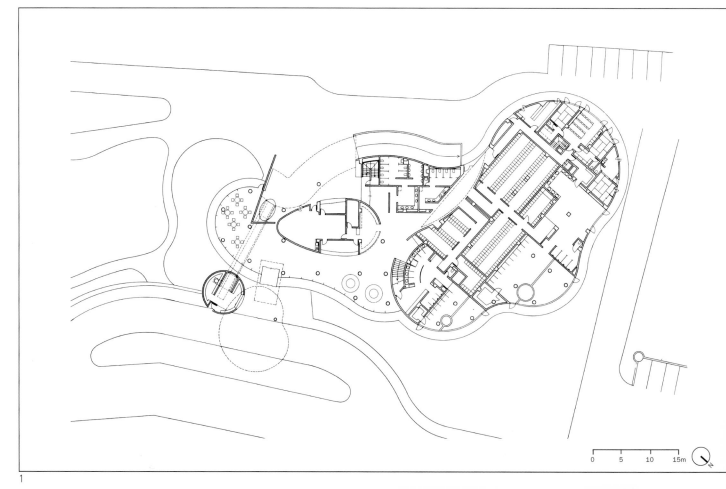

1

0   5   10   15m

2

1   Site plan
2   View of Clubhouse from the green
3   View of lounge on second floor
4   Detail of expansion joint of high-rise and low-rise
5   First floor entrance hall

3

4

5

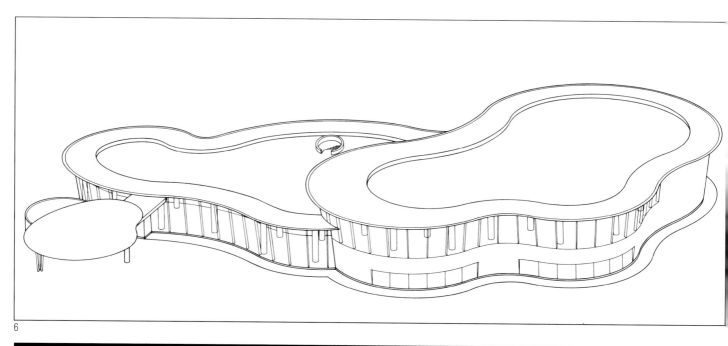

6

7

6   Axonometric
7   View of Mt Fuji from second floor lounge
8   Fractal handrail
9   Ceiling of locker-room
10 Handrail of stairs
Photography: courtesy Kisho Kurokawa architect & associates

8

9

10

Myungwheewon Sports Center

Kunchook-Moonhwa Architects & Engineers

Completion: June 1997
Location: Sadong, Ansan, Korea
Client: Myungwheewon
Area: 3,721 square metres; 40,054 square feet
Structure: Reinforced concrete
Materials: Brick
Cost: US$9.5 million

Myungwheewon established by Lee Bang-Ja, the last queen of Lee dynasty, is a human service agency for disabled children. It consists of a rehabilitation centre, school and dormitory.

Myungwheewon Sports Center which is used as a physical therapy centre, comprises indoor sports facilities and a swimming pool. Due to a very limited budget, it was essential to consider a low-cost construction system. The structure of the building exposed as a finishing material and the effort to reduce the structural weight has been given in the same reason.

To overcome the original location of the building which was hardly seen, the roof is designed as a repeated half-circle shape. On top of the roof, there is a green reinforced concrete tower showing the logo of Myungwheewon Sports Center.

The height of the building is 12 metres (39.37 feet) which is the international standard size for sports games. In order not to block the view to Myungwheewon and Myunghye schools which are two-storeys high, the ceiling height of the stand in the Sports Center is stepped down.

For this same reason, it was unavoidable to locate the Sports Center facing west. To prevent the direct heat of the sun, two facts were considered: firstly louvres and reflecting glass were used; secondly lobbies were opened through the west to the east in order to allow flow-through circulation of air.

To maintain economical costing, columns were placed in the middle. Exterior columns have gothic characteristics, giving the appearance of a modern interpretation of a flying buttress.

There is a triangular-shaped patio surrounded by the Sports Center. The architect intended to bring nature into the patio; this space serves not only for the disabled but also for their families.

1 South elevation
2 Main entrance
3 First floor plan
4 Interior view of swimming pool
5 Interior view of Sports Center
6 Interior view of aerobic room
7 Exterior view of Sports Center

Photography: courtesy Kunchook-Moonhwa Architects & Engineers

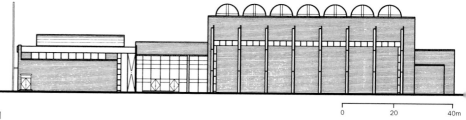

1

0   20   40m

2

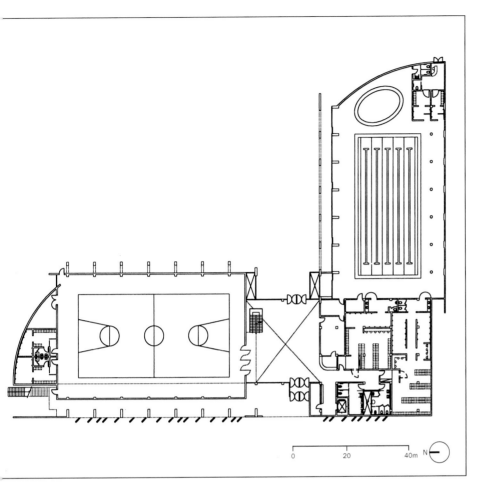

4

5

Osaka City Municipal Central Gymnasium

Nikken Sekkei
in association with Osaka Municipal Government

Completion: April 1996

Location: Osaka, Japan

Client: Osaka Municipal Government

Area: 408 square metres; 4,392 square feet

Structure: Reinforced concrete

Materials: Spherical concrete shell

Awards: Excellent Green-rich Landscaping Award

Designed as a centre for promotion and popularisation of sports in Osaka, the gymnasium is a comprehensive facility that incorporates a main arena accommodating 10,000 spectators, sub-arena, a judo hall, training rooms, meeting rooms large and small, and a sports' information centre.

Environmental conservation and effective use of the park site were the main goals of this gymnasium, which has all its facilities including the main arena, 110 metres (360 feet) in diameter and 30 metres (98 feet) in height, constructed subterraneanly. The rooftop is covered with one metre of brought-in soil, which converts the roof into a hilly, versatile park rich with greenery. The nature-friendly gymnasium adopts such energy conservation measures as the natural ventilation system which takes advantage of the heat insulating effect and constant temperature of subterranean structures, and the system which secures natural ventilation and lighting at various dry areas.

The gymnasium comprises a major challenge on the possibility of utilising a new category of urban space—namely, the huge subterranean space.

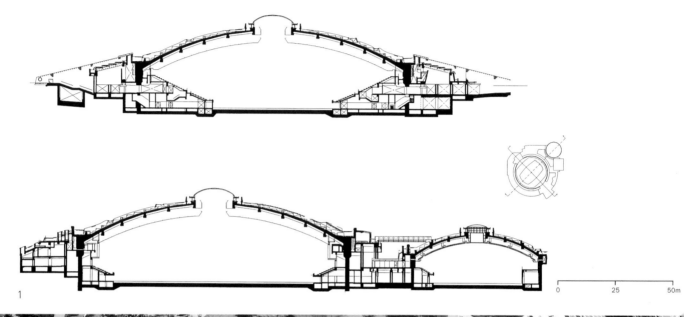

1

2

1   Sections
2   Aerial view
3   Courtyard
4   Third basement lobby
5   Main arena
6   Rooftop of main arena
Photography: Yoshiharu Matsumura

4

5

Pathé Multiplex Cinema
Architektenburo K. van Velsen B.V.

Completion: March 1996
Location: Rotterdam, The Netherlands
Client: Pathé Cinemas
Area: 8,475 square metres; 91,227 square feet
Structure: Steel
Materials: Glass; corrugated polycarbonate panels
Cost: Hfl. 20.000.000

The design for the cinema links up with the new layout of the Schouwburgplein. The large foyer in the building is interpreted as a semi-public area and thus as an extension of the square. The building has been designed as a huge light-giving sculpture, with some corners bevelled off to preserve important vistas.

The facade consists of opal and clear lexan corrugated plates around the white volumes of the cinemas, so that air pipes and fire escapes are partly hidden. The facade material provides relief; the staggered wall surfaces provide changing reflections. In the daytime, the corrugated plats allow sunlight in, while at night the building radiates light.

The cinema is standing on the foundations of the car park, a corner of which has been demolished and laid out as a restaurant. A strip of glass in the lowest level of the

building ensures that it seems to rise above the square. The cinema has seven screens, the biggest seating 760 and the smallest 200. Visitors enter through a single entrance into a hall with the box offices. Broad stairs lead to the foyer, from which all the cinemas are directly accessible, recognisable by their entrances. From this foyer the visitor is led along the stairs to the cinemas and after the film, back again. Above this platform is an abstract play of lines, of stairs and volumes, whilst below are a myriad of vistas. It was attempted when choosing the materials and colours, as well as in the details, to be restrained and thus do full justice to the spatiality.

1

1   Facade
2   Auditorium
3   Interior
4   Foyer
Photography: Kim Zwarts

3

4

Turner Field

Ellerbe Becket

Completion: April 1997

Location: Atlanta, Georgia, USA

Clients: Atlanta Olympic Committee, and the Atlanta Braves

Area: 304,800 square metres; 3.3 million square feet

Structure: Precast concrete

Materials: Brick

Cost: US$207 million

This unique facility was designed as two complete stadiums. In its first configuration, 85,000 spectators watched the 1996 Olympic track and field events, and opening and closing ceremonies. And then in April 1997, the stadium opened as the 48,000-seat Atlanta Braves baseball stadium. This approach established a precedent for future special event facilities by developing architectural and construction techniques that allow a facility to be converted for long-term use after the event.

Design features include grand terraced staircases and escalators gradually rising along both sides which allow direct access to the three seating levels of the facility, and an Olympic Torch Tower. The Tower remains in the converted facility as a memorial to the 1996 Olympics.

The team addressed sightlines, circulation and access, food service, and media requirements, as well as special seating requirements for the Olympic family, VIPs and luxury suites for baseball. In converting the facility to a baseball park, nearly 40,000 temporary seats were removed to create the baseball outfield. New seating, a stadium club, and office space for the team were all added. The Atlanta Stadium Design Team comprised Ellerbe Becket, Heery International, Rosser Fabrap International, and Williams-Russell and Johnson, Inc.

1

1–6 Turner Field
Photography: Aerial innovations

2

4

3

5

6

CentrO Oberhausen

RTKL International Ltd

Completion: September 1996

Location: Oberhausen, Düsseldorf, Germany

Client: Neue Mitte Projektentwicklung GmbH & Co. KG (the limited partnership formed by Stadium Developments Ltd and joint venture partner P&O)

Area: 1 million square metres; 10.7 million square feet

Structure: In situ frame; steel

Materials: Brick and natural stone cladding; granite; steel; aluminium; glass

Cost: DM 2 billion

1 Site plan
2 Main entrance
3 Warner Bros. cinema
4 Warner Bros. cinema interior
5 Centre court atrium
Photography: David Whitcomb

CentrO Oberhausen is situated on an 83-hectare site of an old Thyssen Steel mill 20 km outside Düsseldorf. At the heart of the project is a 230-store retail centre complemented by a variety of leisure components including a waterfront promenade, an 11,000-seat arena and a nine-screen Warner Bros. cinema. Other features include a Planet Hollywood restaurant, CentroPark children's activity park and a 1,200-seat themed Oasis food court.

Current and future developments at the site include a hotel, offices, tennis complex and an aquarium.

CentrO marks the beginning of a new commercial era for the surrounding community. The centre was opened to the public in September 1996 and expects to attract over 30 million visitors a year.

1

2

3

4

5

Fridays Bar and Restaurant
Bligh Voller Nield Pty Ltd

Completion: November 1996
Location: Brisbane, Queensland, Australia
Client: Weller Corporation
Area: 985 square metres; 10,603 square feet
Structure: Concrete
Materials: Granite; stainless steel; sycamore timber veneer
Cost: $500,000

The original Fridays Bar, a restaurant and nightclub had been a presence on the Brisbane hospitality scene for over a decade. Bligh Voller Nield was commissioned to update the venue for both day and night use to present a more timeless image to attract new clientele. The design capitalises on the views of the Brisbane River with a desire to be sympathetic to the original architectural intent of Harry Siedler.

Facilities were rationalised and upgraded with two bars consolidated into one that also serves and encroaches onto the outdoor space. Materials are durable and high quality though inexpensive.

The integration of structure, construction materials, and services has been achieved with a reductionist design language. It uses readily available materials and standardised construction methods. The materials are generally harmonious with the existing building fabric but also contrast with strong colours used to slice through the volume of space emphasising the composition. The interaction of these elements expresses an intimacy combined with openness appropriate to a club/restaurant environment. Darker elements are used on horizontal planes to anchor the space, whilst light finishes are used on vertical elements to avoid detracting from the view.

2

4

1   Central bar at night, external
2   Bar detail and seating
3   Central bar at day, internal
4   DJ Booth
5   Internal dining area
Photography: David Sandison

261

Residential

Ambassador's Residence

The Stubbins Associates, Inc

Completion: May 1996

Location: U.S. Embassy, Singapore

Client: U.S. Department of State, Office of Foreign Buildings

Area: 929 square metres; 10,000 square feet

Structure: Concrete

Materials: Masonry; wood; tile

The Ambassador's Residence of the U.S. Embassy in Singapore is located on a three-acre site in the Leedon Park district of Singapore.

The Ambassador's Residence, like the Embassy must play two roles. It is the Ambassador's private home as well as the principal venue for Ambassadorial entertainment. Singapore's English and Oriental roots combined to create residential designs that expressed these two roles: the lower floor, devoted to entertainment, was formal while the upper floor was vernacular in design and private in function.

1

2

1 Garden front
2 Porte cochére
3 Entry rotunda
4 Veranda
5 Dining room
Photography: Tim Griffith/Esto

3

4

5

Apartment Interior
Peter Forbes and Associates

Completion: January 1996

Location: Boston, Massachusetts, USA

Client: Mr & Mrs Peter Forbes

Area: 116 square metres; 1,250 square feet

Structure: Reinforced concrete

Materials: Fresco plaster; frosted glass; pietra serena

The original plan for this apartment within I.M. Pei's Harbor Towers' complex provided the anonymous, generic living spaces inevitable when an apartment is designed for unknown inhabitants. The renovation responds specifically to the owner's desire for both an uncluttered living environment and storage space for all the belongings they need, but don't want to look at.

Walls were removed to create a series of broad interior vistas into which were placed two objects. The first, a utility core containing kitchen and storage seems to float in the muted greys of the *pietra serena* floor.

The second element, a curved frosted glass screen, defines the bedroom. Reflective and luminescent, it gathers and distributes light to the rest of the apartment.

The perimeter of the space is lined with concealed closets, cupboards, and a study carrel.

Perimeter walls are painted white. Ceilings and core are unpainted fresco plaster. The study carrel is lined in natural cherry.

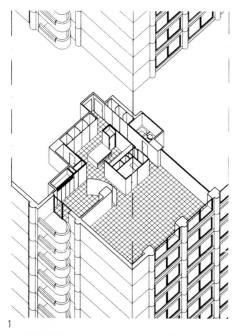

1

2

3

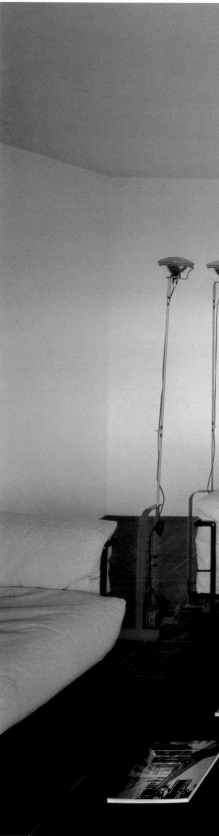

4

1 Axonometric
2 View of dining and edge of bedroom wall
3 Kitchen and bedroom screen wall
4 Living area
Photography: Nick Wheeler/Wheeler Photographics

Casa Torre Paradigna

Architetto Aurelio Cortesi

Completion: November 1996

Location: Parma, Italy

Client: Istituto Autonomo Case Popolari Public Institution

Area: 4,500 square metres; 48,439 square feet

Structure: Concrete pilasters and beams

Materials: Brick; concrete; tiles

Cost: 3.000.000.000 Lira

Casa Torre Paradigna is a 58-unit retirement residence, located in the flat landscape of the north periphery of Parma. The L-shaped site constrained a composition based on the development of the corner condition. The project is broken into fragments: the staircase, the two 11-floor volumes and the two degradating smaller east solids.

The staircase, which recomposes the unity of the building, whirls around the concrete/brick wall that sustains it, gaining height up to the 11th floor, providing a central zone for the wing circulation. The project is articulated through different volumes and presents a different facade from each point of view from the landscape. The idea which sustains the design is to reconstitute the profile of a city, with all the variations and discrepancies which happen when joining together two entirely different volumes.

Balconies and loggias, appearing only at designated floors in order to maintain strict security, become a very important part of the rhythm of the facade, projecting outward and inward; an outside room with a view of the landscape.

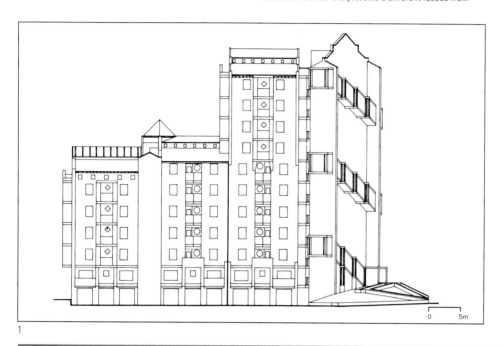

0   5m

1

2

3

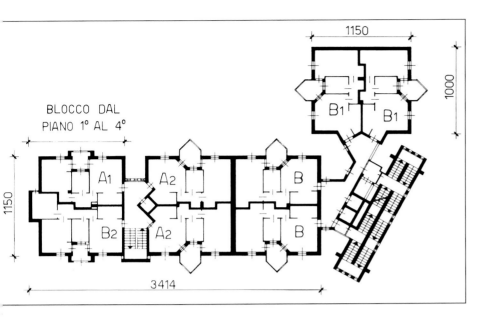

BLOCCO DAL
PIANO 1° AL 4°

1150

3414

1150

1000

A_1 A_2 B

B_2 A_2 B

B_1 B_1

1 North facade plan
2 View of west facade
3 View of interior courtyard
4 Ground floor plan
5 View of north facade
Photography: Davoli & Buzzoni, Vecchi

Chason Residence Addition & Remodel

House + House Architects

Completion: March 1997

Location: San Francisco, California, USA

Client: Audie Chason

Area: 214 square metres; 2,300 square feet

Structure: Wood frame

Materials: Redwood plywood; stainless steel; steel; maple; coloured concrete; birch cabinetry; burnished aluminium; glass

Awards: Renaissance Design Award

1   Axonometric view with floor plans
2   West facade
3   Detail of south facade
4   View of living area from entry

In the shadow of San Francisco's historic landmark Coit Tower, this 1906 earthquake relief home had an awkward plan, low ceilings, dark spaces and a collection of odd and clumsy materials. During the remodel, the structure was completely gutted and 400 additional square feet were added to create a dramatic new contemporary home of high ceilings and flowing spaces all filled with natural light.

Carefully skewed geometry and a sleek palette of materials in sensuous colours complement the drama of space and garden. The surprise hits immediately when one enters and an 18 foot (5.5 metre), high grid of windows embraces an existing Japanese maple tree into the corner of the living room. The curving stairway wraps the bar, defining the kitchen and connects to an open bridge flying above to the secluded master bedroom. An arc of perforated steel off the master bedroom deck recall the radiating forms inside, screening for privacy while filtering rays of sunlight.

Flush overlay birch cabinets are dyed purple for a continuing flow of colour from the carpet. Sculpted walls shape the space and form niches, each washed with light from geometric fixtures, all linked by the rhythm of the steel cable rails. Smooth exterior grade plywood siding stained grey and turquoise provides crisp form on the exterior, at once in scale with the neighbourhood, while denying scale altogether.

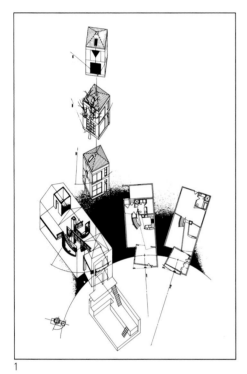

1

2

3

5

5   View of dining and kitchen areas
6   View to living area from second floor
7   View of kitchen
8   View of master bedroom
Photography: Allan Geller

6

7

Choi's Residence (Ikchunggak and Crystal House)

Kunchook-Moonhwa Architects & Engineers

Completion: July 1997

Location: Samchung-dong, Seoul, Korea

Client: Hie-jong, Choi

Area: 455 square metres; 4,898 square feet

Structure: Reinforced concrete; wood frame

Materials: Exposed concrete

Awards: 1997 First Prize Annual Korean-
Architectural Culture Award

1   South elevation
2   Overall view of *crystal house*
3   View toward garden
4   Room with skylight
5   Interior view of Hanok

Photography: courtesy Kunchook-Moonhwa Architects &
Engineers

People say that they are living 'with' Hanok (Korean
traditional style wooden house) rather than living 'in' it.
Although living in Hanok may not be suited to the modern
life style, living in Hanok contains an important meaning,
especially as the traditional life style is disappearing;
it means preserving ancestor's life and trace for future
generations rather than just searching for the identity
of house style or having a stylish life.

The design concept was to combine the western style
house with Hanok. There is an existing Hanok, called Ik-
chung-gak basically made up of *An-bang, Gunun-bang* and
Byulsil, which can be used as a tea room.

Retaining the existing Hanok as much as possible, only
a small *Daechung Maru* (balcony) and a bathroom was
added. The western style house (called *crystal house*)
was located under the ground; utilising the differing
ground levels, the architect placed parking space and the

mechanical room in the entrance level and Crystal House
underneath Hanok.

This house is designed for three generations and can be
divided into four sections. Firstly, Hanok is a space for
the middle-aged couple; secondly, the basement floor is
a living space for children and their future families; thirdl
a divided space for the older couple and children is
basically one big room, which is constructed as a 'built-in
method to enable flexibility of space to suit differing nee
and finally, the fourth section containing both parking an
mechanical space.

Here in this house, west and east coexist without losing
their own identities.

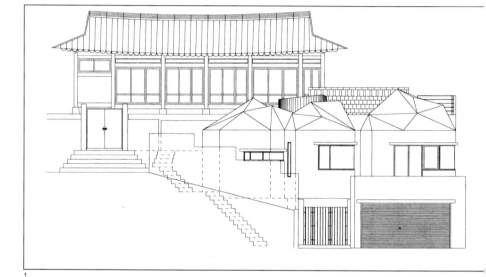

1

2

3

4

5

Conservation to Existing Bungalow at Chatsworth Park

William Lim Associates Pte

Completion: June 1996

Location: Chatsworth Park, Singapore

Client: Keppel Land International Limited

Area: 681 square metres; 7,320 square feet

Structure: Brick; timber

Materials: Brick; timber

Cost: $2 million

Awards: 1997 URA Heritage Award

This conservation project mainly consisted of two major tasks: conservation of the existing house and an extension to suit modern living.

The conservation of the existing house entailed setting the base context for the design intervention by judging whether the various additions carried out throughout the life history of the building contributed to the original quality of the house. Following this study, it was decided to adopt renovation up to 1951 as the base. Other than enlarging the kitchen and reconfiguring the timber staircase, whatever that was recorded up to this period has been faithfully restored and reinstated.

As for the extension and alteration to the conservation house, the design intention was to signal the layering of time to distinctively differentiate the past from the present. To accommodate more rooms, a single storey semi-circular out-house which was detached from the conservation house was introduced both to act as a backdrop as well as allowing for all-round visual appreciation of the existing house.

1

2

1 View of pool area
2 View of bedroom balcony
3 Patio outside dining room
4 First storey plan
5 New extension curve-block
6 View from dining room to patio and rear garden
7 View of kitchen

Photography: courtesy William Lim Associates Pte

3

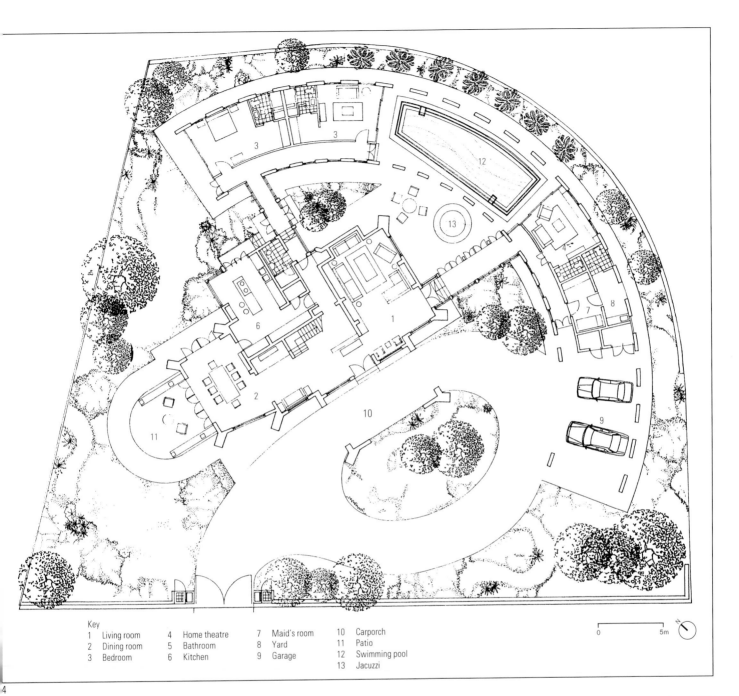

Key
1 Living room   4 Home theatre   7 Maid's room   10 Carporch
2 Dining room   5 Bathroom   8 Yard   11 Patio
3 Bedroom   6 Kitchen   9 Garage   12 Swimming pool
                                                                  13 Jacuzzi

0   5m   N

4

6

7

5

Custom Home
The Steinberg Group

Completion: March 1996

Location: Atherton, California, USA

Area: 734 square metres; 7,900 square feet

Structure: Wood; steel; concrete

Materials: Mount Mariah stone; cedar; zinc

Awards: 1997 Gold Nugget Grand Award, Pacific Coast Builders Conference/Builder Magazine

This 734 square metre (7,900 square foot) private residence with separate pool house is situated on a cul-de-sac terminating a meandering road through a wooded area of heritage oak trees. The curvilinear form of the building permits the preservation of California oak trees on the site.

The arched form of the residence is penetrated by a nine metre (30 foot) high and 46 metre (150 foot) long Mariah stone wall, which is the main organising spine, presenting a powerful architectural feature. The wall subdivides the site into different zones: a welcoming public entry zone which receives the visitor; a warm activity zone, oriented to the southwest, with pool and activity areas; and a cooler zone with north and morning light exposure, accommodating more private activities. The masonry of the wall is laid in irregular, rough patterns to counterpoint the precise and refined detailing of the rest of the home.

The materials and colours used were carefully selected to blend and harmonise with the natural beauty of the site and surrounding oak trees. The interior palette of natural earth tones is achieved through the use of natural materials and colours. The material palette contains wood, zinc and stone to reflect the exterior environment, with broad reliance on natural light and use of glass.

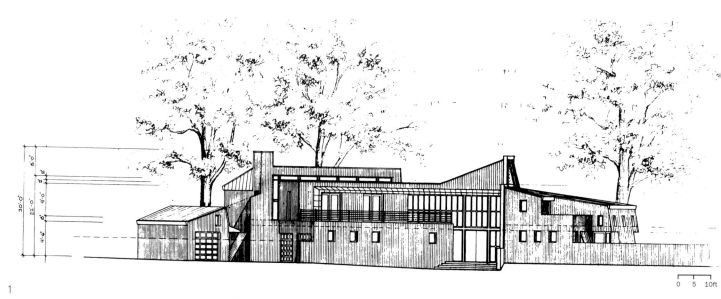

1

0 5 10ft

2

1 Front entry elevation, east
2 Front view of house from cul-de-sac
3 View of main entry
4 Master suite garden near library
5 View of living and dining room from garden

3

4

5

Opposite:
　Living room
7　Master suite with corner doors
8　View of bridge from main lobby
Photography: Richard Barnes

7

8

Dan House

Israel Callas Shortridge associates inc.

Completion: February 1996

Location: Malibu, California, USA

Client: Michael and Cecilia Dan

Area: 464 square metres; 5,000 square feet

Structure: Sand-finished stucco; zincalum; burnished concrete

Materials: Maple; Douglas fir; stainless steel; ceramic tile

Built on a fire site in Malibu, this house replaces an original which was destroyed in the great Malibu fire of 1993. The original foundation defines an armature for the new house from which elements such as the master bedroom, master office and family room extend. Essentially a bar building with a giant hipped metal roof, the Dan House also defines a system of diagonals which tie the composition together. These are covered in stucco and are intended to scale down the rear facade.

Landscaping has been carefully designed to divide the site into separate areas which celebrate sport, entertainment, family gathering and contemplation. The Dan family is a complex whole and this house is intended to recognise their rich diversity and creative spirit.

1   Front wall at entrance
2   Main bedroom pavilion viewed from pool
3   Main bedroom pavilion at dusk

1

2

3

4

5

6

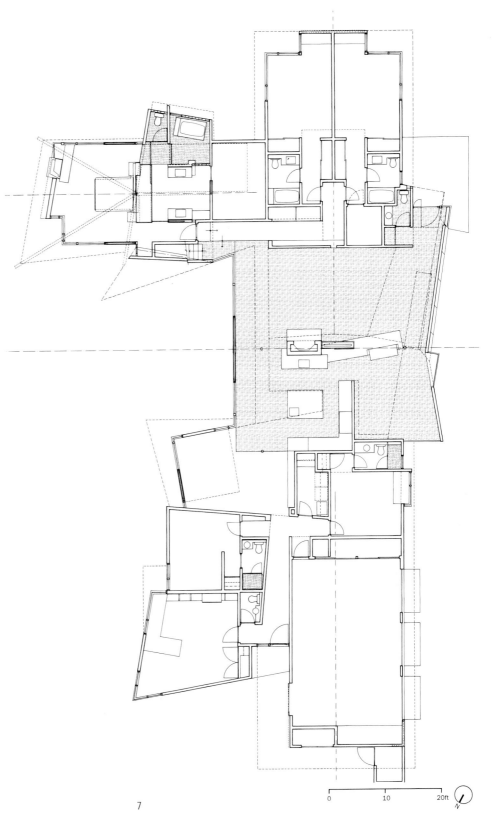

4 Living room with folding ceilings up to skylight
at edges
5 Den looking into open kitchen
6 Dining room looking across to entry and living spaces
7 Floor plan
Photography: Erhard Pfeiffer

Dietz House
Burr & McCallum Architects

Completion: December 1996
Location: Williamstown, Massachusetts, USA
Client: Jack & Maureen Dietze
Area: 260 square metres; 2,798 square feet
Structure: Wood frame
Materials: Wood; stone
Cost: US$400,000

A house for a couple with grown-up children. A limited budget coupled with a desire for a 'New England look' led the architects to a barn motif. Whereas traditional New England houses have pretty columns, fancy detailing, and complex dormers and porches, barns traditionally are simple shapes with simple detailing. The clients could have a New England look uncompromised by any budgetary constraints.

1

1   View from approach road to house
2   Floor plan
3   View of screened porch
4   Detail of entry courtyard
5   View of house from woods
Photography: Ann McCallum

Key
1   Porch
2   Dining area
3   Living room
4   Breakfast room
5   Library
6   Powder room
7   Kitchen
8   Entry
9   Mudroom
10 Laundry
11 Garage
12 Garbage

0   5   10m

3

4

Ellis Residence
Westwork Architects

Completion: May 1997

Location: Santa Fe, New Mexico, USA

Client: Mr David Ellis

Area: 232 square metres; 2,500 square feet

Structure: Wood frame and masonry

Materials: Synthetic finish on stucco on wood frame; exposed masonry; clad wood windows; birch veneer; stained exposed concrete, slate; ceramic tile

A documentary film maker who had lost his home in an earthquake in the Los Angeles area decided to relocate to Santa Fe. He had previously lived in New Mexico and wished to create, as he stated in his program: "a modern house with international influences and southwestern flavour"

The nature of the client's work as a film producer inspired a 'story line' narrative for the design of the house. The story chosen to tell was the journey of the client from the earthquake event in Los Angeles, to his new life in Santa Fe. The plan of the house reflects this journey in its form. At the heart of the plan is a 'timeline' that traces the 'story line' narrative from beginning to end.

The 'story' begins at the entry where a piece of the residence is fractured away from the main body of the house in recognition of the event that set the design of the house in motion. As the journey continues, the 'timeline' passes through the Santa Fe environment, represented here by a simple geometric rectangular form which holds the main living areas of the house.

The 'timeline' traveller, thus modified by both the Los Angeles experience and the culture of New Mexico, occupies a circular tower space for creative work and is finally transformed to a new sense of life in this region as they travel to the end of the 'timeline' and out into the rugged rock strewn hills.

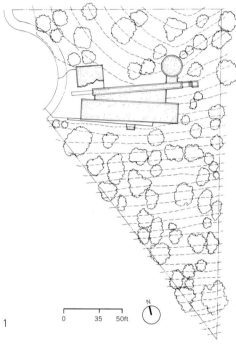

1

0   35   50ft

3

2

4

1   Site plan
2   Entry at front door to 'timeline'
3   Overall view from southeast
4   East elevation where 'timeline' emerges betwen portal and studio spaces
5   Interior of 'timeline' at kitchen
6   Floor plan
7   Interior at living area

Photography: Robert Reck

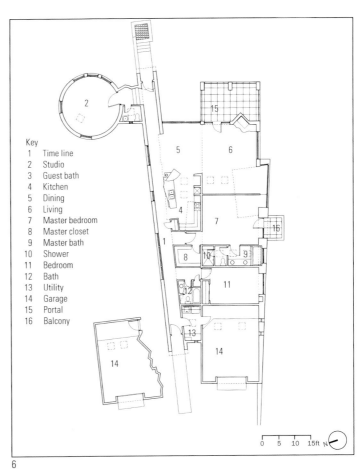

Key
1   Time line
2   Studio
3   Guest bath
4   Kitchen
5   Dining
6   Living
7   Master bedroom
8   Master closet
9   Master bath
10 Shower
11 Bedroom
12 Bath
13 Utility
14 Garage
15 Portal
16 Balcony

0   5   10   15ft   N

6

Ess Residence

Anderson Anderson Architecture

Completion: August 1996

Location: Gig Harbour, Washington, USA

Area: 1,115 square metres; 12,000 square feet

Structure: 2X6 platform framing; post and beam; curtain wall

Materials: Wood; steel; glass

Awards: Southwest Washington AIA Award of Merit

The site for this house is a broad point of waterfront. The owners' lives on this site circle around two primary interests: a large collection of classic automobiles and the beachfront activities of boating, swimming and outdoor entertaining. Following the curve of the beach and taking advantage of the natural topography, the house is sited as an S-shaped wall defining two courtyard areas: an auto court and a waterfront terrace.

The concave curve of the house traps the morning sun and allows continuous glass curtain wall affording sweeping views while at the same time creating an inward focus and sense of self-protection. The auto court provides a welcoming enclosure and displays the auto collection. The curved walls also serve a structural function. The soli outer wall around each courtyard resists lateral forces on the glazed inner curve transferred through the shear diaphragm of the roof. This structural configuration allow continuous glass garage doors opening onto the auto cou and a continuous glass curtain wall onto the water view.

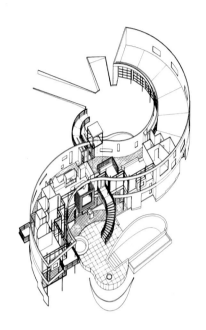

1

2

1   Axonometric
2   View from water front
3   View from waterfront/pool terrace
4   View from master bedroom
5   Approach view of entry and auto court

6

7

9

10

6 Approach view of entry and auto court
7 Entry view, bridge walkway to front door
8 Front entry door with skylight above
9 Overhead view of framing
10 Site plan
11 Interior, solid shear wall and kitchen to right
Photography: Scott Leen (9); Anderson Anderson Architecture

Glanz Residence Remodel

House + House Architects

Completion: February 1997

Location: San Francisco, California, USA

Client: Keith Glanz

Area: 56 square metres; 600 square feet

Structure: Wood frame

Materials: Maple and cherry wood; coloured concrete; stainless steel; limestone; sand-blasted glass

Perched on the eastern slopes of Russian Hill with breathtaking views to the San Francisco skyline and Bay, this newly remodelled 56 square metre (600 square foot) condominium glows with warm colours and sculptural forms. The blend of naturally finished maple and cherry cabinets with subtly coloured concrete and wood counters is complementary to the stark stainless steel appliances. A bold burgundy column is all that is needed to separate the kitchen from the living. A study area was added adjacent to the kitchen within a long wall of sculpted cabinets. It fills a multitude of functions while expanding the space visually.

A bold arch and stepped, staggered cabinet with integral counter areas, flipper doors to hid the TV and stereo, and glass panels with artfully lit interiors add an enormous sense of volume and dimension. The wall between the living and bedroom was cut, shaped and carved to provide space for art, flowers and objects and to filter light throug a thin strip of patterned, sand-blasted glass and matching glass door. The flooring, a specially fabricated plank of recycled wood from Finland, is the colour of California grasses in the summer. What had been a cramped bathroom is now a gracious and comfortable space with a generous shower of limestone walls tapering to an integra seat. The rosy terracotta concrete bath counter, soft yellov walls and limestone floor are infused with richness by beautifully selected and focused lighting.

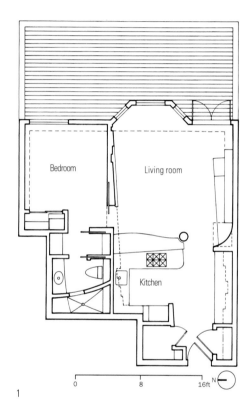

1

2

1   Floor plan
2   View of kitchen from entry
3   Detail of kitchen counter
4   View toward kitchen from living area
5   View of living cabinetry and counter

3

4

6   Detail of study
7   View of bathroom
8   View of bedroom
9   View of living room
Photography: Claudio Santini

9

Great Island Residence

William Kite Architects, Inc.

Completion: July 1996

Location: West Yarmouth, Massachusetts, USA

Area: 450 square metres; 4,844 square feet

Structure: Fieldstone; wood

Materials: Red cedar shingles; mahogany; maple; stone

Awards: Honor Award New Construction Rhode Island Chapter, American Institute of Architects

This comfortable and relaxed summer home is situated in a private development on a peninsula along the Cape Cod/ Atlantic coast. Simple in design and modern in character, it utilises a significant amount of glass to maximise the view of the ocean as a design element. The house is conceived as a grouping of small scale buildings arranged in an informal fashion and linked together by single storey, flat-roofed, transparent connectors. Throughout the interior, simple plaster walls are enhanced by stained mahogany trim. Vernacular building forms are used for the main building elements; gable roofs and dormers with traditional window openings and skylights highlight the ocean vistas.

The building is designed to blend with the environment an emerge naturally from the terrain, presenting a harmonis impression to the viewer, from the land or from the sea. Cedar shingles on roofs and walls have been left to weather. All mahogany windows, doors, and exposed trir are stained transparent red. Fieldstone is used at chimney and secondary structures to complement the shingle building forms. Bluestone terracing, laid in a herringbone pattern in contrasting colours, is used at all outside terraces. The varying hues of tan, red, blue and grey echo the weathered colours of the seaside landscape and resu in a design that is in harmony with its environment and ye comfortably accommodating of the most formal gathering

1

1   Approach from beach
2   View from southwest
3   Ocean-side terrace
4   Site plan
5   Front entrance porch

2

4

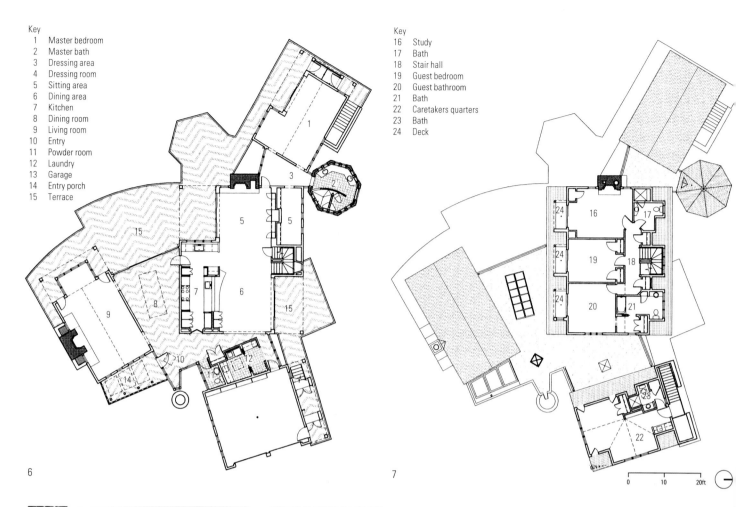

Key
1 Master bedroom
2 Master bath
3 Dressing area
4 Dressing room
5 Sitting area
6 Dining area
7 Kitchen
8 Dining room
9 Living room
10 Entry
11 Powder room
12 Laundry
13 Garage
14 Entry porch
15 Terrace

Key
16 Study
17 Bath
18 Stair hall
19 Guest bedroom
20 Guest bathroom
21 Bath
22 Caretakers quarters
23 Bath
24 Deck

6

7

0   10   20ft

8

6 First floor plan
7 Second floor plan
8 View from northeast showing stone master bath
9 Living room fireplace and view to ocean beyond
Opposite:
   Dining room with view toward main entry
Photography: Aaron Usher, III

9

House in Surry, Maine

Peter Forbes and Associates

Completion: June 1996

Location: Surry, Maine, USA

Client: Dr & Mrs Earl David Nordberg

Area: 353 square metres; 3,800 square feet

Structure: Reinforced concrete; steel; wood

Materials: Glass; granite; cedar; fibre glass; copper; oak; birch veneer

Landscape, geometry, and light interact to define this seaside home, studio and guest house. The site, a meadow bordering a broad pebble beach, is a flood-plain area.

As regulation required concrete piers to support the floor above flood level, these piers, extended up to eave height, carry the roof as well and establish an order of paired columns that bend and shift with the landscape. To the columns are clipped steel beams and rafters creating a continuous pavilion that floats above the ground.

Within the ordering structure, sleeping area, kitchen, storage units and baths are inserted as free-standing objects. A massive chimney of local granite separates the owners' private area from family gathering spaces.

The open site is suffused with intense light, magnified by reflection from the ocean. Light surrounds each component of the architecture, articulating the parts, dissolving the building and creating an elusive, hovering form.

1

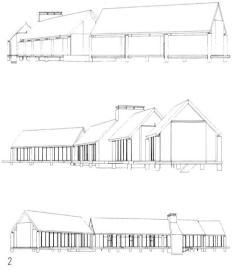

2

1 Exterior
2 Perspectives
3 Division of the two principal sections
Opposite:
   Exterior

3

5

6

5   The 'hinge'
6   End wall appears as a free-standing plane
7   Floor-to-ceiling operable windows
8   Public and private realms of main house divided by
    granite chimney

Photography: Nick Wheeler/Wheeler Photographics

7

House on the Nova Scotia Coast #12

Brian MacKay–Lyons

Completion: May 1996

Location: Nova Scotia, Canada

Area: 308 square metres; 3,316 square feet

Structure: Concrete; timber

Materials: Wood shingle; galvalume; glass

Awards: Lieutenant Govenor General's Award for
Architecture
Governor General's Medal of Excellence for
Architecture

The house consists of two principal elements forming
a southeast oriented courtyard, thereby resolving the
typical conflict between sun and view orientation along
the diagonal axis of Nova Scotia's coast. The garage acts
as a mute retaining wall parallel to the road and the
slope, while the living spaces are contained in a ship-like
cross-slope pavilion.

The passage through the house is punctuated by a series
of iconic or totemic elements. Upon entering, the kitchen
island is a foreground element to the kitchen-in-a-box,
which reorients one to the long axis of the 'Great Room'.
After passing through the dining void, the double-height
sunken living area is punctuated by the hearth and stair.
A two-storey glass bay in the living space appears to
extend the house to the deck and sea.

The concrete base together with four timber frames form
the primary structure for the house. The structure is large
a response to lateral wind loads given the exaggerated
height and narrow width of the building, together with th
totally open tube of the 'Great Room'. The four wind she
frames form rigid rings which wrap around the 'Great
Room'.

The primary structure is completely wrapped by the flush
zero-detailed, shingled envelope creating a northern
climate relationship between structure and envelope tha
differs from the usual warm climate modernist approach.

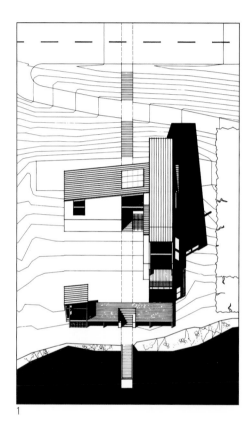

1

2

3

1 Site plan
2 View from sea
3 View from road
4 Entry porch from courtyard
5 Elevation
6 Entry porch

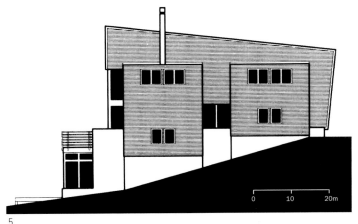

5

7 Axonometric
8 Hearth
9 View from kitchen
10 Great room
Photography: Jamie Steeves

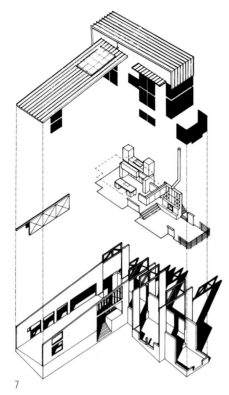

7

8

9

House with Boathouse

Baneke, van der Hoeven architekten

Completion: May 1996

Location: Loosdrecht (The Netherlands)

Area: 170 square metres; 1,830 square feet

Structure: Steel; concrete

Materials: Finnish birch plywood; red brick; glass; zinc; moraines; western red cedar

The house is arranged with the living spaces alongside the garage and garden room. The rooms are placed on a floor with different levels and under a roof with large overhangs, in which round and rectangular openings have been cut. The light-holes are provided with structures of varying heights and sizes, clad in zinc. The sleeping areas are separated from the other spaces by double-walled glass surfaces with aluminium slats. The living area has an open floorplan with an S-shaped timber screen and a totally glazed kitchen.

From a concrete float a ramp leads to the entrance of the house. A fireplace block which protrudes outward has been fitted into a glass surface. There is a glass sliding door in the closed north facade, which provides access to a jetty and a raised path to the boathouse.

1

1 Living room with glass kitchen unit on right
2 South facade and boathouse
3 View of kitchen
4 View of bathroom
Photography: Jeroen van Putten (1); Hans Fonk (2–4)

Indian Point Residence

Arbonies King Vlock

Completion: January 1996

Location: Stony Creek, Connecticut, USA

Area: 702 square metres; 7,554 square feet

Structure: Steel frame

Materials: Wood shingles; Stony Creek granite

The design of this shingle-style residence is inspired by local tradition, materials, and craftsmanship. The exterior is clad in cedar shingles, unstained and allowed to weather. The steeply sloped roofs, articulated belt courses, dormers, and robust eave and rake trim are all New England in character. Massive cleft blocks of Stony Creek granite, laid by local stone cutters, were used to restore the broken sea wall along the Point.

The approach to the house from the land side is intentionally scaled down to be cottage-like and private, with its steeply sloped roofs and minimal fenestration.

On the water side however, the house opens up to take full advantage of the panoramic views. Large divided-light windows afford a welcome transparency—picture frames to the ever-changing scene of birds, boats, islands, and sunsets.

The concept of an interior verandah along the water side allows living spaces to open onto one another. Rather than a series of rooms, Tuscan columns define dining room, living room, library, kitchen and family room. The sense of informality is further suggested in the natural beaded board ceilings, traditional mouldings, and continuous window seats.

Generously sized French doors provide easy access to the outdoor 'great room'—an elliptical shaped deck that wraps the entire water side facade.

1

2

3

1 Exterior, approach to building
2 Exterior, detail of front entry
3 Exterior, water side elevation
4 Interior, detail of living room
5 Interior, detail of dining room
Photography: Timothy Hursley

La Pirca

Antonio H Ravazzani & Associates

Completion: June 1997

Location: Punta Piedras, Punta del Este, Uruguay

Client: Mr & Mrs Abal

Area: 350 square metres; 3,767 square feet

Structure: Concrete

Materials: Fieldstone and cobblestone-clad

Cost: US$250,000

Sited on a beach and supported by existing rock formations, this house blends beautifully with the coastal landscape, successfully incorporating the client's brief for the house to register only the smallest footprint on the landscape, taking advantage of the prevailing winds in cooling the property during the hot summer months.

The colours and textures used reflect the coastal hues, adding to the local perspective.

The main elevation of the property faces the sea, taking full advantage of the panoramic views through well placed windows and natural light. The facade has been created out of the stone originally excavated from the site with the pool area designed to present the house with an almost Arabic setting.

This house represented Uruguay at the Bienal in Quito - Ecuador.

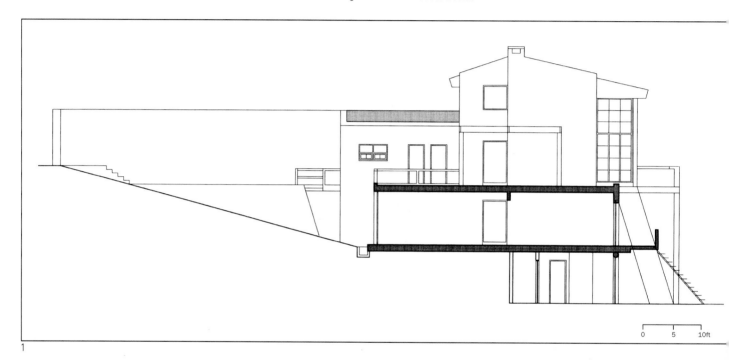

0   5   10ft

1

1 Lateral section
2 Access to swimming pool
3 Underground living area
4 View from beach
5 View of living room/mezzanine

Photography: courtesy Antonio H Ravazzani & Associates

2

3

4

Metrolux Tower 1B (Casa Del Sol)
T.R. Hamzah & Yeang Sdn Bhd

Completion: September 1996

Location: Bukit Antarabangsa, Selangor, Malaysia

Client: Metrolux Sendirian Berhad

Area: 26,903 square metres; 289,590 square feet

Structure: Reinforced concrete frame; sand brick infill

Materials: Masonry; glass; metal; marble

The client's programme was to build 160-apartment units on a green-field site situated in Taman Bukit Antarabangsa in Gombak, Selangor. The 11-storey development faces a valley, hence the semi-circular shape to give views from each apartment.

The building features planted and terraced skycourts that are spatially interconnected and placed in a diagonal pattern, stepping sideways from the slab's centre. These skycourts provide terraces for the adjoining residential units within the same slab. The naturally-ventilated single-loaded corridor access to the apartment units, faces the

hot west-side of the site and buffers the afternoon sun. The corridor is separated from the tower slab by an air gap. This gives privacy and provides opportunities for cross-ventilation through the apartments.

All the apartments are designed with through ventilation. The lift lobbies and staircases that separate the two halves of the curved slab are naturally lit and ventilated.

At ground floor, a small plaza-terrace leads to the clubhouse, poolside and communal space where residents can relax in their immediate surroundings.

1

2

1   Elevations from side driveway
2   West elevation
3   Central stairway
4   Access walkway
Photography: K.L. Ng

3

Morla-De Matron Residence

Inglese Architecture/ Nilus De Matron
Interiors: Jennifer Morla

Completion: January 1997

Location: San Francisco, California, USA

Client: Jennifer Morla & Nilus De Matron

Area: 186 square metres; 2,000 square feet

Structure: Wood frame

Materials: White western maple; cast concrete;
Blomberg aluminium

Cost: US$250,000

The Morla-De Matron home inhabits a singular site perched at the edge of Portrero Hill with an astonishing view of the San Francisco skyline. The clients are both designers; he is an architect by training and she is a well-known graphic and interiors designer. They have two children, many friends and family members visiting from all over the globe., The house and grounds that they designed with Mark English/Inglese Architecture and Jeff Smith/Landscape Architect accommodate public lives while providing for the privacy of family life.

The site is north-facing, steep and located 4 metres below the street. A small house was moved to the site in 1910 and renovated in a minimalist manner in the early 1960s. The challenge was to reconfigure the existing rooms, add a master suite and parking while providing adjacent sunlit exterior space for every living space. The resulting solution locates the master suite below the parking within a new space carved from the hillside and a new terraced garden 'room' tumbling down to a lawn area. Below the generous view terraces the clients have built a painting studio with one of the most unique settings in the Bay area.

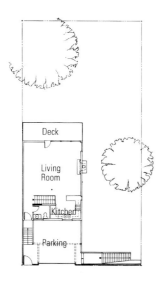

1

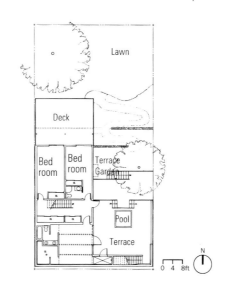

2

3

4

1   Upper level floor plan
2   Lower level floor plan
3   View from north lawn
4   View from south terrace towards San Francisco
5   View of master bedroom
6   View from living room
7   View of kitchen
Photography: Allan Geller

6

New York City House

Tod Williams, Billie Tsien and Associates

Completion: September 1996

Location: New York City, New York, USA

Area: 1,278 square metres; 13,760 square feet

Structure: Steel beams; CMU; poured-in-place concrete

Materials: Indiana limestone; bluestone; Jet Mist granite; cherry wood; glass tiles; glass

Awards: 1996 American Institute of Architects New York Chapter Design Architecture Award 1997 Architectural Record House

Compressed into the 9.2 metre x 30.5 metre (30 foot x 100 foot) footprint of two demolished brownstones in a New York City block, this new townhouse suggests that it is still possible to build a single family house within the super dense urban fabric of Manhattan. The immediate context of this building is a five-storey brownstone to the east and an 18-storey apartment building to the west. In response to the scale of the more intimate building, the central element in the quiet composition of the facade is a hammered limestone wall around which are composed translucent and transparent windows. The wall provides a sense of protection and privacy from the street while at the same time connecting it with surrounding built fabric through material and scale. The composition of glass surrounding this stone wall isolates and abstracts it, while bringing filtered light to rooms within. The rear facade is predominantly glass and is related in its sense of composition to the front of the house. In order to encourage vertical circulation by foot in this six-floor house and to flood the interior of the house with light, a large skylight illuminates and marks the stairway from the basement level to the top floor. Defining the sense of movement and illuminated by the skylight is a monumental wall, one echoing the initial limestone facade.

1

2

3

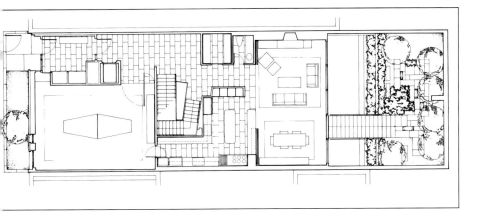

1 Light monitor and stair
2 Front facade
3 View of living room from balcony
4 First floor plan
5 Section
Photography: Michael Moran

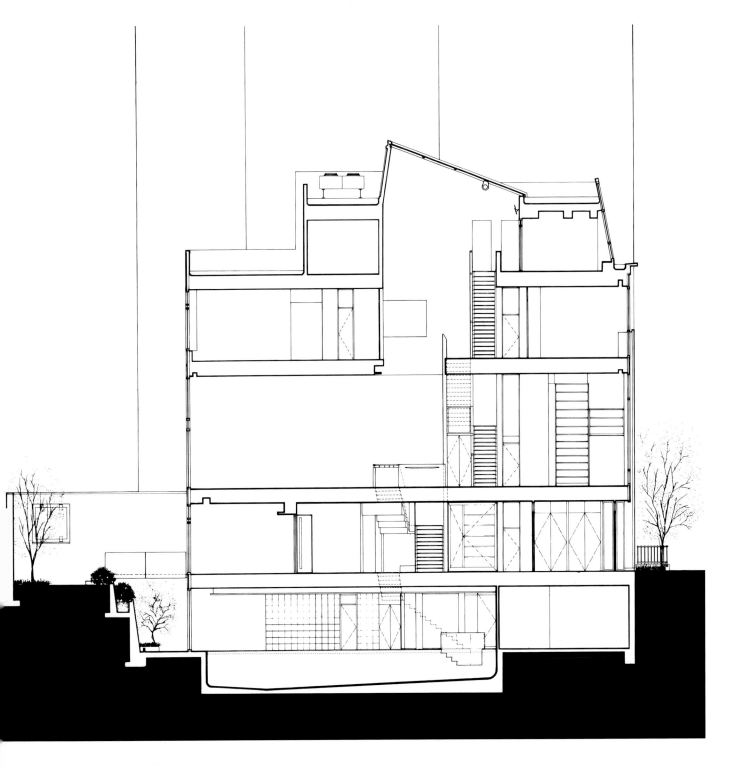

Nokia House

Helin & Siitonen Architects

Completion: March 1997

Location: Espoo, Finland

Client: Oy Nokia Ab

Area: 38,600 square metres; 415,500 square feet

Structure: Glide-cased stair tower; prefabricated columns; reinforced concrete

Materials: Concrete; steel; glass

Cost: FIM 250 Million

Awards: Facade of the Year 1997

Closeness to nature is a key factor in the design of Nokia House. As a contrast to rushing and a hurried pace of work the restfulness and space of the landscape, daylight and the variation of seasons create a backdrop to working. The marine and the island scenery can be viewed from the lobby as well as from the well-lit offices and conference rooms, and from the building's axis of corridors and vistas.

The compact building also blends in with the shoreline site; its reflective glazed facades conceal 1200 workstations and auxiliary facilities. The glass surface has a special ecological value as well; it is a new architectural element which reduces the need of energy for cooling and heating.

Nokia's operations are crystallised by communication. Electronic, informal and intuitive communication was a functional requirement for the design work. The building was made transparent in its inner spaces specifically to facilitate intuitive communication.

Each workstation is an individual territory but the open corridors, conference rooms and lunch facility allow for informal get-togethers and chats, for 'test-driving' ideas.

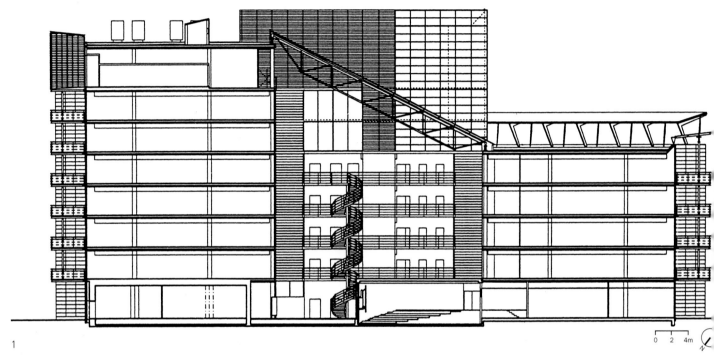

1

2

1   East–west section, facing south
2   East side offices have view to sea
3   Balconies of west facade
4   Main entrance with steel and glass canopy above
5   Steel and glass stairs spire up on both sides of inner court

4

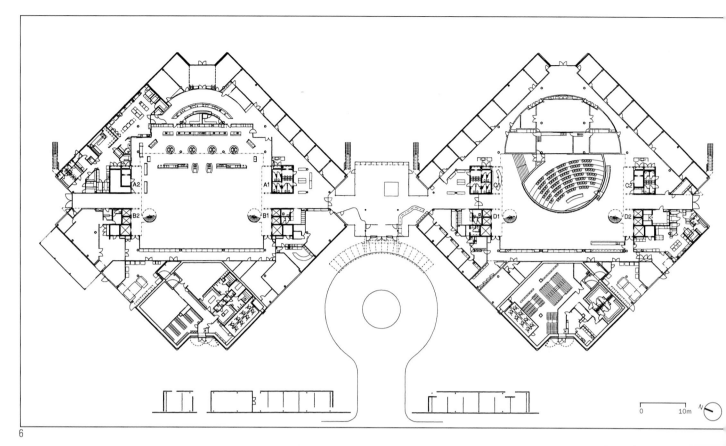

6

7

6   Ground floor plan
7   Seating area by meeting room on ground floor
8   Entrance lobby and curved glass block reception desk
9   Inner court and restaurant
Photography: Jussi Tiainen (2,3,4,5); Voitto Niemelä (7,8,9)

8

Plehn/Marple House

Burr & McCallum Architects

Completion: November 1996
Location: Wothington, Massachusetts, USA
Client: Mr Steffen Plehn & Mrs Harriet Marple
Area: 280 square metres; 3,014 square feet
Structure: Wood frame
Materials: Wood; stone; steel
Cost: US$450,000

This is a house for a recently married couple with grown children. The look is a rationalisation of opposites: her desire for modernity and large windows with his wish for a traditional New England house.

1

2

1   View from northeast
2   South view across meadow
3   East view
4   South side windows
5   View of clavichord in tower room
Photography: Ann McCallum

Sofitel Raja Orchid
Interdesign Company Limited

Completion: January 1996

Location: Khon Kaen, Thailand

Client: Raja Orchid Hotel Co., Ltd

Area: 65,000 square metres; 699,677 square feet

Structure: Reinforced concrete

Materials: Glass; concrete; granite; stucco; terracotta; fibreglass

Cost: 1,300,000,000 BAHT

The Sofitel is a 300-room, five-star hotel in the centre of Khon Kaen, the capital of Thailand's most populous province, located in the unique *Isaan* region. The challenge to the designers was to reflect the distinctive regional traditions in a modern, urban facility.

The building's stepped profile, marked by five prominent vertical shafts on each wing, symbolically alludes to the form of the *Kaen* instrument, intrinsic to the region's indigenous music. Fronting the main tower is a monumental porte-cochére, a modern interpretation of the overlapping roofs of traditional Thai architecture.

The juncture of this grand entrance with the angled main structure forms a vast five-storey lobby space, naturally illuminated by cascading tiers of sloping skylights. Both the entrance and tower structures visibly penetrate this geometrically complex atrium, literally representing the meeting of traditional and modern Thailand.

The principal interior spaces are finished with a variety of Thai hardwoods and native silk fabrics, expressing the hotel's central theme: the transformation of the traditional materials, forms, and craftsmanship of Thai culture into a distinctly modern spatial experience.

With its symbolic form rising 22-storeys above the plains of *Isaan* and its grandly-scaled public space, the Sofitel Khon Kaen provides a modern meeting place for Thailand most tradition-based region.

1

Front entrance from southwest
Section
View of lobby from above
Stairs to banquet hall foyer
Photography: Image Focal

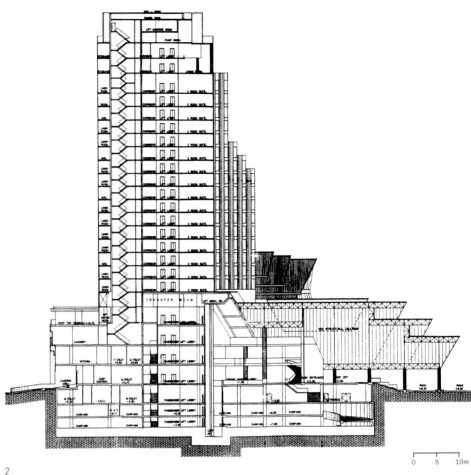

2

3

4

Stone Cloud
Kyu Sung Woo Architect, Inc.

Completion: April 1997

Location: Seoul, Korea

Area: 617 square metres; 6,641 square feet

Structure: Cast-in-place concrete; stone veneer

Materials: Lead-coated copper; aluminium; stainless steel; stone; cherry veneer

The design of the Stone Cloud responds to the conditions of a cultural context both old and new. As reflective of tradition Korean architecture, primary living areas are arrayed around a central courtyard. However, the courtyard of the house is not entirely contained: the exterior space and surrounding rooms open to the east and the urban community below. This notion of the traditional house directed outward represents the evolving state of contemporary Korean culture.

Sited in an established residential neighbourhood in the old city of Seoul, the landscape strategy retains the site's character by preserving prominent Acadia trees and rocky outcroppings. A series of stairs and passages link a garage, a lower level apartment, primary living and bedroom areas on two floors and an exercise room on the roof terrace. The varied and circuitous sequence begins from a grounded and contained position and moves toward an ever increasing lightness and openness to view.

A series of terrace walls which respond to the steep terrain of the site moderate the progression. The final destination of the formal, exterior sequence of the house is the roof terrace where one can view the courtyard below and the urban landscape beyond.

1

2

3

4

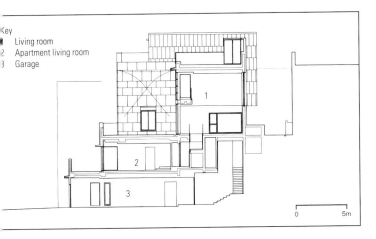

Key
1 Living room
2 Apartment living room
3 Garage

0   5m

7

8

1 View from street
2 Fabric canopy and balcony
3 Interior balcony, catwalk
4 Dining room and fabric canopy at dusk
5 Section
6 Living room and entry
7 Upper lawn, terrace with Acadia trees
8 Rear passage
Photography: Timothy Hursley

Sunny Bay Residence

Anderson Anderson Architecture

Completion: May 1997

Location: Gig Harbour, Washington, USA

Area: 232 square metres; 2,497 square feet

Structure: 2x6 platform framing; steel frame

Materials: Wood; steel

Awards: Southwest Washington AIA Honour Award

This house is a set of three structurally simple shed or gable roof rectangles accommodating the site and basic program of the house, arranged in a rectilinear pattern and then set into and impacted by the complex, contradictory reality of the site with its many overlapping conditions, limits and potentials. The basic order and integrity of the structure is maintained and revealed throughout the house in order that the inhabitants may read and understand the deformations of the building and the reasons for those deformations in the relationship between the clearly expressed rational structure and the sometimes evident and sometimes mysterious forces of nature, site history and human aspiration that have reached in to bend the house to some advantage.

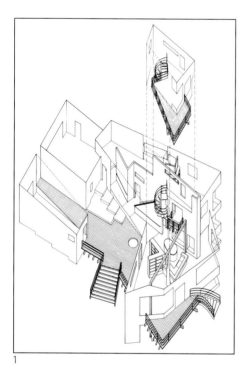

1

2

3

1   Axonometric
2   View of kitchen and living area from master
    bedroom balcony
3   Exterior view
4   View of master bedroom balcony and spiral
    staircase up to tower
5   View of entry alley between garage structures
6   View of kitchen and master bedroom balcony
    beyond
Photography: Eric Browne (2); Michael Scarbrough

6

Telegraph Hill Remodel

House + House Architects

Completion: February 1997

Location: San Francisco, California, USA

Area: 185 square metres; 2,000 square feet

Structure: Wood frame

Materials: Anigree wood; limestone; granite; marble; stainless steel; stucco sheet metal; sand-blasted glass

Hanging on the steep eastern slopes of Telegraph Hill in San Francisco, with spectacular views to the Bay Bridge and Treasure Island, this 185 square metre (2,000 square foot), remodel combines two small condominium units into one sweeping, light-filled space. An open central kitchen links the living and dining areas. The shimmering depth of the anigree wood cabinets is cut with strong reveal lines and complemented by a stainless steel backsplash and luscious green granite counters. Stainless steel pipes pierce the wood corners and a custom stainless steel sink links the two halves of the long, curving wet bar/island.

New limestone flooring throughout provides a neutral, elegant palette for the blend of new and old furnishings. A new maple entry door is detailed with stainless steel and opens onto a stair which ties all of the materials together with strong geometric lines. Custom stainless

steel radiator covers add focal point details to an otherwise unnotable component. Long walls are sculpted with niches and given strong colour as background for ar Glass doors with a sand-blasted geometric pattern provie privacy between the study and dining areas, while allowing maximum light.

A canted, backlit mirror floats above the green marble counters in the master bathroom. An existing light well is filled with plants and the pipes concealed with lattice, transforming a typical dismal urban necessity into a tiny garden in the corner of the bathroom. A new elevator wit windows at each level and a galvanised steel cornice add detail and visual interest.

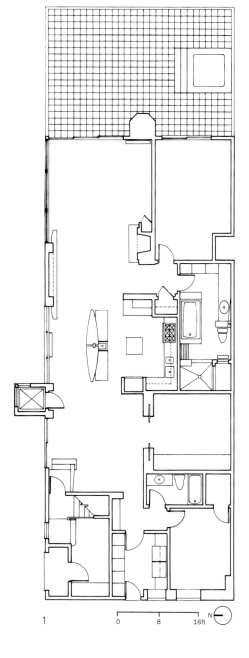

1

2

1 Floor plan
2 Exterior view of new elevator
3 View of kitchen from living room
4 Detail of wet bar
5 View of bathroom
6 View of dining area
7 Detail of entry
Photography: Claudio Santini

4

6

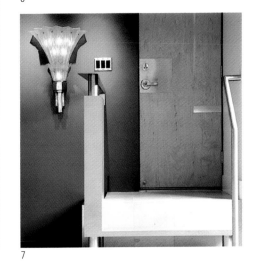

7

Verbena Heights

Anthony Ng Architects Limited

Completion: December 1996, (Phase 1)
Location: Tseung Kwan O New Town, Hong Kong
Client: Hong Kong Housing Society
Area: 150,000 square metres; 1.6 million square feet
Structure: Reinforced concrete
Materials: Ceramic tile
Cost: HK$ 1,000 million

Hong Kong is renowned for its hyper-density; land is at an astonishing premium and high-rise construction (commonly 30-storeys and above), is an economic reality. To combat the chronic housing shortage, major residential projects have been continually developed with standard block forms which are economic in terms of initial construction but often characterless and energy intensive in operations.

In response to the surging concern for sustainable design from local and global perspectives, Anthony Ng Architects Limited is devoted to research and design in the search for appropriate architecture that is responsive to the environmental agenda and the local context.

In the course of designing Verbena Heights, extensive scientific studies based upon computational analysis, wind tunnel modelling, etc. were carried out with a view to optimise the long-term environmental credentials potentially achievable through planning and architectural design. In addition to energy minimisation, the environmental studies covered material use, water conservation, waste management, and other local concerns such as traffic noise mitigation.

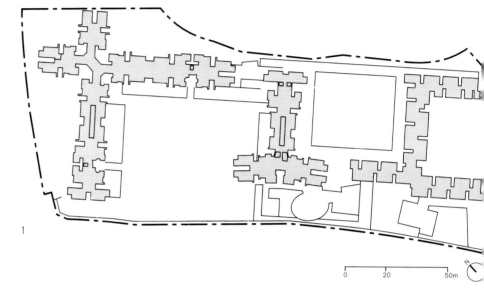

1   Master layout plan
2   Stepping housing blocks and podium noise screen
     viewed from south
3   Southwest elevation
4   Entrance canopy for control of pedestrian level wind
     climate
5   External solar shading screen
Photography: Keith Chan (2,4); K.S. Wong (5)

1

0   20   50m

336

2

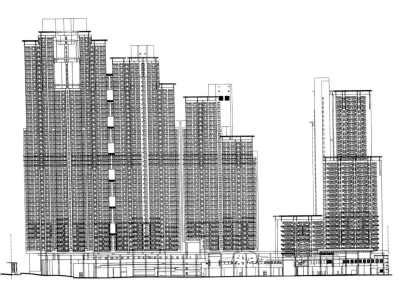

4

Vorio Residence

Arbonies King Vlock

Completion: January 1997

Location: Stony Creek, Connecticut, USA

Client: Tom and Diane Vorio

Area: 260 square metres; 2,800 square feet

Structure: Wood

Materials: Wood shingles; Stony Creek granite

Located in Stony Creek, a village on the Connecticut shoreline famous for its pink granite, this compact house is perched atop a steeply sloping site surrounded by woods, punctuated by boulders and rock outcroppings.

It has magical views of an old granite quarry, now filled with water, and a waterfall. Conceived of as a 'tree-house in the woods', the design is deceptively simple. Its perfectly square plan, with a soaring, light-filled two-storey living space, simplicity of form, and use of natural materials allow its natural setting to energise the interior.

The central position of the kitchen with its generous counter space and magnificent 12 foot island is designed for entertaining. Lighting of the open plan living space is choreographed to suit many activities and moods, drama or intimate.

The most astonishing feature is its core of four 40 foot timbers which serve as the structural and visual centre of the house. With only the bark removed, these massive, natural columns reflect the adjacent wood and reach upward from the bedroom level to the cupola.

1

1 Exterior building view
2 Interior detail of dining and kitchen
3 Interior living space, view to entry
Photography: Timothy Hursley

100 Wozoco's

MVRDV
in collaboration with Bureau Bouwkunde, Rotterdam

Completion: March 1997

Location: Amsterdam-Osdorp

Client: Housing Co-operation Het Oosten

Area: 7,600 square metres; 81,808 square feet

Structure: Reinforced concrete; steel

Materials: WRC; eternite board; aluminium; glass; perspex; perforated steel

Cost: US$5 million

Awards: Merkelbach Award Amsterdam Fund for the Art

Within the densifying garden city in the western part of Amsterdam (Westelijke Tuinsteden) a slab with 100 apartments for '55+'s' was placed. The existing zoning envelope and the north–south orientation of the building made it impossible to position the 100 apartments in a slab; only 87 were able to fit in. The solution was to cantilever the remaining 13 apartments on the north

facade of the slab with steel trusses in such a way that each hanging apartment would get sun via an east- or west-facade. (It is not acceptable in Holland to build north facing apartments). In this way the open ground plan, characteristic for these neighbourhoods, remained as open and green as possible.

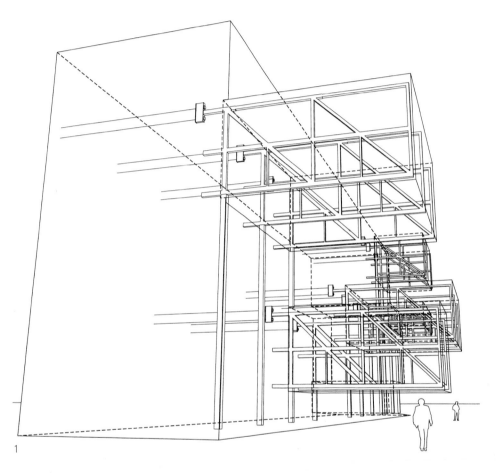

1

2

3

1 Perspective
2 South facade
3 Fragment south facade
4 North facade
5 View from gallery (at north facade)
Photography: Hans Werlemann

5

Century Mahkota Hotel, Melaka
Arkitek MAA Sdn Bhd

Completion: December 1996

Location: Melaka, Malaysia

Client: Ayer Keroh Resort Sdn Bhd (member of the Lion Group)

Area: 84,000 square metres; 904,198 square feet

Structure: Reinforced concrete; timber

Materials: Marble and sandstone; ceramic tiles; quarry tiles; concrete roof tiles; timber

Cost: RM94 million

Century Mahkota Hotel sits on a 9-acre seafront site at the historical city of Melaka, and is conceptualised as a sprawling complex of 617 units of service apartments and hotel rooms organised around an elongated central landscaped courtyard on an east–west axis with the apartment blocks orientated north–south generally.

The buildings are staggered progressively in height, from three storeys at the western boundary to 19 storeys at the eastern boundary. The blocks sited along the southern boundary are purposely kept low in order to maintain maximum sea views for the higher blocks at the rear.

The various buildings are visually tied together by facade treatment derived along a Mediterranean theme, with major influences from traditional Malaccan urban buildings, and physically linked by covered walkways at ground level.

The central landscaped courtyard serves as the internal focus and activity area of the development and has been extensively landscaped with lush tropical vegetation. It features two large swimming pools, barbecue areas, children's playgrounds, jogging tracks, water features, a mini-golf course and a tennis court. The lobby and first floor public areas of the hotel block are designed to achieve a long vista of the courtyard along the east–west axis, which presents a spectacular view and all service apartment blocks have direct access to this courtyard at ground level.

1   Overall view from sea
2   Entrance porch and facade detail
3   View of hotel block from courtyard
4   Water feature detail
Photography: courtesy Arkitek MAA Sdn Bhd

1

2

3

4

Enismore Gardens Mews House

John Pawson

Completion: May 1996
Location: London, UK
Client: Sophie Canmoerkerke
Area: 150 square metres; 1,615 square feet
Materials: Cherry wood; stainless steel; Yorkstone

A traditional three-bedroom Victorian mews house in London was the subject of a complete internal restructuring that transcended the spatial limitations conventionally associated with homes of this kind. The whole of the ground floor has been opened up to create a single space. A cherry wood floor has been used throughout.

A fireplace wall with a Yorkstone hearth hides a new staircase, while a second new wall defines, but also conceals the kitchen. Most of the upper floor is occupied by a studio bedroom. Two folding panels provide possible subdivision. The result is two rooms, each with their own access.

1 Ground floor plan
2 Second floor plan
3 Studio bedroom
4 Stairway to first floor studio
5 First floor, view from studio to bedroom
Photography: Christoph Kicherer

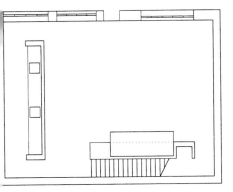

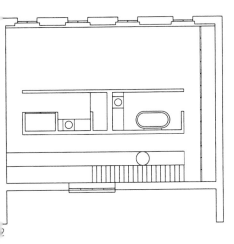

House in Higashi-nada
Waro Kishi + K. Associates/Architects

Completion: May 1997
Location: Higashi-nada-ku, Kobe, Japan
Area: 72 square metres; 775 square feet
Structure: Reinforced concrete
Materials: Cast-in-place concrete

This house is located in Kobe's Higashi-nada ward. The site conditions were stringent—70 square metres (753 square feet) with a 4.2 metre (13.8 foot) frontage. Across the road on the north side however, was a park, a precious pocket of greenery in the dense urban surroundings. It was sought to create a relationship with this park as the theme in developing the design.

Keeping the heights of the first and second levels lower than usual, the ceiling of the third floor dining room where residents gather, was raised as high as possible, to 3.9 metres (12.8 feet). At the south, this space with its lofty ceiling faces on the void of the terrace and court, which are connected by means of a staircase with a gentle incline. An aperture in the north side opens the full breadth of the building from below. By fully opening the north side the third floor is experienced as a semi-exterior space, facing the park, while winds circulate through the building from south to north.

The residents live in contact with nature, in the depths of a metropolis—the result of providing direct experience of the park's greenery whilst high above ground on the third floor.

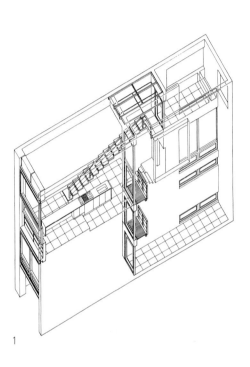

1

1 Axonometric
2 Narrow courtyard
3 Facade
Photography: Hiroyuki Hirai

2

3

House in Higashi-osaka

Waro Kishi + K. Associates/Architects

Completion: April 1997
Location: Higashi-osaka, Osaka Prefecture, Japan
Area: 116 square metres; 1,248 square feet
Structure: Steel
Materials: Precast cement

The building stands in a monotonous expanse of residential buildings sliced by private railway lines, in the suburb of Osaka.

The main structure has a frontage of two 3.6 metre (11.8 foot) spans and a depth of three 3.4 metre (11 foot) spans. A terrace and a staircase has been placed within a single span section, on the side fronting the road. Behind the main structure a single span section is devoted to a court with a stairway. This court has been opened to the south through an aperture at its top level, the only such opening on the south side.

From there, one enters the third floor living/dining room with its 4 metre (13 foot) high ceiling. The room is partly roofed with semi-transparent material, so that the spatial transition from the court to the interior of the room, from exterior to interior, is orchestrated around the experience of gradual change.

The main floor is only a few metres above ground, yet this slight difference in elevation produces a character of space that is at once removed from the city yet open to it.

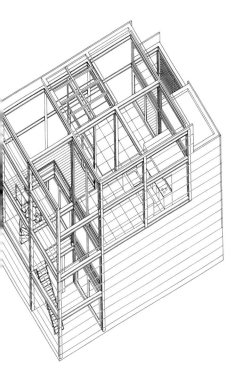

Axonometric
Third floor living/dining room looking to courtyard
Facade
Third floor living/dining room
Photography: Hiroyuki Hirai

2

4

Panelized House Prototype

Anderson Anderson Architecture

Completion: July 1996
Location: Tsuruga, Japan
Client: Amerikaya Construction
Area: 111 square metres; 1,194 square feet
Structure: 2x6 platform framing; post and beam
Materials: Wood; steel
Awards: Southwest Washington AIA Award of Merit

Designed for a construction company in Japan, this prototype is a part of a series of single- and multi-family housing designs intended as affordable, high quality alternatives to contemporary developer housing.

In contrast to the traditional wood houses of Japan, typical current housing construction maintains little of traditional design and cultural values. The comparatively low cost of 2x4 style construction has created a large industry importing materials and housing design from foreign countries. Much of this import housing equally fails

to value traditional Japanese design and construction quality or the best qualities of modern materials and fabrication processes.

This series of semi-modular, panelised housing prototype provides rational prefabrication, integrated indoor and outdoor living spaces, natural light and materials, and an open flow of space. The designs introduce disabled accessible units and flexible spaces to accommodate rapidly changing family living patterns while still providing traditional entries, bathing spaces, and tatami rooms.

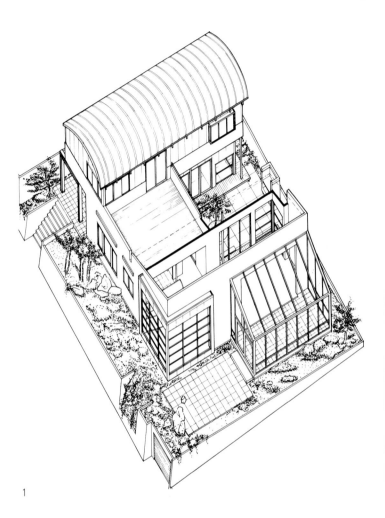

1

2

3

4

1   Axonometric
2   View from street
3   Tatami room and courtyard beyond
4   View of deck beside dining area and sunroom
Photography: Amerikaya Co., Ltd.

Redevelopment of Lam Tin Estate (Phases 1–3)

Hong Kong Housing Authority

Completion: December 1996

Location: Lam Tin, Hong Kong

Client: Hong Kong Housing Authority

Area: 4.68 hectares; 11.56 acres

Structure: Reinforced concrete

Materials: Ceramic tiles; glass mosaic tiles; textured paint

Cost: HK$1.1 million

Redevelopment of Lam Tin Estate Phases 1—3 is part of the whole Lam Tin Estate redevelopment which spans over 10 years with the final phase completed in 2005. These three phases provide 5,433 rental flats for the lower income sector.

Facilities include a shopping centre with approximately 2,000 square metres (21,528 square feet) of retail shops, restaurants, fast food and market stalls and carparking spaces. Educational facilities include two primary schools and two kindergartens, welfare facilities such as sheltered housing for the elderly, a day care centre for both elderly and children and a youth centre.

All the domestic blocks, shopping centre, schools and carpark are interconnected by a system of covered walkways which also link to the Transit Railway Station.

Due to the hilly topography, escalators and link-bridges are also provided to interlink the various building platforms.

1 Shopping centre in Phase 2
2 Domestic block in Phase 3 constructed on suspended platform
3 Covered walkway between domestic blocks
Photography: courtesy Hong Kong Housing Authority

3

Redevelopment of Lower Wong Tai Sin Estate # (Phase 9 and 11)

Hong Kong Housing Authority

Completion: September 1996

Location: Wong Tai Sin, Kowloon, Hong Kong

Client: Hong Kong Housing Authority

Area: 56,700 square metres; 610,333 square feet

Structure: Reinforced concrete; precast concrete facade

Materials: Glass mosaic tiles; textured paint

Cost: HK$519 million

This project is located in Lower Wong Tai Sin adjacent to the Morse Park. It comprises seven 26-storey Harmony 3 (option 1) Blocks providing a total of 3,094 domestic flats with a total design population of 11,375.

Facilities include one single-storey carport of 97 parking spaces, a carport podium roof garden with hard landscaping, a feature wall, pools and water features. Large amounts of passive and active open spaces with planting areas, children play areas, sitting areas, and the estate plaza provide pleasant environments. All domestic blocks are connected by a covered walkway for safe and easy access.

This is the first housing project with mandatory external facades of the domestic units, in those blocks designed and constructed in precast concrete panels by the contractors, in accordance with the 'drawings and specifications'. This construction method is to ensure the quality of concrete works and finishing works of the facades. Aluminium window frames are cast in situ with the precast facade in traditional window fixing method to eliminate possible leakage problems.

1

2

1   Evening view of Harmony Blocks from Cascade
2   Overview of estate plaza with performance stage in front
3   View of Harmony Blocks from Morse Park
Photography: courtesy Hong Kong Housing Authority

3

The Boyd Hotel

oning Eizenberg Architecture

ompletion: December 1996

ocation: Los Angeles, California, USA

lient: Skid Row Housing Trust

rea: 1,765 square metres; 19,000 square feet

tructure: Steel; wood; concrete

Materials: Cement plaster; aluminium; ceramic
e; terrazzo paving; corrugated metal panels

ost: US$2.2 million

The Boyd Hotel is a 61-room, 4-storey single room occupancy hotel located in downtown Los Angeles. Its design draws on Los Angeles' rich tradition of urban commercial and residential buildings from the 30s. The design presents a welcoming face to the street, and side elevations are simple but articulated. The plan highlights shared public space, an exterior courtyard and common areas for social interaction. Air conditioning is not an economic option and comfort is achieved with passive energy strategies such as exterior window shading, cross ventilation and maximisation of natural light to both corridors and guest rooms.

3

1   Lobby looking to street
2   Lobby looking to lounge and courtyard
3   Street view
Photography: Benny Chan

University of Arizona Colonia De La Paz Residence Halls

Moule & Polyzoides Architects

Completion: January 1996

Location: Tucson, Arizona, USA

Client: University of Arizona

Area: 11,148 square metres; 120,000 square feet

Structure: Brick exterior; sand-blasted concrete interior

Materials: Poured-in-place, coloured and waxed concrete floors; slat wooden ceilings; dry wall partitions between rooms

Cost: US$12 million

The firm's campus plan for a Highland District created a new southern gateway for the campus of the University of Arizona and links several student living-related facilities together through close clustering based on extreme hot weather, self-shading, indigenous building and open space types. Within this district, is the completed design of the first two residence halls.

The architectural approach was to conceive of the building and its gardens as an integrated figure. The foundation of the design was in the definition of a memorable figure of open space around which buildings could be arrayed. This matrix of open space is composed of 11 courtyards.

Along the streetfront, an arcade defines the building's edge and becomes part of a new campus entrance arcade system on Highland Avenue.

The project is organised as a hybrid of two typical American campus residential types; the major shared living, dining, and study spaces located around two large courtyards and the multiple entry building where student rooms with bathroom facilities are gathered into suites oriented around intimate gardens, courts, covered exterior living rooms called *iwans* and stair entries. Each suite has its own entry from a courtyard giving it privacy and identity

1   Entrance court
2   Front arcade on Highland Avenue
3   Courtyard

Photography: courtesy Moule & Polyzoides Architects

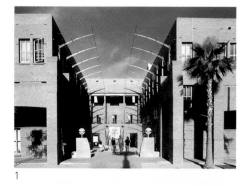

1

2

3

Valley Park Condominiums

TSP Architects + Planners Pte Ltd

Completion: April 1997

Location: River Valley Road/Kellock Road, Singapore

Client: River Valley Properties Pte Ltd

Area: 110,000 square metres; 1.2 million square feet

Structure: Reinforced concrete

Materials: Curtainwall; texture coating

Cost: S$218 million

The development comprises five blocks of 20/15-storey condominiums with full facilities.

The project makes use of curves, waves, arcs and circles in the design and, as a whole, shows certain typical TSP Architects + Planners characteristics, notably the precast scoop-shaped balconies and the complex plan form, in which, what appear to be simple circular envelopes, turn out to be clusters of three and four modules linked at the centre. The folds and clefts breaking up the plan form are used to light and ventilate the kitchen and service areas.

Two of the blocks are designed as one S-curve block. The process of working with the developers shows their concern to maximise the number of apartment types, even to the extent of knocking off a corner here or there or of a room in a carefully worked out plan. The concern for privacy of every unit is also naturally achieved by the use of circular profile plans of the blocks, which minimises direct frontal overlooking of units, but at the same time affords a 'wide angle' view from each of the units.

1 Swimming pool deck with clubhouse
2 Poolside condominium block
3 Curves on balconies and clubhouse
Photography: Hans Schlupp

Retail

Ever Gotesco Shopping Complex

G&W Architects, Engineers, Project Development Consultants

Completion: June 1996

Location: Cainta, Philippines

Client: Gotesco Properties Incorporated

Area: 60,000 square metres; 645,856 square feet

Structure: Reinforced concrete

Materials: Polycarbonate sheets; stainless steel

The client's brief was for a shopping complex which was both attractive and inviting to the customers which resulted in a unique character attained by the mixture of modern and classical elements such as traditional columns, decorative handrails, arcades and eye-catching storefronts.

The mall's wide aisles provide maximum exposure for all stores and the fountain located inside the central mall enhances the festive atmosphere.

The 60,000 square metre (645,856 square foot) mall provides complete shopping facilities and introduces modern features such as the 360 degree circular cinema which is the only one of its kind in the Philippines.

1

2

3

1   Shopping complex facade
2   Skylight leading to main entrance of mall
3&5   Shopping mall atrium
4   Lobby of circular cinema
6   360 degree circular cinema is one of the main attractions of the mall

Photography: RRL Photography, Inc.

5

Times Square Building

Nikken Sekkei

Completion: October 1996

Location: Tokyo, Japan

Client: Rail City East Development Co., Ltd.

Area: 12,732 square metres; 137,050 square feet

Structure: Steel reinforced concrete; reinforced concrete; steel

Materials: Granite; precast concrete

The project involves redevelopment of the former site of a Japan Railways freight depot adjacent to Shinjuku, the largest commercial district in Japan. Times Square Building was designed to play a leading role in the urban reorganisation of the area around the south exit of the enormous Shinjuku Station. With Takashimaya Department Store as its main tenant, the commercial complex was the first among those in an urban setting to combine merchandising functions with a wide range of entertainment facilities. Creating buildings of a long-life span was a major objective of the project. The buildings are also flexible to future changes, with their expansive and attractive open spaces, highly durable exteriors, reinforced structures and high ceilings.

The facade is highlighted with windows arranged in a grid shape. The innovative double glazing used for the windows brings the dual benefits of inviting controlled sunlight indoors while alleviating the overpowering feeling that comes from the huge walls. When indoor illumination lights up the complex at night, one is reminded of an 'andon'—a traditional Japanese oil lampstand with a wood frame and paper shade. The result is a dramatic transformation of the complex's appearance from day to night.

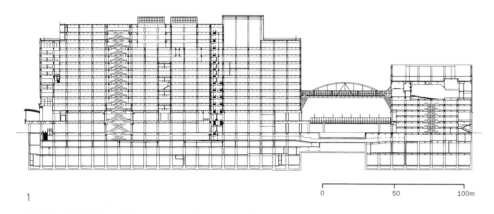

1

2

3

1   Section
2   Aerial view
3   Night view, west facade
4   Exterior view
5   Open space, south side
6   Sales area
Photography: Seiichi Motoki (3); Shinozawa Architectural
Photography Office

Tourneau 'TimeMachine'
Levi, Sanchick and Associates

Completion: June 1997
Location: New York, New York, USA
Client: Tourneau
Area: 1,500 square metres; 16,200 square feet
Structure: Steel
Materials: Granite; wood; stainless steel

Tourneau's 'TimeMachine', their new four-level flagship store for selling fine watches and jewellery, was designed by Levi, Sanchick and Associates with consulting architect John Defazio. Exterior identification is an open stainless steel truss carrying clocks representing great cities of the world and their time zones, juxtaposed against the taut-skinned granite and glass office tower behind and above.

The triangular interior, with entrances from the street and a much-used public atrium, turns the entire street level into through circulation. To take advantage of this, the upper levels carrying 'high-end' merchandise, required unification and visibility, achieved by carving out a half-circle from the second floor, inserting a mezzanine and

creating a rotunda. The lower concourse, served by escalators, has its own aesthetic for sport and 'fun' watches, and houses an 'event space' and the 'gallery of time'. All levels are connected by an open stairway and an elevator.

Each of the store's levels is like a separate watch armature. A single existing column, two storeys high, rises up like a pinion gear. Gear geometries are carried into the ceilings, with murals of watchworks continuing the illusion.

1 Street view
2 Street floor
Opposite:
  Rotunda from street level

1

2

Opposite:
Antique church clock over street
entrance
5 Rotunda from second floor
6 Lower concourse
7 Second floor
Photography: A. Michael Hoiland

6

Palace Mall/Salisbury Garden

Kwan & Associates Architects Ltd

Completion: June 1997
Location: Tsim Sha Tsui, Hong Kong
Client: New World Development
Area: 13,140 square metres; 141,442 square feet
Structure: Reinforced concrete; glass
Materials: Aluminium cladding; granite

Hong Kong's first underground shopping mall, this project consists of four basement levels housed completely beneath a grand glass-house structure which is integrated with the landscaped Salisbury Garden open space adjacent to the Cultural Centre and serves as a forecourt to this monumental building. Both the curvilinear roof and transparent anatomy of the glass structure assure its landmark status.

The retail component at basement levels one and two is reached by an escalator system commencing in the glass volume. The transparent atrium allows maximum levels of natural light to permeate the mall. Beneath the retail levels

is a 250-space two-storey car park which is accessed via the neighbouring New World Centre car park, obviating the need for a ramp. This car park is designated for the use of Cultural Centre patrons.

Pedestrian subways connect the mall to the New World Centre, the Peninsula Hotel and the Sheraton Hotel, anticipating the time when pedestrian crossings at grade will no longer be possible in this busy area of Tsim Sha Tsui.

1 Site plan
2 Aerial vista
3 Facade and entrance
4 Glass house brings daylight into basement shopping mall
5 Escalators bisect space, reflecting the atrium roof
Photography: courtesy Kwan & Associates Architects Ltd

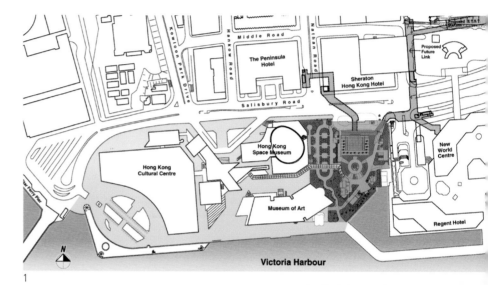

1

2

4

3

5

Shui Wai Area 13 Phase 2

ng Kong Housing Authority

mpletion: April 1997

ation: Tin Shui Wai, NT, Hong Kong

ent: Hong Kong Housing Authority

a: 6,048 square metres; 65,102 square feet

ucture: Reinforced concrete

terials: Ceramic tiles; textured paint

st: HK$37 million

The shopping centre is located at the main vehicular and pedestrian access of the estate at the northwest corner.

The shopping centre is a two-storey building with a roof garden. Facilities include shop premises for a wide range of trades including general retail stores, a supermarket, restaurant, cafe, convenience store, barber shop, bank etc. A multi-storey carparking facility is also provided nearby.

The shops at ground floor are facing the bus terminus and shops at 1/F are linked to the adjacent Tin Yiu Estate by a footbridge.

2

View from Tin Shing Road

Footbridge linkage to Tin Yiu Estate

Steel truss at commercial centre

'Entrance Gateway' to commercial centre

otography: courtesy Hong Kong Housing Authority

4

Other

Ahtiala Social and Health Center

Paatel & Paatela, Architects Ltd

Completion: March 1996
Location: Lahti, Finland
Client: The City of Lahti
Area: 2,500 square metres; 26,911 square feet
Structure: Prefabricated reinforced concrete
Materials: Brick; concrete; tiles; metal; glass
Cost: FIM 20 million

The Ahtiala Social and Health Center provides the inhabitants of Ahtiala area, a suburban centre of the city of Lahti, with primary healthcare and social services. The building has two floors with easy access to all units for aged and disabled persons.

On the ground floor next to the lobby and information desk are the child health consultation unit, the home service and home healthcare unit, the coffee shop and staff dining area, together with the administration and service functions.

The first floor contains the central patient waiting area—partly open to the ground floor entrance lobby—the doctors' examination and treatment facilities, the laboratory and EKG room and consultation rooms for the daycare and social service workers.

The main lobby is partly open to the first floor central are thus the natural roof light—from the east in the morning the northwest in the evening—makes an ideal climate in the interior spaces made of glass, wood and tiles, for bot clients and staff throughout the day.

The exterior is made of white concrete surfaces, tiles and glass and a red tiled roof. With the plantation growing on the site, the surroundings will age to be an harmonious part of the surrounding suburban area of the same nature

1 Section
2 Site plan
3 Facade south
4 Facade east
5 Detail of facade
6 Main entrance

Photography: Timo Kaupp

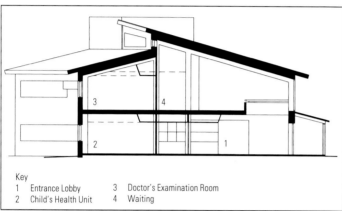

Key
1 Entrance Lobby
2 Child's Health Unit
3 Doctor's Examination Room
4 Waiting

1

3

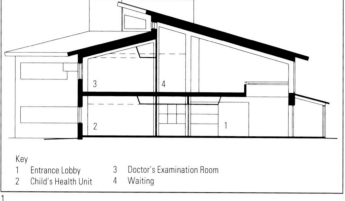

Key
1 Main Entrance
2 Lobby
3 Information
4 Home Health Care
5 Home Service
6 Child Health Consultation
7 Cafe
8 Administration
9 Services

Parking

Service Courtyard

2

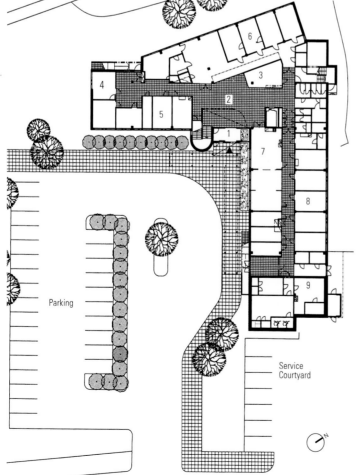

4

5

2. KERROS
LABORATORIO
LÄÄKÄREIDEN VASTAANOTTO
SAIRAANHOITAJAT
SOSIAALITYÖNTEKIJÄT JA KANSLISTIT

1. KERROS
NEUVONTA
KOTIPALVELU
KOTISAIRAANHOITO/AIKUISNEUVONTA
LASTENNEUVOLA
PÄIVÄHOITO
ÄITIYSNEUVOLA

Class of 1951 Observatory
Roth & Moore Architects

Completion: May 1997
Location: Poughkeepsie, New York, USA
Client: Vassar College
Area: 258 square metres; 2,780 square feet
Structure: Laminated timber; light steel
Materials: Aluminium; bluestone; quarry tile
Cost: US$1 million

This astronomical observatory at Vassar College, a liberal arts college in upstate New York, has been planned for use by undergraduates. The facility replaces an antiquated observatory built in 1860, now placed on the National Register of Historic Properties. The original masonry structure was hampered by poor 'seeing' conditions due to its massive, uninsulated construction and exposure to excessive light pollution from nearby buildings and site lighting.

The new complex is located on the highest point of the campus, affording unobstructed access to the night sky with minimal threat of light or thermal pollution. Included are two domes housing 32-inch and 20-inch remotely operated reflecting telescopes; a support building with

computerised control room, classroom, and faculty work space; an observation terrace with permanently fixed mounts for portable telescopes; and a third smaller dome housing an older manually operated telescope.

The laminated timber structure of the support building is clad in lightweight, low thermal-mass aluminium sheathing and standing seam aluminium roofing; heated spaces are super insulated to minimise night-time heat pollution adjacent to the domes. The unheated motor operated domes are of light steel construction clad in aluminium sheathing.

1

Motor operated bi-parting shutters
Site plan
Two 22-foot diameter domes

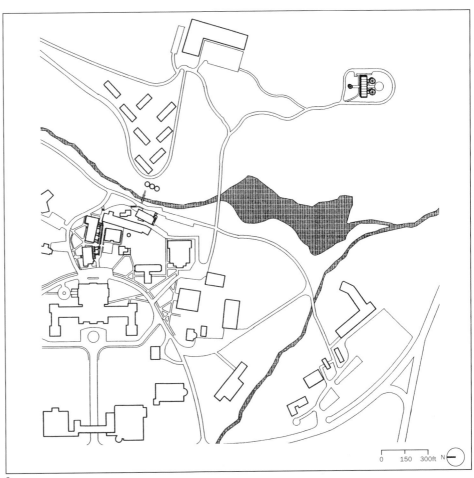

2

3

369

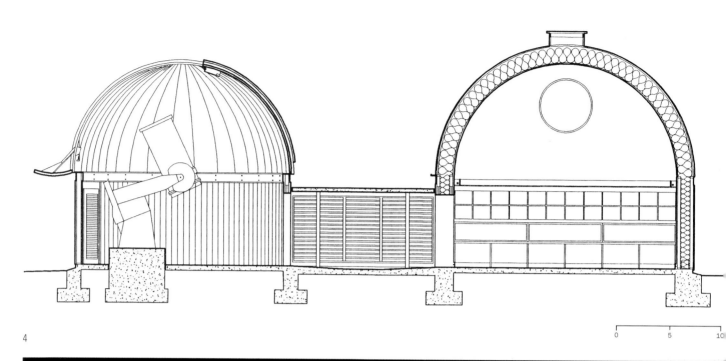

4

5

4 Section
5 Louvred passageways connect domes to support building
6 Recessed entrance to complex is trimmed in bluestone
7 Control room houses computerised telescope equipment
8 Vaulted classroom
Photography: Robert Benson

7

8

Hong Kong Temple

Liang Peddle Thorp Architects & Planners Ltd

Completion: April 1996

Location: Kowloon Tong, Kowloon, Hong Kong

Client: The Church of Jesus Christ of Latter-Day Saints

Area: 2,560 square metres; 275,556 square feet

Structure: Concrete; stone cladding; triple/double-glazed glass

Materials: Regina White granite; Tiger Red granite

Cost: HK$180 million

Awards: 1996 HKIA Annual Award, Certificate of Merit

Owing to the small given site (1,240 square metre; 13,347 square foot) available, this mid-rise complex houses three different uses under the same roof. There is a chapel with ancillary offices for Sunday services and social activities, and staff quarters that occupy both first and second floors. The Temple which is used for special functions such as marriages and *'family bonding'*, takes up the third, fourth and fifth floors. Separate entrances and lobbies are maintained for the Temple and the chapel, as well as separate vertical circulation.

The Temple is expressed both externally and internally to distinguish it from the chapel below where Temple floors and external walls receive more articulate architectural elements with classical reference than the chapel. The whole building is clad predominantly in white granite with earthy red marble for its base and fence wall. The stone finish projects an image of permanency, stability and eternity of the church's belief. The whitish colour symbolises purity and heavenliness; the darker reddish base represents the connection of heaven to the congregation. On the ground level, a heavily landscaped garden is created at the front area of the site to provide a transition zone.

At the main entrance facing the bustling Cornwall Street, an elaborately designed waterfall feature wall dramatis the sense of entry and acts as an acoustic and spatial barrier between the serene temple complex and the nois outside world.

1 East side ornate entrance gate
2 Night view of building exterior
3 South elevation
4 East elevation
5 Exterior

Photography: Keran Ip

1

2

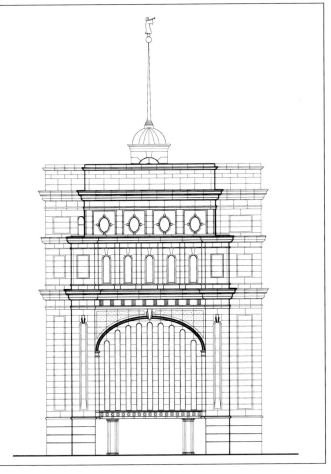

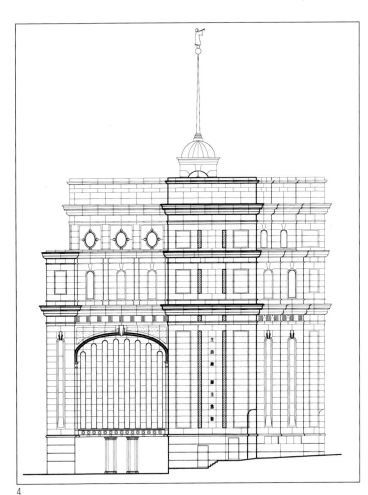

4

Kook Min Corporate Training Center
Tai Soo Kim Partners

Completion: June 1997
Location: Yong In, Korea
Client: Kook Min Insurance Company
Area: 9,660 square metres; 103,982 square feet
Structure: Steel
Materials: Granite; lead coated copper
Cost: $15 million

This corporate training facility is nestled in a mountainous area and is designed to reflect the rolling terrain. A series of terraces and retaining walls serve as a foundation to anchor the complex. In contrast, playful curving rooftop structures and curved exterior walls mirror the mountains' silhouettes. The playful curves are carried into the interiors with two serpentine walls defining circulation space and controlling acoustics.

To facilitate the owner leasing out the Center when not otherwise in use, the educational program is separated from housing. The one-storey 3,000 square metre (32,393 square foot), educational building provides auditoriums, classrooms, breakout rooms and a cafeteria. The 6,600 square metre (71,044 square foot), dormitory provides over 250 beds.

1

2

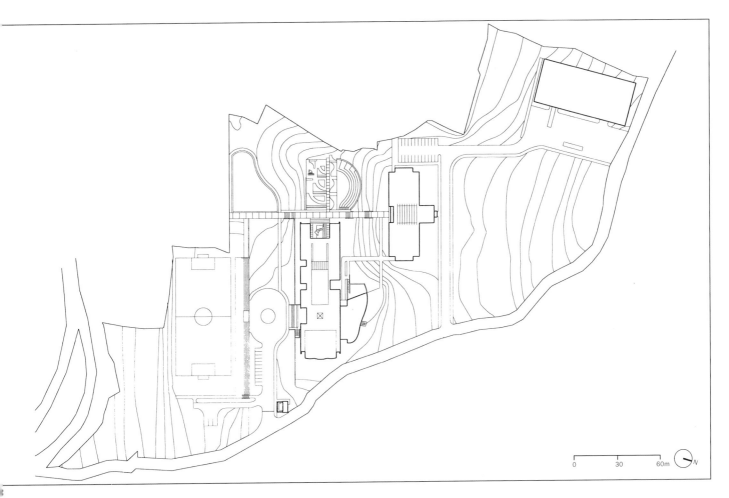

1 View of educational building
2 Site features a reflecting pool and terraced gardens
3 Site plan
4 Rigid steel structure opens onto terraced gardens
5 Ceremonial colonnade marks the entry

4

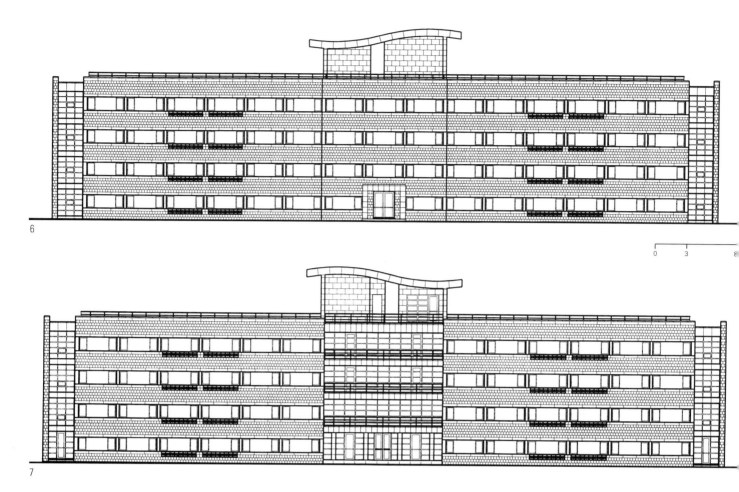

6

7

0   3   8

8

6   North elevation, dormitory
7   South elevation, dormitory
8   Rooftop structures
9   Serpentine walls define corridors and auditoriums
10   Seminar rooms
Photography: Timothy Hursley

Miyazaki Airport Station
RTKL International Ltd.

Completion: June 1996

Location: Miyazaki City, Miyazaki Prefecture, Japan

Client: JR Kyushu

Area: 225,000 square metres; 2.4 million square feet

Structure: Reinforced concrete; steel

Materials: 'Lamda' concrete panels; porcelain; 'Acrotec' aluminium; flamed/polished granite

This railway station adjacent to Miyazaki, Japan's regional airport is a functionally and visually distinctive portal to this resort city and its surrounding region, affording comfortable and accessible passage in a vibrant, stimulating environment.

In addition to providing convenient access to the client's extensive railway network, the station's economical design intentionally harmonises with the client's previously built station in downtown Miyazaki, also designed by RTKL International Ltd. The Air Station adopts the senior facility's exuberantly louvred frame, which shields the train platform and carries along on illuminated spires, invigorating the station's image during evening hours.

From a distance, the terminal establishes itself as a bold landmark, with towers shaped like the inverted wings of an aeroplane and wave-like canopy. Inside, curved shapes soft monochromatic colours, and light-hued materials reinforce the host city's resort character, while complementing the existing white air terminal's structure per the airport authority's request.

The architecture of Miyazaki Air Station conveys both the area's established tropical, airy appeal and its streamline ultramodern aspirations for the future—thus ably fulfilling its vital role in the region's development.

1

3

1 Exterior entrance
2 View of train terminal at platform
3 Dramatic night view of *bofu* screen (windscreen)
4 Lobby view
Photography: Nacasa Studio

4

St Andrews Multi-Purpose Anglican Church

innovarchi pty ltd

Completion: January 1996

Location: Gracemere, Queensland, Australia

Client: Anglican Church of Australia Diocese of Rockhampton

Area: 560 square metres; 6,028 square feet

Structure: Segmented timber portal frames

Materials: Laminated veneer lumber; rendered and lime-washed concrete; aluminium; zincalume

Cost: $350,000

A church with a uniquely 'Australian' character and reflecting the beauty of the natural landscape, the scheme was conceived as a complex of three elements: an existing church (relocated and converted to Sunday School); the new multi-purpose hall and an interlinking courtyard. A tripartite spatial concept has also been reflected by the grounding of the timber portals into the gently undulating landscape, a glazed enclosure and a sheltering roof hovering overhead.

The first building of its kind, the industrial laminated plantation pine (LVL) portals have been constructed with an innovative segmented jointing system developed by

innovarchi pty ltd. Short curved pieces connected to less expensive straights, gives potential for an endless variety of cross-sectional shapes.

ESD principles and the use, where possible, of environmentally sensitive products are essential to the design which maximises natural day lighting, passive cooling, ventilation and recycling of roof water into a landscape of native plants.

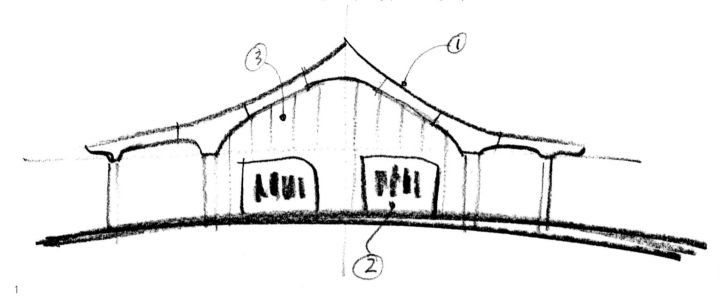

1

2

5

1   Sketch elevation
2   View of entry from eastern approach
3   Hovering roof provides protection for verandah entry
4   Free-standing altar wall
5   Timber structure and masonry entry
Photography: K Ireland (2); J Linkins (3,5); K McBryde (4)

Ventilation Building #7/Ted Williams Tunnel

TAMS Consultants, Inc. Architects, Engineers & Planners
Preliminary Design: Wallace, Floyd, Associates, Inc. & Stull and Lee, Inc.

Completion: January 1997

Location: Logan International Airport, Boston, Massachusetts, USA

Client: Massachusetts Highway Department

Area: 9,500 square metres; 102,260 square feet

Structure: Cast-in-place concrete; steel frame superstructure

Materials: Architectural concrete; aluminium rain screen panel system; exposed structural steel

Cost: US$15 million

Serving the new 2,500 metre (8,202 foot) long Ted Williams Tunnel beneath Boston Harbor, Ventilation Building #7 acts as a colossal respirator comprised of 24 enormous exhaust and supply vans. Its distinct and forceful appearance also serves as an icon of Boston's new urban infrastructure.

Comprised almost entirely of air-moving machinery, the building is divided into two primary wings. The larger exhaust system section occupies the northern end of the building and is distinguished by 14 stainless steel-capped exhaust stacks that rise prominently above the roof.

The smaller supply wing to the south contains 10 air supply fans which dispense fresh air to the tunnel through a manifold system of exposed concrete ducts emerging from a wall of giant-scale louvres.

The visual and tectonic expression of the structure is a direct reflection of its mechanistic purpose: concrete, steel and aluminium building components are distinctly articulated and boldly scaled to address the grand sweep of the harbour and airport skyline.

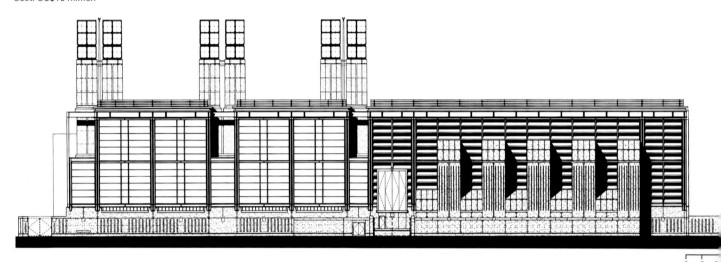

1

0 3 6

2

382

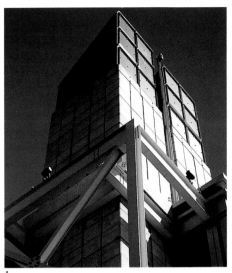

4

5

6

1 Elevation
2 Illuminated building at dusk
3 Detail of exhaust stacks, rainscreen and concrete wall
4 Exhaust stack detail
5 Detail of exhaust stacks and stainless steel terminations
6 Supply fan room, detail of fans
Photography: Peter Vanderwarker (2,3,5,6); Chris Iwerks (4)

Digit Digit
Arkitech

Completion: January 1996
Location: Causeway Bay, Hong Kong
Client: Digit Digit Post-Production Ltd
Area: 450 square metres; 4,844 square feet
Structure: Concrete
Materials: Semi-transparent glass
Cost: HK$3.1 million

A first floor office building with a 5 metre (16 foot) high ceiling, without any partitions or columns in the 450 square metre (4,844 square feet) space, gives a strong feeling of a loft-house or industrial space utilised for a high-tech post-production facility, equal to those at NASA.

By covering the existing windows with a layer of semi-transparent glass, the problem of a poor view and importantly, the bad *Feng Shui* of the original building, was overcome.

Extending this same skill to the internal raw concrete walls, they were clad with a semi-transparent glass thereby creating another spatial mystery in this intriguing renovation.

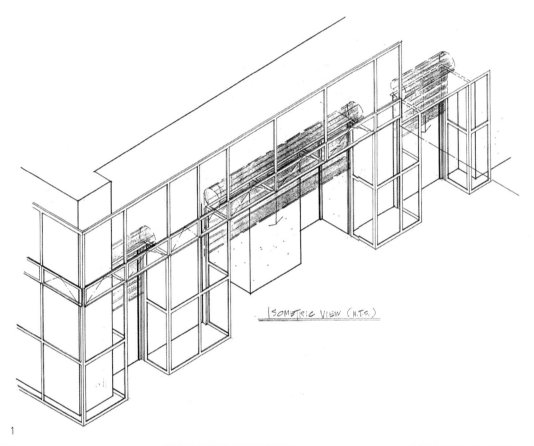

ISOMETRIC VIEW (N.T.S.)

1

2

3

4

5

6

1 Isometric view
2 Detail of concrete walls
3 Sculptural staircase leading to mezzanine
4 Roller shutters hidden in semi-transparent glass
5 Lift entrance
6 Canteen style reception area welcomes guest
Photography: Allan Kwan/Arkitech

The Florida Solar Energy Center

Architects Design Group, Inc.

Completion: January 1996

Location: Cocoa, Florida, USA

Client: Florida Board of Regents

Area: 5,017 square metres; 54,004 square feet

Structure: Steel; concrete slab on grade

Materials: Insulated metal; specialised glazing

Cost: US$7.2 million

Awards: 1996 AIA State of Florida Award for Design Excellence

AIA, Orlando Chapter Award for Design Excellence

Architects Design Group, Inc. (ADG), was selected from a large field of highly technical, specialised firms to perform master planning and architectural services for the new Florida Solar Energy Center (FSEC), complex.

The new complex contains approximately 5,017 net assignable square metres (54,004 square feet), and incorporates specialised applications of solar systems and energy conservation building techniques. The facility provides modern, state-of-the-art laboratories for research and testing as well as an education-oriented Visitor's Center devoted to disseminating information concerning renewable energy applications.

ADG's design for the new complex was an intrinsic element aiding the continuation of FSEC's pioneering research in building concepts for hot, humid climates, photovoltaic applications, etc. The facility was planned to develop and implement solar standards, solar collector testing and certification, consumer education and development of energy education and training programs.

1 Southeast corner Visitor Center
2 Overall view of west stair
3 West facing exterior Visitor Center exit stair
4 Visitor Center interior
5 View into HVAC equipment space
Photography: Kevin Haas

2

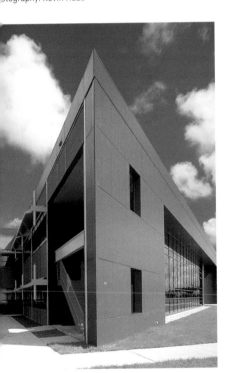

3

5

Orange County Landfill Operations Center

Architects Design Group, Inc

Completion: December 1996

Location: Orange County, Florida, USA

Client: Orange County Board of Commissioners

Area: 4,831 square metres; 52,002 square feet

Structure: Steel; concrete slab

Materials: slab-on-grade; steel; recyclable steel

Cost: US$7.4 million

1995 AIA Florida Unbuilt Design Award
1995 AIA Orlando Unbuilt Design Award
1997 AIA Florida Excellence in Architecture
1997 Metal Construction Honor Award

Designed for the study of alternate operating techniques in areas of high water table, this facility is located in an area of indigenous pines bordered by wetlands that buffer the site from nearby residential development. The Center accommodates numerous functions, including administration, training, supply and vehicle maintenance.

The design team had as its goal the premise of sustainable architecture, defined as 'architecture that sustains human utilisation for a variety of functions with a minimal impact on the environment, that uses recycled and recyclable materials, that is energy efficient and that incorporates materials that have a useful life of one hundred years or more'.

Examples included resilient flooring throughout made fr flaxseed plants and linseed oil; with ceramic tile, furnitu fabrics and upholstery manufactured from various recyc materials.

Colour played an important role in the total design conce Here the palette actually reflects the environment; thus green is the primary building skin. Accents of blue, red and yellow, seen in bales of recycled waste materials at the landfill, are used to define specific functional elements.

1   Exterior maintenance bay area
2   Detail of entry site wall
3   Interior maintenance bays
4   Detail administration core
Photography: Kevin Haas

1

2

3

4

Biographies

hrends Burton and Koralek

rrends Burton and Koralek (ABK), established 1961 has won numerous awards for design d technical achievement and has a wide nge of experience in the United Kingdom, eland and Europe. Each commission is a ique response to a specific brief, an terpretation and evaluation that grows out of titudes and standards that are the cumulative oduct of shared thought and feeling and of e conviction that the character of the vironment cannot be dissociated from the ality of life.

BK makes extensive use of the most advanced chnology at all stages of the design process, r CAD, contract documentation and project ministration.

enowned for its work in the fields of lucation, healthcare and the arts, the actice's imaginative approach has led to cclaimed buildings in many fields, from the ergy saving St Mary's Hospital on the Isle Wight to 11 new stations for the Docklands ght Railway in London. Current and recent ojects include the new British Embassy in oscow, a new wing for the Dublin Dental ospital, a learning resource centre for Selly ak Colleges, new departmental buildings for e University of Loughborough, headquarters fice buildings for WH Smith, and extensions r the Whitworth Gallery in Manchester.

he practice offers skills in architecture and lated fields such as urban design and anning, interior and furniture design, and has onsiderable experience in design for energy onservation.

kira Kuryu Architects & Associates

kira Kuryu Architects & Associates was ounded in Tokyo in 1979 by Akira Kuryu who ad worked for Fumihiko Maki Associates. he company currently has 14 staff and is ctively engaged in creative architectural lanning and design in a wide range of onstructions from public museums, city ffices, private housing, condominiums to xhibition facilities and total city plans.

ne of its representative designs is seen in Carnival Showcase', a private recreation acility, which received the Japan Institute of rchitects Award for the Best Young Architect 1989.

kira Kuryu was one of the master architects f the World City Expo Tokyo planned in 1995.

1996, the 'Uemura Naomi Memorial Museum' was completed and its total design oncept incorporating building, landscapes,

furniture and exhibitions was highly evaluated to receive the Annual Award of Architectural Institute of Japan Design Prize of the same year.

Akira Kuryu is a professor for the Technology Department (Architecture Faculty of Chiba University) and also teaches in Tokyo University and Waseda University.

Allford Hall Monaghan Morris

Allford Hall Monaghan Morris was formed in London in 1989 after five years of collaboration between the partners, in both practice and education.

Current large scale projects in the office and on site include competition winning schemes for a bus-station, two theatres, an art gallery and a school—the latter a prototype for 'sustainable development'. The office is also building a theatre in Hampshire, an apartment block for the Peabody Trust, a tennis club in Highgate, a medical centre in Croydon, a health club in London's West End and three offices in Central London.

The completion of a number of award winning buildings has resulted in the emergence of the office as one of the UK's leading young practices and recent projects have been featured in publications in Britain, France, Germany and Japan. The partners teach at The Bartlett School of Architecture and have lectured extensively on their work worldwide.

Anderson Anderson Architecture

Anderson Anderson Architecture—with offices in Seattle and Honolulu—began in 1984 as a construction firm building finely crafted modern buildings. With a skilled team of architects and construction workers, the firm has designed and built numerous projects in the United States and Asia. Firm principals Peter Anderson and Mark Anderson lecture frequently about their design work and construction research projects at universities and conferences in the U.S., Europe and Asia.

Their projects have won numerous design awards and have been widely published. Current projects include residences, a church, and a tree canopy research and interpretive structure in the United States; prefabricated home prototypes in Japan; a museum and residence in Odawara, Japan; a multi-family housing project near Tokyo; and on-going research projects in prefabrication and new media-based construction technology.

Andrews Scott Cotton Architects Limited

Established in 1953 and renamed Andrews Scott Cotton Architects in 1992, the practice operates from an historic building in central Auckland. Andrews Scott Cotton Architects provides architectural and interior design services for projects throughout New Zealand.

A creative response to client needs and aspirations is met by an experienced staff numbering 40 to offer a full range of planning; architecture, interior design, cost planning and contract management services. The result is high quality buildings with budgets and programming targets held firmly in view.

Each project is seen as deserving an individual response to client and user requirements. A sustained thorough analysis and understanding of these requirements is fundamental to the success of each project.

With an ongoing commitment to Quality Management Andrews Scott Cotton Architects operates in an open studio environment so that directors and project team members work side by side to ensure maximum creative input and coordination of a highly competent team.

This, along with a dedication to design excellence and cost effectiveness, facilitates the creation of distinctive buildings individually tailored to express the client's requirements.

Ann Beha Associates, Inc.

Ann Beha Associates, Inc. is dedicated to architecture as a means to support, expand and enrich community life. Founded in 1977, the award-winning firm provides planning, design, and historic preservation services to cultural, community, and academic clients across the United States. The firm is led by three principals, with staff architects specialised in design for cultural organisations, museums, religious buildings, libraries, civic and academic facilities. The firm's design work has been widely recognised for integrating craft and traditional materials with modern requirements as well as its experience in planning and design, building technology, interior design, and materials conservation.

Notable projects include renovations for the Isabella Stewart Gardner Museum; Boston's Symphony Hall; the Ringling Museum in Sarasota, Florida; the Portland Art Museum in Oregon, and the design of the new Haffenreffer Museum of Anthropology at Brown University. The firm is also known for providing planning and designs for academic buildings for Trinity, Wellesley, and Williams Colleges, and public and private libraries: the Nantucket Atheneum, the Malden and Woburn Public Libraries, the Research Center for Fort Ticonderoga, and the research library at the Clark Art Institute.

Anthony Ng Architects Limited

Anthony Ng studied architecture in the University of Hong Kong, and then acquired post-graduate study in urban design in Rome. He was the founding director of Kwan & Ng Associates (first established in 1979) and KNW Architects & Engineers Ltd. (first established in 1982). In 1991, Anthony Ng Architects Limited was established, providing a professional practice with emphasis on architectural and urban design.

The project architects and designers of Verbena Heights included: Kitty Au, Stuart Berriman, Vincent Chang, Richard Hay, Henry T.H. Ho, Jacky K.K. Lam, N. Matsuda, Anthony Ng, David Y.W. Ng, James W. Pierce, George Strome, Andy H.W. Wong, David W.P. Wong, Guymo Wong, Kenneth K.C. Wong, and K.S. Wong.

The team of consultants were: Arup Acoustics, ERM (HK) Ltd. in association with ECD Architects and Energy Consultants (U.K.) and Vipac Engineers & Scientists Ltd. (Australia), Levett & Bailey Chartered Quantity Surveyors, Maunsell Consultants Asia Ltd., Meinhardt (M&E) Ltd., and Urbis Travers Morgan Ltd.

Antoine Predock Architect

In his work, Antoine Predock Architect makes choices which come from the spirit and from an understanding of the actual world around him, both in terms of the present and the past. He responds to the forces of a place—to geology, culture, myth and ritual—and evokes these qualities in his buildings.

In the studio, connections are explored between the earth and the sky, as in the Turtle Creek House which has a ramp that aims toward the sky, establishing a trajectory that one follows on ascent. The buildings in the desert often suggest an analogous landscape. The American Heritage Center in Wyoming is an abstraction of land forms in the area—an 'archival mountain' in the landscape, with a village, the art museum, at its base.

The built work, for almost three decades, expresses these initial physical and spiritual impulses. Antoine Predock Architect's practice includes projects throughout the United States, and in France, Spain, Morocco, and Denmark. In the United States, projects include sites in Massachusetts, New York, Florida, Texas, New Mexico, Arizona, Nevada, Washington and California. The work includes housing,

museums, theatres, academic buildings, hotels, libraries and civic buildings.

Antoine Predock is a Fellow of the American Institute of Architects and a Fellow of the American Academy in Rome.

Antonio H Ravazzani & Associates

Antonio Ravazzani graduated from the Faculty of Architecture and City Planning of the University of Buenos Aires, Argentina, where he also did postgraduate studies. He has won a number of prizes for his public and institutional projects in Buenos Aires.

Antonio Ravazzani moved to Punta Del Este, Uruguay in 1972 and began his own office there in 1978 and continues to work on projects in Brazil and Argentina. A new office was opened in 1992 in Aspen, Colarado, USA.

His designs are a result of an in-depth study of the landscape and surroundings, of the needs and psychology of each client and of the possibilities and potential of the labour available in respect to materials used.

His most important works could be classified within a trilogy of materials: houses of wood, stone and brick, with a different treatment in each case.

Arbonies King Vlock

Arbonies King Vlock is a Connecticut-based firm with projects and clients nationwide. Specialising in the planning and design of art museums, college and university buildings, and custom residences, their work is inspired by local traditions, materials and craftsmanship and has been published internationally.

What distinguishes this award-winning firm is its client-centred, collaborative style of working. In public or campus building projects, group collaboration is the beginning point of design. As a result, clients often see their building as a reflection of a collective vision and the 'signature of many'—not the singular expression of the architect alone.

For residential projects, Arbonies King Vlock's innovative design solutions and attention to detail come out of a close personal collaboration between the architect and client.

Architects Design Group, Inc.

Architects Design Group, Inc. (ADG), was established in 1971 by I.S.K. Reeves V as a full-service architectural and planning firm and is located in Winter Park, Florida. The majority of their work is in the United States but includes commissions in the Middle East and Central America.

Their projects are highly contemporary in character and utilise technology to create facilities that are both environmentally sensitive and energy efficient. Their work includes research centres; cultural facilities (museums, science centres); governmental/administrative complexes; transportation centres and law enforcement facilities (courts, police, correctional/detention facilities).

Colour is an important aspect of their work and has contributed toward their success in being recipients of several national (U.S.), state and regional awards for design excellence and publication in numerous architectural and technical journals in the United States, Japan and Italy.

Architektenburo K. van Velsen B.V.

Koen van Velsen stated his own practice in 1977. His work covers a wide range of design disciplines including architecture, interior design, urban planning and landscaping. The scale and complexity of the commissions realised by his office gradually developed from private houses to larger public buildings in complex urban environments.

In the last two years the office completed a multi-plex cinema in Rotterdam, municipal office buildings and landscaping in Terneuzen and a museum for the University of Utrecht.

Van Velsen does not cultivate a personal aesthetic; each new project is analysed and its specific features, contextual or programmatic, form the basic arguments for a design concept. Great care is taken for a precise and lucid realisation of the design with the knowledge of building techniques and details playing a major role in this process as does the input of external engineering.

Van Velsen has won a number of prizes for his work including the 'Mart Stam Prize' awarded by the city of Amsterdam, the 'A.J. van Eck Prize' for his public library in Zeewolde and recently the 'Rietveld Prize' for the University Museum Utrecht.

Architetto Cortesi

Aurelio Cortesi (born in 1931) established his architecture firm in Parma in 1957. His professional activity ranges across a variety of projects including residential (private and public constructions), commercial (from single shop to commercial centres), office buildings, institutional constructions and master plans for urban developments.

As well as his professional activities, he has been leading an academic career, teaching Architectural Composition at universities, beginning with the Politecnico of Milan (where he studied) as an associate professor. Since 1983 he has been teaching as an established professor at the Architecture University of Florence and Genova.

He has participated in various competitions, including Piazzale della Pace in Parma (1972, first prize ex-equo); 'L'Opera Bastille' in Paris 1987); 'Una Porta per Venezia' (1990); 'Le Forum de Les Halles' (1978) which led to the publication of the '*L'Ivre da Pierres*' (1981) and the exhibition of the project at the Paris Museum of Modern Art (1982).

More recently, he participated at the Architecture Venice Biennale (1993) and the Milan Triennial (1995). The exhibition in Venice was entitled 'Sacred Space in Modernity', with the project presented to the S. Ilario Oratory, a chapel designed in Parma for a religious institution. The 'Theatre Gallery' in Corsico (Milan), a museum about theatrical representations, was presented to the exhibit 'Il Centro Altrove' at the Milano Triennial.

Aurelio Cortesi frequently participates in various lectures, conferences and publications. He is currently a member of the Managing Committee of the European Architecture Review 'Area'.

Arkitech

Allan Kwan, a founder member of Arkitech Ltd Hong Kong since 1986 is a three-times winner in commercial, restaurant and corporate categories of Asian First Pacific Design Awards of Hong Kong from 1990–1992 respectively.

Kwan graduated from the Graphic Design Faculty of Hong Kong Polytechnics in 1976 without actually studying interior design. But, after trying his hand at a number of other disciplines including graphic design, illustration, fashion design, window display, garment merchandising, set design and art direction with the field of advertising for 10 years, he has over the past 10 years, settled firmly into the art of interior design.

Kwan's projects are mainly located in southeast Asia including PRC, Taiwan, Singapore and Hong Kong with the projects varying from resort hotels, restaurants, discotheques, hair salons, fashion boutiques, corporate offices and private residences.

However the categories vary, his solutions are never repeated, his style remaining consistent and *modern*, *chic* and *conceptual* being the key words.

Arkitek MAA Sdn Bhd
The practice of Arkitek MAA Sdn Bhd (MAA), was established in 1965 in Kuala Lumpur, Malaysia under the style of Malaysian Associate Architects. The architectural works are located mainly in West Malaysia and include large scale housing, commercial, industrial and institutional projects, both in the public as well as private sectors. MAA has also undertaken assignments in East Malaysia, Singapore, Brunei, Thailand, Indonesia and the Philippines.

A recent joint venture office has been established in Beijing under the style of M&A Architects & Consultants International Ltd. The Beijing office' works comprise of projects throughout the whole of China, a substantial number of which are under construction.

With the firm's long and established professional history and a track record for consistently winning architectural awards, MAA has the depth of professional talent to respond to projects of any size and complexity. The practice is built on a tradition of personal attention and individual commitment and at the helm of MAA are 11 directors, heading a staff of around 100. MAA's specialisations are in the fields of architecture and master planning.

Baneke, van der Hoeven Architekten
Baneke, van der Hoeven Architekten in Amsterdam is a small firm with approximately 10 highly educated staff members.

The work done by the firm varies greatly; new buildings are being alternated with renovating projects and interior design. Building types range from small residential to offices and complex laboratories.

Works are being designed and constructed both in and outside The Netherlands.

The firm's projects are characterised by the unusual solution to the Program of Demands; the guiding principle in this is the devlelopment of a spatial concept. In this concept the routing and different types of usage in the building play an important role.

The office pays much attention to the way materials and natural and artificial light are used to obtain dynamic spatial results.

Benthem Crouwel Architekten BV bna
Characterised as sober, practical and functional—in keeping with Dutch tradition—Benthem Crouwel's work is also acclaimed for its expressive and aesthetic qualities. This apparent contrast may well hide the most important quality of its work.

Functionality and internal logistics are important priorities in the buildings. The firm continuously look for good, though not always obvious, solutions to design problems, applying modern technology in a user-friendly way.

An independent bureau, Benthem Crouwel approaches every commission, large or small, with an open mind, working as a team in close collaboration with the client and using the brief always as the point of departure.

The firm believes that to obtain an 'optimal outcome' the business side must also run perfectly. Its reputation for sound management of the building process, both in terms of cost control and time, is cherished.

Benthem Crouwel has established many long-standing relationships with a number of clients working on highly varied commissions such as architecture, urban design, infrastructure and interior design.

Bligh Voller Nield Pty Ltd
Bligh Voller Nield Pty Ltd is one of Australia's major architectural practices with experience in a wide range of building projects. It is a third generation practice, noted for its innovative architecture and collaborative approach developed over 71 years of continuous practice. The firm has 11 principals; Michael Adams, Christopher Alcock, Graham Bligh, Christopher Clarke, Robert Gardner, Neil Hanson, Lawrence Nield, Phillip Page, Phillip Tait, Shane Thompson and Jon Voller, with nine practice directors and 13 associates, and a technical and administrative staff of 145.

Offices are located in Brisbane, Sydney, Canberra and Melbourne, with joint ventures in Cairns, Hong Kong, Malaysia, and Papua New Guinea with a specialist Health Group, Bligh Nield Health and a specialist joint venture as Bligh Lobb Sports Architecture. The practice has a particular reputation for the successful completion of major and special projects.

Significant projects include the Australia Stadium for the Sydney 2000 Olympics, Brisbane Airport International and Domestic Terminals, World Expo '88 Brisbane, National Science and Technology Museum Canberra, 111 George Street State Government Office Tower Brisbane, Queensland Conservatorium of Music for Griffith University, Westmead Children's Hospital Sydney, and the Overseas Passenger Terminal Redevelopment Sydney.

Bligh Voller Nield has been recognised by their receipt of over 60 awards by extensive national and international publication and exhibition of their work and by their prominence within the Australian Architectural community.

Boarman Kroos Pfister Vogel

Boarman Kroos Pfister Vogel & Associates (BKPV), is a Minneapolis based full-service architectural, interior design and engineering firm that provides complete design services ranging from planning to construction administration. BKPV's professional staff of over 50 architects, interior designers, engineers, graphic artists, marketing professionals and specialised support personnel, provide total in-house project services.

Since the firm's inception in 1978, its goal has been to become a nationally recognised innovator and leader. BKPV is a design oriented group of professionals that base their problem solving on clear statements of functional need and aesthetic goals. While the firm's values and experiences are important factors in shaping a design, it is the users' needs that define the basis of the problem, and the client's aspirations that provide the measuring stick for evaluation. BKPV believes that good design is the result of the attitude of the client and the architect rather than the size of the budget. Through the dedicated efforts of its collective professional staff, BKPV offers clients dedicated years of experience and a wealth of talent.

Brian MacKay–Lyons Architecture + Urban Design

Brian MacKay–Lyons Architecture + Urban Design practices out of a former gas station in Halifax, Nova Scotia, Canada. The firm has focused on houses, public buildings and urban design commissions, which have steadily accumulated to form an extensive and consistent body of work in Nova Scotia.

The use of his native landscape as a laboratory for design and building within the Master-Builder tradition has led to Brian being described as 'The Village Architect' *(Design Quarterly 165)*. His modern, regionalist architectural language combines the use of archetypal forms with local building practices that grow out of material culture and climate.

As a result, the work has both a local and international audience, as evidenced by more than 60 publications, including profiles of the firm in *Progressive Architecture (PA)*, *Design Quarterly (DQ)* and *Architectural Review (AR)*. In addition, his buildings have received some 40 awards for design, including four Governor General Awards (three Medals), and three Canadian Architect Awards of Excellence.

Brian (B.Arch., T.U.N.S., M.ARCH., U.C.L.A.) has lectured or taught at several schools of architecture, including DalTech (Dalhousie University) where he is a professor, and Harvard G.S.D. where he has been a visiting professor.

Burr & McCallum Architects

The firm of Burr & McCallum Architects has brought a high standard of design to a wide variety of projects since its inception in 1982.

Clients range from colleges, towns, museums and commercial enterprises to individuals building their own houses.

Their work has been recognised nationally and internationally through publications, exhibitions and awards.

Ann McCallum was the 1989 recipient of the international Andrea Palladio Award.

Buttrick White & Burtis

Buttrick White & Burtis was established in 1963 as Harold Buttrick, Architect. Today it is a full-service architectural firm with a staff of over 30 professionals. The practice is diverse but the projects are unified by a high level of design which has been recognised by numerous awards and publications in professional journals. The firm has been described by Paul Goldberger of *The New York Times* as being among the city's best 'contextual architects'.

Commissions include new construction, renovations and master planning for institutional, commercial and residential clients.

In the office, located on the west side of midtown Manhattan, is state-of-the-art CADD capabilities and one of the most complete architectural and interiors' library in New York.

The size of the firm enables it to provide clients with the specialised expertise necessary to handle major projects, yet is small enough for the partners, Harold Buttrick, FAIA; Samuel G. White, FAIA; and Theodore A. Burtis, AIA, to maintain day-to-day involvement and control resulting in design excellence, high quality of construction and adherence to project budgets and schedules.

Architects Domenig-Eisenköck

The working team Domenig-Eisenköck is a Graz based firm. The office is fully equipped by a staff of 20 architects including principals Domenig and Eisenköck and five other office staff.

The office performance profile is based on: execution of architectural projects and supervision of works and project management for all fields of building construction; adaptation of architectural works in engineer buildings; design of exterior spaces and squares; provision of expertise; counselling; planning and supervision of interior design; planning activities for exhibitions; and successful participation in national and international architectural competitions.

Douglas Roberts Peter Loebenberg & Partners cc

Established in 1964 the firm now has over 50 members in Cape Town and Johannesburg offices. The partners, while all South African, have worked and studied in various countries including England, Italy and the USA.

Projects have been completed in all the major South African cities, and African centres including Dubai, Harare, Bulawayo, and Windhoek. Projects have also been built in China and Thailand.

Current and recently completed work includes specialty shops, retail malls, corporate office blocks, wholesale distribution depots, warehouses and private hospitals.

While the staff complement includes specialists in construction management, interior design and town planning, the main thrust is architecture and the specialist skills available are used to support the architectural teams.

The practice has established good working relationships with British and American architectural firms, and have worked jointly on a number of projects.

Ellenzweig Associates, Inc.

Founded in 1965, Ellenzweig Associates, Inc. has built a reputation for innovation in the architectural design of academic and research facilities. With a staff of 60 operating from a single office in Cambridge, Massachusetts, the firm provides comprehensive professional design services including programming, feasibility studies, master planning, and full architectural services—schematic design, design development, contract documents, and construction administration.

Ellenzweig Associates specialises in complex, technically challenging projects—state-of-the-art teaching facilities for academic clients; research facilities for academic, medical and corporate clients; and transportation-related facilities such as parking structures and subway stations for municipal clients. Initial commissions at Harvard University and the Massachusetts Institute of Technology launched the firm's continuing focus on academic facilities.

llenzweig Associates' commitment to design xcellence and client satisfaction is reflected in s long-term relationships with many clients hroughout the United States. The firm has won ver 60 design awards in the last eight years, nd its work has been featured in *Architecture, rchitectural Record,* and *Progressive rchitecture,* among other journals.

llerbe Becket

llerbe Becket is one of the oldest (1909) and argest architecture, engineering and onstruction services firms in the United States, roviding integrated services ranging from trategic planning through post-construction. 1996 revenue totalled US$122 million.

Vith nearly 800 employees, the firm has 10 ffices in the United States and overseas: ansas City, Mo.; Minneapolis; Phoenix; San rancisco; Washington, DC; Jakarta, Indonesia; Moscow; Seoul, South Korea; Tokyo; and Vakefield, England—a joint venture with David Lyons & Associates.

ecent or ongoing work includes: Mayo Clinic ractice Integration project in Rochester; Minnesota, Carlson School of Management at ne University of Minnesota; Yonsei University everance Hospital in Seoul, Korea; Olympic tadium/Turner Field (Atlanta Braves) in tlanta, Georgia; and Alfa Arbat Center in Moscow.

lliott + Associates Architects

stablished in 1976, Elliott + Associates architects is a full-service architectural firm f licensed architects, interior and graphic esigners and support personnel. The firm has esigned 98 award winning projects for orporate clients, various arts' organisations, useums and public spaces.

he design philosophy of the firm is shaped rom the theory that a space reflects the unique ersonality of the owner, coupled with unctionality. Elliott + Associates Architects reates special environments—portraits— revealed as expressions of the client. xamining together who the client is, where e is going and what he wants to accomplish; efining the essence of who he is and his bjectives enables the development of oncepts to address the issues forming the asis of the portrait.

he sketch book is where the ideas gleaned rom clients become concepts. The presentation oard puts concept into physical form and final xpression becomes the blueprint from which ne building will spring. The idea is shaped, efined, detailed and executed. The portrait ecomes architecture.

Eric Parry Architects

The practice was founded by Eric Parry. It has developed a reputation, both in the United Kingdom and internationally for producing inventive designs. The directors and project architects have been working together from the establishment of the company and form part of a core of 16 people working in London. The practice also has an office in Kuala Lumpur, Malaysia.

Eric Parry Architects' approach to design is underlined by the belief that the art of architecture is a culturally situated discipline and because of this the practice has avoided being typecast by style or fashion whilst the work has found its own voice.

The range of projects undertaken includes the Sussex Innovation Centre; an office building at Stockley Park, Heathrow; a fitout of the Ministry of Sound nightclub; Animation Studios in Soho; and Artists' Studios for Antony Gormley and Tom Phillips.

Current projects include the New Master's Lodge and Student Accommodation Building for Pembroke College, Cambridge; the refurbishment of the Mandarin Oriental Hyde Park Hotel; a master plan for Abington Science Park in Cambridge; mixed-use warehouse and public square in Convent Garden, London; private residences and a 30-unit luxury apartment building in Kuala Lumpur.

Dr. Farouk Elgohary Architects

The practice was started in Egypt by Dr. Farouk Elgohary in 1966, with an earlier start in England with Sir Basil Spence in the Royal Cavalry's building in Hyde Park, London.

Practicing for more than 30 years, the experience matured a special architectural flavour that cultivated the company name deeply in the world of Egyptian architecture.

Its clients have varied enormously, among them presidents, rulers, princes, governments, private-sector investors, companies, banks and laymen.

The buildings have varied from top security to highly technical; functional office complexes and religious structures. The scale has varied from small buildings to urban planning as well as open and closed spaces for leisure centres and social clubs.

The firm has dealt with large scale projects totalling costs of more than one billion Egyptian pounds.

Flad & Associates

Flad & Associates was founded in 1927 and has operated successfully as an architecture,

engineering and interiors firm since that time. Today an employee-owned business, Flad staff number approximately 225 people nationwide. The mission is to service key knowledge-based industries around the globe, assisting in all areas of planning, design and ongoing facility strategy and management.

The practice is dedicated to servicing national and international knowledge-based organisations with specialised facility needs. Discovery and innovation in work process, streamlined methods for research and production, and high performance, technology-driven environments characterise the client facilities the firm designs.

Key industries serviced include research and development and advanced technology organisations, whose specialised design needs include laboratories, process, production and manufacturing facilities; global corporations in all areas of campus planning and design, from new headquarter facilities to office expansion, data centres, training facilities, and all other advanced technology facilities; healthcare organisations in community-based and managed care systems, including hospitals, clinics and ambulatory care environments; and academic and university research facilities at private and public colleges.

In support of its work efforts throughout the United States, Flad has five office locations: Madison, Wisconsin; Stamford, Connecticut; San Francisco, California; Research Triangle Park, North Carolina; and Gainesville, Florida.

Fox & Fowle Architects

Robert F. Fox, Jr. and Bruce S. Fowle formed Fox & Fowle Architects in New York City in 1978. From its inception, the firm's practice has been diverse, with much repeat work in such primary areas as the planning and design of investment grade office buildings, corporate and institutional interiors, and various cultural and institutional facilities.

Today the firm employs 50 people. Current work in New York City includes the critically acclaimed 48-storey Condé Nast Building at Four Times Square and adjacent subway station, the Knowledge Union for the New School for Social Research, renovation of the American Bible Society headquarters, and a new residential building in Greenwich Village.

Fox & Fowle has been active in Asia since 1990. Projects there include the interiors of the Senayan Convention Center in Jakarta; two major office towers currently under construction in Shanghai, the headquarters of the Industrial Commercial Bank of China and Shanghai Jawha Headquarters; and three prototype houses for the new capital city of Malaysia, Putrajaya.

The firm provides a complete range of multi-disciplinary architectural, master planning, and interior design services ranging from feasibility studies, program analysis and site selection through post-occupancy evaluation, for projects of every size and scope.

Frank O. Gehry & Associates, Inc.

Frank Gehry established the architectural firm of Frank O. Gehry & Associates in 1962. Located in Santa Monica, California, the architecture studio has a staff of over 65 people, which includes a group of senior architects who are highly qualified in project management and in the technical development of building systems and construction documents, as well as extensive model-making facilities and a model building staff capable of executing everything from scale architectural models to full size mock-ups.

The firm employs a network of sophisticated computer aided design workstations in the development of projects and in the translation of design ideas into the technical documents required for construction. The firm uses CATIA, a 3-dimensional computer modelling program originally designed for the aerospace industry. This program is supplemented by more traditional 2-dimensional CAD programs.

G&W Architects, Engineers, Project Development Consultants

G&W Architects, Engineers, Project Development Consultants (G&W), has maintained its position of leadership as a company which engages virtually in every type of project investment and engineering design, construction supervision and management.

G&W has a network of 10 divisions serving throughout the country and abroad. The most recent of which is the International and Foreign Clients Division II (IFCD II) and the Advanced Design Technology Division (ADTECH). The company has grown steadily but dramatically throughout the years under its maiden name Gilbert C. Yu * Willie C. Yu Architects and Associates. Built on the solid foundation of versatile staff whose depth and diversity of experience are its principal assets, G&W has attained the capability and flexibility of assembling the most appropriate team to handle any project with speed, efficiency and sustained quality to live up to the company's thrust for architectural excellence.

As the global community becomes a reality, G&W is preparing for success and growth in a new century through a continuing commitment

to meet the needs of mankind. Operating under a collaborative and multi-disciplinary team approach to design, team work and organisational efficiency are the keys. Each completed project management system undertakes an indepth analysis of the social fabric, functional and economic aspect of every project.

Committed to growth and progress they encourage their people to be involved which keeps concepts free and original. The experience, guidance and leadership of its senior members helps create a working environment for design excellence. The firm is not identified with any particular architectural design style, it is attuned to trends, but foresight makes the designs lasting.

This approach to problem solving has laid strong foundations for the company's growth and persistent effort has become the source of the company's remarkable progress and dynamic character.

Helin & Siitonen

Since Helin & Siitonen's founding in 1979 its work has included cultural institutions, offices, commercial and recreational development and housing. The scale of projects range in size from summer cottages to corporate headquarters of 50,000 square metres (538,215 square feet) and master plans for multi-functional centres.

The work is committed to creative design, backed up by particular research in every project, and thorough knowledge of processes and technology in the field of building.

The emphasis is in the quality of the design, careful supervision of the execution and the close collaboration with the client. Each project is given the same individual attention and is treated as a unique opportunity to improve conditions of space for a certain function.

The office is fully equipped with modern CAD facilities, by a staff of 12 architects including principles Pekka Helin and Tuomo Siitonen, and 12 other office staff.

Herbert S. Newman and Partners P.C.

Since its founding in 1964 Herbert S. Newman and Partners P.C. has been based in New Haven, Connecticut and has carried out architectural projects throughout the United States. The firm has a national reputation for the design of new structures as well as the renovation of existing structures and the restoration of landmark buildings. The firm has won over 50 awards for design excellence and has been published in architectural journals in the United States and abroad.

It is the position of the firm that just as it is the task of architecture to provide shelter and accommodate human activity, it is also the task of architecture to dignify and to enrich the lives of those who experience it. Herbert S. Newman and Partners believes that certain core properties are inherent to architecture and they seek to found their design on them: the primacy of space, clarity of path and structure, the luminance of natural light and the humanising quality of natural materials. Herbert S. Newman and Partners strives to execute solutions which are stimulating and harmonious.

Hideto Horiike & Urtopia

Hideto Horiike & Urtopia (HH&U), established in 1979 is a design firm focusing on services ranging from architecture, urban design, interior design, furniture design and architectural consultation. Experiences of the firm includes office buildings, health care facilities, hotels, corporate headquarters, factories, public buildings, residential buildings and urban planning.

HH&U is affiliated with offices in New York, Los Angeles, Paris and Berlin. There are 15 full-time employees in Tokyo headquarters of which nine are registered architects in Japan. The firm is equipped with 3-dimensional systems and CAD programs.

The philosophy of the firm is as to the 'Machina' of the manifestation of a man's will. They are concerned that architecture exists and plays a role as a device in the urban context. Therefore, the act of the creation of architecture is the martial art to the globe.

Hodder Associates

Hodder Associates is a Manchester and London based practice with a growing reputation. In 1992 it received the Royal Fine Art Commission Sunday Times 'Building of the Year Award' for Colne Swimming Pool in Lancashire. This resulted in the appointment to extend Arne Jacobsen's Grade I Listed St Catherine's College, Oxford.

It was selected as one of six practices by Lord Rogers and the former President of the RIBA, Dr Frank Duffy, amongst others, to represent the emerging generation of British Architects in an exhibition at the Architectural Institute of Japan in Tokyo in October 1994 and was awarded the Grand Prize at the Royal Academy Summer Exhibition in 1995 for the panels presented as part of the submission for the Manchester City Art Gallery competition.

The development continues and, most recently, it received the most important award in British chitecture, the inaugural RIBA/Sunday Times uilding of the Year' Award, the Stirling Prize Architecture for the Centenary Building, niversity of Salford.

ong Kong Housing Authority

e Hong Kong Housing Authority, which as established in 1973, is a statutory body sponsible for coordinating all aspects of blic housing developments in Hong Kong. rough its executive arm, the Housing epartment plans, designs, builds and manages blic rental housing estates, Home Ownership heme (HOS) estates and interim housing to eet the various needs of the people.

e Housing Authority is currently holding a using stock of around 750,000 flats, housing most half the population of Hong Kong. Under e policy of continuous improvement, the using Department is committed to endeavour achieve the goals both in terms of production d quality.

meet the government's housing quirements, the annual production target to complete at least 50,000 flats a year. The nual housing production will reach a record gh of 115,000 flats in the year 2000/01.

e quality policy is to provide quality ofessional services that satisfy customers' pectations and enhance the built vironment of Hong Kong, and which have a uality system meeting the requirements of O 9001. The Vision, Mission and Core Values the Housing Department are used for idance in the delivery of services.

iven all the new housing challenges ahead, e Housing Authority has already prepared for e future by stretching the planning horizon to 010 and is exploring new frontiers and novative solutions with the aim of meeting e rising expectations of the community on blic housing in Hong Kong.

ouse + House Architects

teven and Cathi House and their associates ndeavour to create beauty, serenity and nazement in their work and in the process of chitecture. They find their greatest inspiration the subtleties of each site and in the deepest cesses of their client's souls—and with timate analysis discover how to mould each oject into that unique environment that mbodies magic and harmony. In each project ey find new opportunities to lift themselves d their clients to a higher level of perception f the world ...not through the latest chnology, but through their skilful anipulation of form, light and texture.

Recognised for their innovative work, House + House Architects has designed projects ranging from custom homes throughout the San Francisco Bay area, the Sierra Nevada mountains, Los Angeles and Hawaii, to state-of-the-art retail facilities, to a Caribbean Island resort. They have received numerous design awards and have been published extensively.

Steven and Cathi House have co-authored 'Mediterranean Indigenous Architecture - Timeless Solutions for the Human Habitat', a major exhibition which has travelled throughout the United States. The poetic quality of their work derives from the simpler side of life ...the magic sparkle of sunlight raking across a textured wall...

Hubert-Jan Henket bna architecten

Hubert-Jan Henket qualified with honours (Aldo van Eijck) at the Delft University of Technology in 1969. He studied urban design at the Otanlemi University in Helsinki, meanwhile he worked for Reima Pietilä.

From 1970-1976 he worked in London for Castle Park Dean Hook. In 1976 he started his own practice in the Netherlands. He is professor of architecture at Eindhoven University and the founder and president of DOCOMOMO. He is the architectural supervisor of Amsterdam Airport Schiphol. Among the buildings his office has realised so far are the Missionary House for the White Fathers in Dar es Salaam, the pavilion for Museum Boymans-van Beuningen in Rotterdam, the extension of the Teylers Museum in Haarlem, the Town Hall in Wehl, the Law Court of Middelburg, the Maastheater in Rotterdam and the restoration of the Rietveid School of Arts in Arnhem.

Currently he is working on the restoration and extension of sanatorium Zonnestraal (1928) by Johannes Duiker in Hilversum.

Ingenhoven Overdiek Kahlen und Partner

Düsseldorf is home to the main office of Ingenhoven Overdiek Kahlen und Partner. Established as a joint firm of architects in 1992, it is headed by Christoph Ingenhoven, Jürgen Overdiek and since the beginning of 1997, Hans Kahlen, as well as partners.

A team of approximately 75 architects, five interior designers, numerous draughters and model makers as well as a further 15 staff members who look after overheads, accounting and secretarial duties.

The planning and realisation of the projects is carried out by an architectural team made up of a chief director and professional support staff.

The main themes of the projects are office and administration buildings, head offices of large corporations and insurance companies, high-rise projects in Germany and abroad, department store projects and urban design projects, traffic facilities, landscape architecture, as well as project development and design. What is more, the firm handles all aspects of project development and facility management.

All projects go through a draft design stage, which is designed to create integrated plans through close collaboration with engineers and consultants. The make-up of a project is always judged according to criteria of ecological responsibility, ecological use of resources and technical feasibility. This results in architecture characterised by the use of innovative technology that meets the needs of the people living and working in the buildings. In this way, the architects not only pay attention to aesthetic visions, but reflect their responsibility for the environment.

Inglese Architecture

Inglese Architecture is a young firm engaged in all aspects of fine residential, commercial and civic architecture. Mark English and his associates follow a hands-on approach to design with talented sculptors, finishers and builders involved as resources from the beginning of the design process through completion.

Each project is specifically tailored to the needs and personality of the client, place and resources. This process produces work with a variety of 'styles' but with consistent attention to natural and artificial light effects, colour and material explorations. The work strives to engage the senses as well as the intellect.

Current works include residential and civic work in California and Mexico.

innovarchi pty ltd

innovarchi is a prize-winning design and research based practice which seeks to create the best possible architectural solution for each application through studying design issues from first principals. Drawing on extensive experience with internationally renowned architects such as Herman Hertzberger, Renzo Piano, and John Andrews International, the aim of directors Stephanie Smith (M.Arch) and Ken McBryde (M.Arch) is to generate architecture with purpose. The requirements of the users, brief and site create the framework for designs which captivate the resonance of light/shade, sound/movement, structure and space. Concurrently, innovarchi pursues ecologically sustainable design principles through a sensitive use of materials, appropriate climatic solutions and integration with landscape.

Project experience includes a wide variety of building types including residential, entertainment, ecclesiastical, educational, sporting, commercial and airport terminals.

innovarchi also undertakes Research and Development specialising in the appropriate applications for innovative technology and exploring the implications of cultural diversity in design.

Interdesign Company, Limited

Interdesign Company, Limited (Interdesign), was established in Bangkok, Thailand in 1971 as an independent firm of architectural design and planning consultants. The firm provides a comprehensive range of architectural, planning, engineering and construction management services. Its projects encompass a variety of areas, including residential, commercial, office, hotel, resort, and urban planning. Particularly recognised for its thorough understanding of all aspects of hotel and resort planning, Interdesign has played a prominent role in developing complete physical facilities for Asia's rapidly expanding hospitality industry, from downtown urban hotels to coastal and country resorts.

Since its founding, Interdesign has taken a wholistic approach to architectural design and construction services, combining the abilities of a variety of professional specialists into a coordinated team. The firm has extensive experience on international collaborations with other highly-qualified architectural and engineering practices. Solidly grounded in modern building construction technology, Interdesign also possesses expertise in producing architecture reflective of the distinctive local culture and traditions of Southeast Asia. The pre-eminent goal of the practice is one of providing solutions for the functional needs created by human activity and environmental requirements. The firm focuses on being closely attentive to the desires of its clients through a process of continuous collaboration.

Notable past projects of the firm include the Shangri-La Hotel Bangkok, the Sheraton Grande in Phuket, the Novotel Mandalay, the Sofitel Yangon, and the first Central Plaza Complex, Bangkok. Interdesign's professional activities now extend to other countries of Southeast Asia, involving developments of increasing scale and complexity.

Israel Callas Shortridge associates

Israel Callas Shortridge associates has been in existence since 1993. Before that time, both Steven Shortridge and Barbara Callas were senior architects in the parent firm of Franklin D. Israel Design Associates in Beverly Hills.

Among the recent institutional works of the firm are the UCLA/Revlon Breast Centre; the renovation of the School of Public Policy Building at UCLA; and the Southern Regional Library Phase II at UCLA. The firm is currently working on a Fine Arts Building at UC Riverside.

Previous residential projects include the Dan House in Malibu; the Strick House in the Hollywood Hills; and the Jupiter House in Florida. Current out-of-state residential projects include a house in Taos, New Mexico; and one in Sea Grove Beach, Florida. Presently the firm is involved in several international projects: multi-unit housing in the Hague, The Netherlands; eight loft units in Covent Garden, London; and the Belldegrun Penthouse in Tel Aviv, Israel. Current local projects include the Rochman Residence in the Pacific Palisades and the Brown House in San Francisco.

Articles on the firm's work have been published in *Architectural Digest, Metropolitan Home, Progressive Architecture, The Architectural Record, The New York Times* and other journals and magazines in this country and abroad.

James Stirling Michael Wilford and Associates

James Stirling began the practice in 1956 and was joined by Michael Wilford in 1960. The Stirling/Wilford partnership was established in 1971 and continued until James Stirling's death in 1992. Michael Wilford, Laurence Bain and Russell Bevington formed a new partnership in 1993 under the name of Michael Wilford and Partners.

Professional Objectives: the office has an international reputation for producing buildings of the highest architectural quality which satisfy the requirements of the client's brief and respond to the opportunities of site and context. They are eminent as 'design' architects, fully involved in all phases and aspects of the work.

The firm's work over 38 years of practice includes the design of buildings for many clients: institutions such as museums, universities, central and local government, New Town corporations, United Nations and corporate clients such as Olivetti, Siemens, Bayer, B Braun Melsungen, City Acre Property Investment Trust, Chelsfield and Olympia and York.

Their buildings and projects have been illustrated extensively in publications and included in exhibitions throughout the world.

Jestico + Whiles

Jestico + Whiles is an architecture and urban design practice formed in 1977. The principals are Tom Jestico, John Whiles and Tony Ingram.

Early industrial projects at Epsom (1979) and Waltham Cross (1982) demonstrate a preoccupation with adapting off-the-shelf systems and automotive technologies to create advanced thin-skin structures.

A belief in the designer's obligation to use resources with care is demonstrated in low-energy projects for Friends of the Earth (1981 and 1986), Policy Studies Institute (1986) and research commissioned by the Department of Energy (1992).

For the British Council in Prague (1990) and diplomatic buildings for the Foreign and Commonwealth Office in Riga (1994) and Sofia (1996), and Housing 21 (1997) near London, these interests are further merged with the concept of the workplace as a social focus.

A sense of place and identify are also a primary concern in developing the mixed-use urban project. Bruges Place (1995) combines small flexible workspace with low-cost housing to bring back into use an otherwise redundant site, and Carlow Street (1989) and Burrell's Wharf (1995) further explore this approach.

John Pawson

John Pawson's distinctive approach to modern architecture has attracted international attention. The work has been built in Spain, Japan and America as well as Britain. His designs explore fundamentals—space, light and materials and avoid stylistic mannerisms.

Pawson came to architecture relatively late. Educated at Eton he worked for seven years in his family's Yorkshire textile mill, before spending a long period travelling around the world, most notably in India, Australia and Japan, where he spent four years teaching. He went on to study at the Architectural Association in his early thirties.

The breadth of his previous experience is reflected in the maturity and confidence of his early projects. Pawson's work ranges from art spaces to domestic interiors, from shops to restaurants, new houses to offices.

His completed projects include several art galleries in London and New York as well as apartments for Hester van Royen, Doris Saatchi, Victoria Miro and a house for

ans Neuendorf in Majorca. His designs for
tarkmann (a company headquarters), Wakaba
a Japanese restaurant) and Calvin Klein's
Madison Avenue Store have each been a
hallenging redefinition of a familiar building
rpe.

urrent projects include proposals for the
oung Vic Theatre in London, a hotel in Covent
arden as well as a number of private houses in
merica. His designs have been extensively
atured in publications around the world and
s book, *Minimum*, recently published by
haidon Press, puts his approach in an
storical context.

awson's designs are based on making spaces
at are sensual. Architecture creates a mood
nd a setting, rather than drawing attention to
self.

allmann McKinnell & Wood rchitects, Inc.

allmann McKinnell & Wood Architects, Inc
MW), is a 60-person firm based in Boston,
lassachusetts. The firm began in 1962 when
e City of Boston selected the design by
erhard Kallmann and Michael McKinnell for
e new Boston City Hall. A 1976 national poll
f eminent historians and architects voted
oston City Hall the 6th greatest building in
merican history and called in 'one of the
roudest achievements of American
rchitecture'.

addition to a variety of university projects for
ients such as Harvard, Yale, Princeton,
Vashington University and Nanyang
echnological University in Singapore, KMW's
ortfolio also includes: The American Academy
f Art & Sciences; Becton Dickinson Corporate
eadquarters, the U.S. Embassy in Bangkok;
nd the Organisation for the Prohibition of
hemical Weapons in the Hague.

mong the honours KMW has received are
even Honor Awards from the American
stitute of Architects (AIA). In 1984, KMW
ceived the prestigious AIA Firm of the Year
ward. The citation notes the firm's "*capacity
 produce work of human value and lasting
gnificance. Its continuing exploration of the
otential of architecture to serve public needs
ill ensure the place of this small firm as a true
iant of American design.*"

atsuhiro Kobayashi + Design Studio rchitects

atsuhiro Kobayashi was born in Fukui
efecture Japan, in 1955. After studying
chitecture at the University of Tokyo (received
.D in 1985), and Columbia University, N.Y.
982-84), he established his own architectural

atelier in Tokyo, Design Studio Architects, in
1991 as well as teaching as associate professor
at Tokyo Metropolitan University since 1988.

Among his major achitectural works are
C-wedge (1991); Auberge Le Cloître (1992);
Tokyo Water Front Incineration Plant (1994)
and Niigata Port Corridor Towers (under
construction). He has won many prizes in both
national and international architectural design
competitions and his major writings include
Art Deco Skyscrapers (Japanese, 1990); and
Contemporary Japanese Architects (English,
French, German 1993).

Kengo Kuma & Associates

Kengo Kuma founded Kengo Kuma &
Associates in 1990 and the firm is based in
Tokyo. Its work concentrates on creative
architectural design and planning, and on close
supervision of execution. It emphasises
experimentation with techniques and materials
to create unique spaces for each project.
Kuma's work has won many prizes, most
recently the Grand Prize of the Architectural
Institution of Japan and the First Prize/
Residential Dupont Benedictus Award, both
in 1997.

Experience of the firm is varied, including office
buildings, public amenity buildings, corporate
headquarters, residential buildings, sports and
entertainment facilities, etc—its approach is
mainly derived from the traditional Japanese
concern in interior/exterior relationship. It aims
to provide design solutions that are primarily
concerned with the relation of man-to-nature,
consequently resulting in an architecture that
seeks to mediate between the architectural
object and landscape through the play on
screens and frames, and on the intricate inter-
layering of spaces and landscape, achieving a
sort of transparency that blurs clear edge, melts
architecture to its surroundings and defies the
'containing' nature of architectural space as we
know it.

Kuma's theoretical works have a definite
influence on the firm's approach to design,
especially in its use of multi-media tools in both
process and presentation (virtual and CAD
projects combined with other media-like videos
etc.), and in its constant experimentation on
space and on the interior/exterior relationship
that is at the core of its work.

KISHO KUROKAWA architect & associates

Kisho Kurokawa, the founder of KISHO
KUROKOWA architect & associates, is one of
the most prominent architects in Japan today,
taking an active part in the architectural field of

15 different nations around the world. His
distinguished works are recognised around the
world, and are constantly receiving worldwide
attention.

KISHO KUROKAWA architect & associates is a
firm with Kurokawa as the architect; six
associates with more than 20 years experience
at KISHO KUROKAWA architect & associates,
organising and controlling 100 architects; 50
urban planners and 50 CAD centre staff. All of
KISHO KUROKAWA architect & associates'
works, from residential design, museum design,
airport design to urban planning, receive high
appraisal as works of best quality.

Koning Eizenberg Architecture, Inc.

Koning Eizenberg Architecture, Inc. was
established in 1981 by Julie Eizenberg,
president and Hendrik Koning, FAIA, FRAIA, vice
president. Koning Eizenberg is a Santa Monica
based *women-owned* architecture and planning
firm known for its imaginative, site-specific and
people-oriented design approach. Both
principals are licensed as architects in
California and Australia and hold degrees in
architecture from the University of Melbourne,
Australia and the University of California in
Los Angeles.

Koning Eizenberg Architecture has achieved
recognition for its ground-breaking work in
housing and community-based projects
receiving the *Progressive Architecture* First
Award in 1987 for affordable housing in Santa
Monica and National AIA Honor Awards for the
Simone Hotel (1994) and the 31st Street House
(1996). The firm was elected as one of the
Domino's 30 Leading World Architects in 1989.
Other projects have also been recognised with
awards including the Westside Urban Forum
Prize for Urban Design for the Farmers Market
Historic Preservation (1991), the Los Angeles
Business Council Beautification Award for the
Electric ArtBlock (1993) and Sepulveda Gym
(1996), AIA Los Angeles Chapter Merit Awards
for the 909 House (1991) and Tarzana House
(1992), and AIA California Council Honor
Awards for the Sepulveda Gym (1996) and
31st Street House (1994).

Koning Eizenberg's work, remarkably diverse
in appeal, has been widely published in both
international professional journals and general
interest publications and has just released a
monograph titled *Koning Eizenberg Buildings*
published by Rizzoli.

Kunchook-Moonhwa Architects & Engineers

Kim Young-sub who is well known in Korea as a specialist in church architecture, was born in Mokpo in 1950. He studied at Sung Kyun Kwan University and graduated there in 1974.

After establishing Kunchook-Moonhwa Architects & Engineers in 1982, he has been awarded several prizes for various projects and his work was shown at 'SIAC' in Rome in 1986. As a guest lecturer he was invited to teach History of Western Arts and Interior Design at Myungi College (1982-985) and Kuk-Min University (1986-994), History of Western Music at the National Museum of Modern Art (1991-1996), Church Architecture at Catholic University (1997~) and History of Western Arts at Suk-Myung University (1997~).

His interests have been reflected in various fields including art and music. He is a president of the Committee for Holy Music in Myung Dong and a consultant in music for MBC radio FM.

He is not only an architect who is theoretical as well as practical, but also a music columnist.

Recent awards include First Prize in the Annual Korean Environmental Design and Architectural Culture Award for the Catholic University Library and Lecture Hall (1995); Bronze Prize in the Annual Seoul Metropolitan Government for Bam Boo House and Bam Boo Gallery (1996); Third Prize in the Annual Korean—Architectural Culture Award for Myungheewon Sports Center (1997); and First Prize in the Annual Korean-Architectural Culture Award for Choi's Residence (1997).

He wrote *The Architectural History of Myung Dong Cathedral* in 1984, and from 1995-96 held a solo photography exhibition at the Bam Boo Gallery entitled 'Architecture through Old Lens'.

Kwan & Associates Architects Ltd

Kwan & Associates Architects Ltd was founded in June 1991 by Mr Dominic Kwan. The practice offers full architecture, master planning and space planning services.

The team has developed a reputation for good, skilful design and efficient project management across a wide spectrum of high quality projects both at home and abroad. The house portfolio features residential, office, hotel, institutional and industrial design.

Historically, the practice evolved from KNW Architects & Engineers Limited (KNW). The latter was established in 1979 with Mr Dominic Kwan as a founding director. The firm soon flourished and was rewarded for outstanding architectural achievement by the Hong Kong

Institute of Architects: the Silver Medal for Excellence in Architecture in 1983 and 1984; the Certificate of Merit in 1987 and the Silver Medal in 1989.

After the dissolution of KNW, most of the staff stayed on board and completed outstanding major assignments: Tai Po Hospital; Pristine Villa at Tao Fung Shan; Hong Kong University Phase V; Salisbury Garden underground shopping/carparking complex at Tsimshatsui; a housing development at Kwai Shing Circuit and the ASD Minor Works Term Consultancy.

The practice has avoided the adoption of a distinctive house style, believing instead that each project should be treated innovatively, and that creativity should draw on the team's diverse experiences and insights. Each building is designed contextually, and with the client's needs and objectives uppermost in mind. Special care is also taken to meet the budget and to complete design and construction on time.

The firm has formed a joint venture company with Percy Thomas Partnership in Hong Kong which practices in the name of Kwan-PTP Architects & Hospital Planners Limited and provides both public and private sector clients with services ranging from health planning studies and development plan proposals to the complete design, contact administration and commissioning of hospitals, health centres, research centres and facilities and medical schools.

With a workforce of 200, the firm has the resources to meet the requirements of virtually any architectural assignment.

Kwan Henmi architecture/planning, inc.

Kwan Henmi architecture/planning, inc. is one of the more dynamic and innovative architectural firms based in San Francisco, California. Recognised nationally and internationally with numerous design awards, the firm is responsible for architectural and interiors work on such high profile civic projects as the new baseball stadium for the San Francisco Giants, Fisherman's Wharf Pier 45 Commercial Seafood Center, San Francisco's New Main Library, and several projects at the San Francisco International Airport. Many of these projects have involved collaboration with other firms of international renown.

Founded by partners Sylvia Kwan, AIA and Denis Henmi, AIA in 1980, Kwan Henmi was recognised by *Architectural Record* as one of the United States Best Managed Architectural Firms.

Not only do they specialise in the design of large scale civic projects, but Ms. Kwan and Mr. Henmi have also actively worked with government agencies to make building codes more flexible for people with special needs. This has resulted in projects such as affordable housing, single-room occupancy hotels, housing for the disabled, and an AIDS hospice. They have also designed a number of other urban educational facilities, mixed-use commercial and retail/entertainment developments, high technology centres, and transportation facilities.

Kyu Sung Woo Architect Inc.

Born in Seoul, Korea in 1941, Kyu Sung Woo received a Bachelor of Science and Master of Science in Architectural Engineering at Seoul National University. He came to the United States in 1967, where he studied architecture at Columbia University and received a Master of Architecture in Urban Design at Harvard University, 1970. Prior to establishing Kyu Sung Woo Architect Inc. (1990), he worked for Josep Lluis Sert at Sert, Jackson & Associates (1970-1974). He was an Urban Design Consultant for Harbison New Town, South Carolina (1973-1980), Senior Urban Designer for the Mayor's office of Midtown Planning and Development, New York, N.Y. (1975), and Principal of Woo and Williams, Architecture, Landscape Architecture (1979-1990). He was an associate professor at M.I.T. and has also taught at Harvard University. He is a member of the Advisory Board for the East Asian Architecture and Planning Program, and the Whanki Foundation, New York, N.Y. and is a Fellow of the American Institute of Architects.

Notable projects include the 1988 Seoul Olympic Athletes' and Reporters' Village and current projects Keum Jung Sports Park, 2002 Pusan Asian Games and the Arts of Korea Gallery at The Metropolitan Museum of Art.

Levi Sanchick and Associates

Levi, Sanchick and Associates was founded in 1983, originally as Walter E. Levi + Associates. Prior to that time Walter Levi had been in continuous practice as a principal in several firms, since 1958.

The firm has a varied practice, including large scale retail projects, and department stores, smaller specialty stores, educational and other public buildings. Services provided during planning and design are comprehensive; programming, investigative work, feasibility studies and regulatory analyses. All architectural contract documents are produced in-house on computers using the latest version of AutoCad, by the firm's 15 person staff.

a Sanchick, a principal since 1992, heads up ᵊecialty store projects. Clients include Tiffany Co.; Tourneau, Inc.; Brooks Brothers and ʳuno Magli as well as others. The firm's ᵊecialty stores have been widely published in ᵇoks and magazines.

ᵐong other projects designed by Levi, ᵃnchick and Associates and their predecessor ʳms are numerous department stores for Sears ᵈnd JC Penney, a campus for the New York ᵗate University College at Oneonta, several ᵊw schools for the New York City Board of ᵈucation (including Edward R. Murrow High ᶜhool) and major science building ᵐodernisations for the City University of New ᵒrk.

ⁱang Peddle Thorp Architects & ⁱanners Ltd

ⁱnce its establishment in 1982, Liang Peddle ᵗʰorp Architects & Planners Ltd (LPT), has ᵐerged as one of Hong Kong's prominent ᵃrchitectural practices with major commissions ᵗroughout Hong Kong, China, Thailand, ᵊtnam, Malaysia, Singapore and Indonesia. ᵗ is the company's philosophy to effectively ᵃlance and blend design, construction and ᵈministration skills, and it is this that has ᵘnderpinned our success.

ᵘlly computerised and employing over 100 ᵊcialised staff, the company enjoys ᵍnificant involvement and influence across a ᵛerse range of market sectors. LPT offers a ᵒmprehensive range of design and project ᵐanagement services for a broad range of ᵛerse market sectors including hotel, ᵖartment, and retail developments, ᵒmmercial/office buildings, industrial ᵗstallations, major refurbishment projects and ʳban planning.

ᵖT focuses on the importance of the client as ᵃn integral part of the ultimate concept and ᵈsign. Through rigorous application of this ᵉlief at all levels of architecture, LPT ensures ᵉ client's needs and aspirations remain the ᵉntral influence.

ⁱchael Graves, Architect

ⁱnce its establishment in 1964, the Princeton, ᵊw Jersey office of Michael Graves, Architect ⁱGA), has designed a wide variety of projects ᵇoth the United States and abroad, ranging ᵒm large, multi-use urban development to ⁱvate residences, and including numerous ᵒrporate headquarters, hotels, and ᵈucational and cultural facilities. Michael ʳaves, the design principal of the firm, has ᵉen in the forefront of architectural design ʳ 30 years, winning over 100 design awards.

Paul Goldberger of *The New York Times* has described Graves as "the most truly original voice that American architecture has produced for some time." His work has directly influenced the transformation of urban architecture from the abstractions of modernism toward more contextual compositions. Graves has demonstrated his ability to create original designs sympathetic to the general program of use and the character of the context. The firm has a staff of 60 which provides full services in architecture, interiors, and the design of consumer products. MGA also offers pre-design services such as master planning, programming, and feasibility studies.

Mitchell/Giurgola Architects

Mitchell/Giurgola Architects was formed in 1958 and established an office for general practice in New York City in 1968. The practice offers a comprehensive range of architectural services including master planning and urban design, research and programming, new buildings, renovations and additions, interior design and graphic design.

Mitchell/Giurgola has practiced in a wide geographical area including 21 states in the United States and seven foreign countries. Recent commissions include The Lighthouse Headquarters in New York City, the Ciba-Geigy Pharmaceutical's Life Sciences Building in Summit, New Jersey and the Belvedere, a new waterfront park at Battery Park City in Lower Manhattan, as well as a new elementary school for the New York City School Construction Authority.

The practice has been characterised by a constant commitment to an architecture based on humanistic principles. Values inherent to a particular program and a particular locale and culture are explored and celebrated, resulting in a unique architectural solution for each project.

Mitchell/Giurgola received the Architectural Firm Award of the American Institute in 1976, the highest honour bestowed upon an American practice, and the Medal of Honour Award from the New York Chapter of the AIA. The firm has received over 75 professional honour awards for its architecture and planning work. The Life Sciences building on the Ciba-Geigy Pharmaceutical's campus in Summit, New Jersey received *R&D Magazine's* Lab of the Year Award. The Lighthouse Headquarters is the recipient of a National AIA Honour Award for Interior Design. The Belvedere is the recipient of a National New York State and New York City AIA Honour Award winner for

Urban Design, as well as the recipient of the Waterfront Center's International Award for Excellence on the Waterfront.

Current commissions include a new 23,225 square metre (250,000 square foot) elementary/middle/high school complex in Aviano, Italy; a new undergraduate science teaching laboratory facility for the University of Maryland system; and laboratories for senior researchers at Cornell University Medical College in New York City. Master plans are in progress for Queens College, City University of New York; and Teachers College, Columbia University.

Moshe Safdie and Associates, Inc.

Moshe Safdie first established his architectural practice in 1964 in Montreal to design and supervise the construction of Habitat '67. Today the principal office is in Boston, Massachusetts, with branch offices in Jerusalem and Toronto. The firm provides a full range of planning and architectural services. Currently, the firm is engaged in activities ranging from the design of public institutions—including museums, performing arts' centres, and university campuses—to the design of airports, housing, mixed-use complexes and new communities.

The firm has won numerous awards for its designs, including the Governor General's Medal for Architecture of the Royal Architectural Institute of Canada (1992) and the Prix d'Excellence en Architecture by the Ordre des Architectes du Quebec (1988) for the Quebec Museum of Civilization; the Rechter Prize of the Association of Architects and City Planners of Israel (1982) for the Hosh complex; the Urban Design Concept Award by the U.S. Department of Housing and Urban Development (1980) for Coldspring New Town; and the Massey Medal of the Royal Architectural Institute of Canada (1967) for Habitat '67.

Moshe Safdie has been the recipient of numerous awards including the Order of Canada (1986) and the RAIC Gold Medal (1995) as well as several honorary degrees and served as Director of the Urban Design Program at the Harvard University Graduate School of Design from 1978 until 1990. He has also taught at Yale, McGill, and Ben Gurion Universities. He has published numerous articles and books including, most recently, *The City After the Automobile* .

Moule & Polyzoides Architects

Elizabeth Moule & Stefanos Polyzoides, Architects and Urbanists was founded in 1982 in the interest of providing the finest, most comprehensive and most personal architecture and urban design services to our clients. It is our belief that such services are founded on respect and support for client needs and aspirations, close collaboration with the most qualified consultants, and the practice of strong project management.

Moule & Polyzoides is an unusual office where the principals are actively involved in research and design as well as management of projects. The organisation of the firm is built around project teams that are made up of both principals and project managers that execute the work from inception to realisation. At the centre of the practice is a dedication to clearer ideas, integrity, a high degree of efficiency, accountability, strict budgets and schedules, and therefore, a superior service.

As co-founders of the *Congress for the New Urbanism*, Moule & Polyzoides have pioneered a new approach to architecture and urbanism, focusing on physically reconstructing the American metropolis, rebuilding a sense of community, and addressing the environmental and economic issues. Its aesthetic root is in the exploration of design in the context of cultural convention and of nature. The work is known for its respect for historic settings and its engagement with the existing city and the landscape.

The firm has an international reputation for design innovation and its work has been published all over the world.

Murphy/Jahn

Murphy/Jahn is a truly unique architectural firm. With 20 years of 'organisation building', the firm has succeeded in combining DESIGN CREATIVITY and CORPORATE PROFESSIONALISM. This integration sets Murphy/Jahn apart from those firms commonly known either as 'design studios' or 'corporate architects'.

The growing national and international reputation of Murphy/Jahn has led to commissions across the United States, Europe, Africa and Asia. The firm's projects are administered from their offices in Chicago and Munich, Germany. The firm is committed to design excellence and the improvement of the urban environment; its projects have been recognised globally for design innovation, vitality, and integrity.

The diversity of their work—high-rise buildings, airport master plans, transportation facilities, urban planning and low-rise commercial projects—stimulates a cross-fertilisation of ideas and encourages an intellectual freshness derived from addressing and resolving new architectural challenges. In order to succeed in

this endeavour, it has established a policy that each commission receives the full attention of Helmut Jahn.

In addition to Helmut Jahn, all key individuals in the firm are sensitive to the importance of these issues from the client's point of view and further understand that the continued success of the firm in the future depends on its record of client satisfaction.

The firm prides itself on a solid record of performance in delivering architectural service in a manner consistent with each client's pragmatic concerns in terms of document clarity, scheduling and cost control. There are a number of recent examples of work that successfully unite the client's desire for a significant architectural statement with a disciplined approach to maintaining the project budget and schedule.

MVRDV

MVRDV was founded in 1992 by Winy Maas, Jacob van Rijs and Nathalie de Vries and is based in Rotterdam. Their work ranges from large scale to small and is extremely varied in nature covering designing and realisation of buildings as well as master planning, interior design and furniture design.

MVRDV brings together knowledge and experience of projects covering the whole range of spatial design disciplines. The traditional demarcation lines between the different disciplines are absent. Practical experience of realising designs has shown that this sort of cross-fertilisation leads to fruitful solutions. A commission for work on an interior can be approached as if it were a piece of town planning, principles drawn from the field of landscape design can be applied to a piece of architectonic design.

To allow a wide range of commissions to be handled, special design teams are put together for individual commissions. These teams are assisted by advisers in the fields of building and installation technology; building sciences, building management and building costs. In this way MVRDV's generalism and verve is lined with the specialisations and thoroughness of the other team members.

MVRDV also sees the design process for each new commission as an occasion for carrying out a systematic piece of spatial and organisational research. The research methods range from trial and error to highly systematised; the results are applied to the design immediately. Apart from this, long term research is carried on into subjects not directly related to specific commissions. This research sometimes takes input from the problems raised by a particular

commission. Conversely, the results of the research can be applied to the solution of specific design problems.

Nikken Sekkei

Nikken Sekkei is the oldest and largest architecture firm in Japan. Descended from its predecessor firm which was established in 1900, Nikken Sekkei was incorporated into the present form in 1950 and has since grown to its present strength of some 1,700 architectural, engineering, and planning professionals.

Since its establishment Nikken Sekkei has steadfastly upheld its commitment to contributing to society and people all over the world through creation of superior architectural products and urban planning, while maintaining their strict principles as professionals and guarding their integrity as designers through their policy of fiscal self-sufficiency and ideological neutrality. Having all necessary disciplines in-house, Nikken Sekkei renders society and their clients the highest service, responding to the continuous and increasingly complex newly emerging requirements of contemporary development.

Each project is implemented by a special team assembled from the various departments and sections of the company, selected to bring together the particular talents most appropriate to carry out the work under the specific conditions of each project, such as the nature of the building, scale of construction site conditions, and the objectives of the client. The quality of their work is attested by the numerous national and international awards received and their success in open competitions.

P&T Group

The P&T Group, formerly known as Palmer and Turner Hong Kong, is probably the oldest and largest international architectural and engineering practice in South East Asia. With over 700 staff, working from offices located in Hong Kong, Macau, Thailand, Taiwan, Singapore and China, projects are undertaken also in most other Asian countries.

Palmer and Turner was first established in Hong Kong around 1886, and since its inception, has proved a major contributor to the physical development of this region, responsible for many of its old and new architectural landmarks.

The P&T Group offers the full range of architectural, engineering and planning services, with full support from inhouse interior and graphic design divisions. A model-making

ction, extensive computer facilities and full
ministrative support, completes this service
total design.

e P&T Group is committed to the pursuit of
cellence in the architectural and engineering
ld and aims to improve the quality of life by
ntributing to the design of the physical
vironment. Professional emphasis is placed
visual and functional elements of design, to
ate buildings that are aesthetically pleasing,
mpathetic to their surroundings and of a
meless quality.

e P&T Group's growth is a reflection of the
creasing number of large-scale projects
manding the creativity and expertise of many
ofessionals. The reputation of The P&T Group
sts on providing the highest quality in design,
chnical knowledge, professional service to
ents and experience as acting as lead
nsultants. The success in this is
monstrated by the numerous number of
sign awards received from the regional
chitectural institutes of Hong Kong,
ngapore, Taiwan and Macau for the
cellence in design and energy efficiency.

atela & Paatela, Architects Ltd

e name Paatela has been connected to
althcare architecture in Finland for over
years. Founded in 1915 by Professor Jussi
atela, the firm is now run by the third
neration of the same family.

e largest healthcare institutions in Finland,
ch as Helsinki and Turku University Central
spitals, have relied on the professional
pertise of Paatela Architects throughout the
ars of practice. Today, the staff consists of
veral architects with over 20 years of
perience in functional planning and
chitectural design of healthcare buildings.
e projects have varied from large new
spital complexes to small renovations;
m municipal and district hospitals to
vate rehabilitation centres.

addition to healthcare sector, the firm has
signed a variety of projects for research,
ucation, corporate and industry sectors.
sides complexes implemented in Finland,
atela & Paatela Architects Ltd. has designed
ojects in the Middle East, Africa, Russia and
ina, as well as many in Finland.

day, the firm utilises the latest computer
ded design methods to provide constantly update drawings and bills of quantities for each
oject.

Peter Forbes and Associates

Peter Forbes and Associates was founded in
1980 by Peter Forbes, FAIA, with the office in
Boston, Massachusetts.

Since that time the firm has become celebrated
for their architecture of rigorously simple forms,
meticulously detailed and carefully sited in the
landscape.

Peter Forbes and Associates has been selected
to design a variety of building types:
commercial, institutional and public as well as
being one of the few firms to focus on
residential architecture at the highest level of
design. The common denominator of these
commissions and the resulting architecture has
been imperative to evolve innovative solutions
to design problems that have few, if any,
precedents. The firm approaches design
without preconception, achieving new solutions
to complex situations from within the needs
and desires of the client, the dictates of site
and their own rigorous formal discipline.

For this work Peter Forbes and Associates has
received over 30 design awards and has been
extensively published in America, Europe and
Asia.

R.M.Kliment & Frances Halsband Architects

R.M.Kliment & Frances Halsband Architects
was founded in 1972 in New York City.
The work of the firm includes master planning;
buildings for institutional, commercial and
public clients; houses; new buildings, additions,
renovations, historic preservation; interiors,
furniture and lighting.

From the inception of the partnership to the
present, the firm has been characterised by
the direct and continuing involvement of the
two founding partners in all aspects of the
work. From the beginning, those partners have
worked collaboratively with small groups of
colleagues, three of whom have been with the
firm for at least 15 years, and are now partners.
All partners collaborate in the management and
design development of projects, and in the
management and administration of the firm.
All have shared intentions, and all work
together to realise them.

"We intend our projects to be clearly conceived
and carefully made places that engage the past
and imply connections to the future. We believe
it important that they engage the existing
cultural and physical context, so that they
become integral components of it; that they
give direction to future uses and development,
so that change and growth can be natural and
coherent; that they fully develop the

requirements and opportunities of program,
so that they work well; and that their
construction is congruent with available skills
and funds, so that they are built well.

We try to realise a design coherent in its parts,
in the relation of its parts to the whole, and in
the relation of the whole to the larger organism
of which it is to become an integral component.

We strive to make each project specific in
relation to its cultural and physical context,
coherent within itself and consistent with the
essential intent of our work."

Riken Yamamoto and Field Shop

Riken Yamamoto and Field Shop was founded
by Riken Yamamoto in 1973. The practice now
comprises full-time architectural staff of 29
with two administrative staff.

Its work has included individual houses, public
housing, commercial and housing complexes,
a psychiatric clinic, a community centre, and
schools, innovative compositions of which are
always derived from its re-analysis of each
building's purpose and role.

Over the years, the work of the firm has
changed drastically in scale from individual
houses to public housing and universities.
It has received its recent major projects through
winning competitions such as Competition for
Iwadeyama Junior High School (1993); Saitama
Prefectural University of Nursing and Welfare
(1995); Hiroshima Nishi Fire Station (1996); and
Hakodate Municipal College (1997).

Since GAZEBO's winning Kajima Award (1985)
and Architectural Institute of Japan Award
(1988), its work has been widely acknowledged
as a radical solution which challenges what is
conventionally accepted norms.

Roth & Moore Architects

Harold Roth, FAIA and Williams F. Moore, AIA,
both graduates of the Yale School of
Architecture, are the principals of the firm Roth
and Moore Architects located in New Haven,
Connecticut. Following his association with the
office of Eero Saarinen where he was the lead
designer on CBS Headquarters building and the
Ford Foundation building, both in New York,
Mr Roth was founding principal of the firm in
1965. A member of the design faculty at Yale
for many years, he is currently secretary of the
College of Fellows of the American Institute of
Architects.

Amongst the many projects completed over the
past 33 years are the Seeley G. Mudd Library,
the Arthur K. Watson Hall for the department of
computer science and the Joseph Slifka Center
for Jewish Life, all on the Yale University

campus; the employee recreation centre for the Cummins Engine Company in Columbus, Indiana, and the Cummins Parts Distribution Center in Mechelen, Belgium.

Current work of Roth & Moore includes dormitories and dining facilities at the Choate Rosemary Hall School, a visitors' centre at the New Canaan Nature Center, a synagogue complex for the Central Reform Congregation in St. Louis, an academic arts centre for Drew University, a natural resources laboratory for the University of Connecticut and the Lincoln-Bassett elementary school in New Haven.

RTKL International Ltd.

RTKL International Ltd. (RTKL) is amongst the largest and most comprehensive design firms in the world. The firm is headquartered in Baltimore, and maintains offices in Washington DC, Dallas, Los Angeles, Chicago, London, Hong Kong and Tokyo. The staff of 550 includes architects; planners and urban designers; structural, mechanical and electrical engineers; interior designers and architects; environmental graphic designers; and landscape architects.

The portfolio of RTKL is diverse, with projects located in 45 countries around the world. These include major mixed-use developments; retail centres; entertainment venues; hotels and resorts; office buildings and other corporate facilities; healthcare facilities; and government buildings. International work comprises one-third of the firm's revenues.

RTKL's reputation for high-quality design and attentive client service has earned the firm more than 100 awards of excellence and a long roster of repeat clientele. A strong proponent of globalism in design services, RTKL is committed to creation of definitive designs of enduring quality.

Architect Rüdiger Lainer

Established in 1985, Architekt Dipl. Ing Rüdiger Lainer designs and implements an extremely wide range of projects, including housing, schools, industrial facilities and refurbishments as well as urban design exercises.

Some major works include the Former Airfield Aspern (Vienna's largest City Development Zone) an invited competition win which led to the award of the contract, and is still on the drawing board, and was awarded the prestigious American Institute of Architects' Award 1995/UK Chapter London for Penthouse Seilergasse.

The firm has recently widened its scope to include projects of an academic nature, by undertaking a research project into Computer Aided Design of Artefacts.

International publications and exhibitions have included being elected twice (1991 and 1996) to join the Biennale of Architecture in Venice.

The office is very much concerned with the development of projects that start with a conceptual basis to the synthesis of this base as a realised built entity that combines theory with the reality of modern day building.

The S/L/A/M Collaborative

The S/L/A/M Collaborative is a full-service architectural firm with 140 dedicated professionals, known for planning and designing institutional projects throughout the United States. The firm's areas of expertise include campus master planning, research facilities, educational facilities, healthcare environments, corporate facilities, criminal justice projects, and other complex assignments. In addition, it has in-house interior design, structural engineering and landscape architecture studios. Staff members also teach architecture at levels ranging from secondary schools to graduate courses at Yale University.

The S/L/A/M Collaborative's projects range from small renovations and additions to large, highly technical complex buildings. Organised into design studios, the firm commits consistent team resources to a project from inception to completion to insure continuity and personalised service. It has created a synergy of team, talent and ideas, enabling them to draw from a deep pool of collective experience to meet the needs of the clients.

The staff have the expertise and experience necessary to ensure projects are completed on time, without cost overruns. The S/L/A/M Collaborative are well acquainted with regulatory agency procedures and provide facilities' planning that saves operational costs, incorporates advanced technological systems, and provides the most efficient utilisation of space. Because of the firm's ability to understand the planning and design requirements of its institutional clients, it is able to help administrators understand the unique qualities of the campus. This helps form action plans that will provide long-range direction for the facilities' programs. In addition to familiarity with technical design issues, the firm is extremely knowledgeable about the related concerns which face administrators during a building program. The firm also provides master planning services to many organisations to optimise use of existing buildings and to improve campus circulation.

Throughout the years many of The S/L/A/M Collaborative's projects have been honoured for design excellence. Recently the firm was

ranked among the top design firms in the country by several publications, including *Building Design & Construction; Engineering News Record,* and *Modern Healthcare.*

Schwartz/Silver Architects Inc

Schwartz/Silver Architects Inc was founded in 1980 by Warren Schwartz and Robert Silver following the partners' expansion of the historic East Cambridge Savings Bank in Cambridge, Massachusetts. The project received national attention and to this day, serves as a model for the renovation and expansion of landmark buildings. Robert Miklos was named a principal of the firm in 1988.

During the past ten years, Schwartz/Silver has focused on the design of buildings for educational and cultural institutions. Schwartz Silver's architecture is widely recognised for its authenticity, appropriateness, and vitality.

Through its inventive work, Schwartz/Silver has earned recognition as a new and reasoned voice in American architecture and interior design.

The firm's work has been featured in leading design publications internationally. Recent awards include three National Honor Awards from the American Institute of Architects, six Honor Awards from the Boston Society of Architects, two Gold Medals from the Boston Society of Architects for the most beautiful buildings in the Boston area, six regional architecture awards, and four national awards for interior design.

The Stubbins Associates, Inc

Established in 1949, The Stubbins Associates (TSA), has successfully completed an unusually broad range of projects both nationally and internationally. Professional services include feasibility studies; programming and master planning; architectural, interior, and landscape design; and technical services including construction documentation and construction administration. The firm utilises the most advanced CAD technology, including 3-D modelling, on all projects.

Directed by six principals, the firm's highly qualified and experienced professional staff take pride in their teamwork with clients, consultants, and contractors. The size and structure of the firm are designed for active, hands-on participation by a principal-in-charge who is assisted by a project manager and project designer to ensure a high degree of communication, coordination, and continuity for each and every project.

he firm believes in working with each client to explore the full potential for a project, whatever ts site, program, budget, or schedule. TSA does ot impose preconceived design solutions or tyles. The design process is tempered with a eep respect for the client's needs, aspirations, nctional requirements, and constraints. or all of their clients, TSA seeks to provide omething special—the immeasurable quality at lifts the human spirit.

SA is one of the few firms to have been warded the prestigious 'Architectural Firm ward' by the American Institute of Architects, lacing it at the highest echelon of the rofession. In addition, TSA's projects have on more than 150 awards for design xcellence, both nationally and internationally.

tudio*downie*

raig Downie worked for the Terry Farrell artnership, and Foster Associates, forming his ractice in 1992. His projects include a alifornian lakeside house, French Treasury ffices, galleries in France and London, overnment Agency information centres, a ublic square, Sheffield, and recently a ompetition win for a rare book library, visitors' entre and conservation workshop. He is also n interior design adviser at Heathrow for the ritish Airports Authority.

is interests include the study of ocean waves. e has been invited to teach at schools of rchitecture in Denmark and Cyprus and eaches at the Architectural Association, ondon. His work has been exhibited and ublished in France, Scotland, Japan, London nd Switzerland, the latter for a shortlisted ban design entry for a French lakeside town, dged by Dominique Perrault. In 1994 he presented "Emerging UK Architects", an RIBA xhibition and seminar series chaired by Kisho urokawa at the Architectural Institute of apan, Tokyo.

R. Hamzah & Yeang Sdn Bhd

R. Hamzah & Yeang Sdn Bhd was formed in 976 by Tengku Robert Hamzah and Dr Ken eang, following their graduation from the AA rchitectural Association) in London. eadquartered in Kuala Lumpur, Hamzah & ang is regarded as a design-emphasis firm, hose expertise is in ecologically-responsive gh-rise buildings and large-scale projects. is expertise is complemented by the firm's ofessional management and organisation to ocument and deliver these large-scale ojects.

e firm employs over 90 personnel of an ternational nature with projects worldwide.

Underlying the buildings and projects, is a programme of cutting-edge research, design and development, focussing on a new building type, the 'bioclimatic skyscraper'—the tall building whose architecture derives from the systematic understanding of the role climate can play in finding new forms and technologies that are energy efficient, that enhance the quality of life for occupants and are ecologically-responsive.

A 'total design' philosophy is pursued and a strong belief in a multi-disciplinary (design team) approach has developed in a close understanding with many engineering-specialist collaborators worldwide.

A balanced approach is adopted for each project, reconfiguring progressive design-thinking with practical experience in order to connect a client's building programme and budget with a rewarding design and building solutions.

The practice's work has won many awards and has been widely exhibited in Europe, Asia and the United States.

Tai Soo Kim Partners

Tai Soo Kim Partners was established in 1970 in Connecticut as the Hartford Design Group. In 1991, the firm was renamed to reflect the creative leadership of its founder, Tai Soo Kim, FAIA, and to recognise Mr Kim's collaboration with Ryszard Szczypek, AIA and T. Whitcomb Iglehart, AIA. Today, the firm has a staff of 20 in the U.S. and a 10-person affiliated office in Korea.

The firm has a diverse portfolio of projects in the U.S. and Korea. The work is recognised for its unique simplicity and sensitivity to natural and cultural conditions. The firm has won a number of design awards and international design competitions including Korea's National Museum of Contemporary Art; and the L.G. research and Development Park also in Korea.

Among its award-winning projects are the U.S. Naval Submarine Training Facility; the rehab and expansion of Hartford's historic Union Station; the Middlebury Elementary School; the Recreation Center for Miss Porter's School in Connecticut; Persson Hall for Colgate University; and the Helen & Harry Gray & Court for the Wadsworth Atheneum.

Current projects include: a headquarters expansion for the Daewoo Group; the Central City Development in Seoul; and The Learning Corridor, an urban educational campus in Hartford, Connecticut.

TAMS Consultants, Inc. Architects, Engineers & Planners

Established in 1942, TAMS Consultants, Inc. Architects, Engineers & Planners (TAMS), is a collaborative design practice, drawing on the interdisciplinary talents of in-house architects, engineers and planners for projects world-wide. With offices in Connecticut, Illinois, Massachusetts, New Jersey, New York, Virginia, London, Bangkok and Abu Dhabi, TAMS' staff of 450 have developed a reputation for excellence in the planning, design and construction of complex transportation, aviation, education and urban infrastructure facilities.

The projects featured in this publication were produced by TAMS's 65-person Boston office, under the design direction of Chris Iwerks, AIA and Deborah Fennick, AIA. TAMS' Boston office has a diverse practice covering a wide range of facility types and sizes. Principal specialisations are in public and private projects for airport terminals, intermodal transportation facilities, schools, courthouses, institutions and urban infrastructure.

TAMS' aesthetic orientation is concerned with the expressive potential of current and emerging construction techniques. Traditional stereotomic materials (load-bearing solids, primarily strong in compression) composed interdependently with isotropic materials (materials equally strong in all directions) form the basis of TAMS' design sensibility and evolved visual language.

The Steinberg Group

The Steinberg Group (TSG), established in 1953, is an architectural, planning and interior design firm involved in a broad spectrum of building types, including senior, multi-family, single-family and custom residential, civic, educational and commercial facilities. Based in Silicon Valley, TSG is sensitive to the rapidly changing demands of dynamic communities as well as adhering to the needs of clients, local municipalities and historical and social precedents.

TSG's staff of 75 highly trained architects, designers and support personnel is committed to providing quality design. The corporate structure is comprised of four studios (civic, commercial, residential and educational), each assigned the responsibility for specific projects from pre-design through construction administration and move-in. The principals of the firm personally commit their own talent in overseeing every project to its successful completion.

TSG strives to create outstanding design, while maintaining budgets, function and the surrounding environment in order to fulfil their clients' needs and goals.

The Wischmeyer Architects, Inc.

The Wischmeyer Architects, Inc. is committed to creating well-planned, cost effective architectural solutions. An extensive scope of experience is the result of projects for schools, colleges, laboratories, hospitals, long-term care facilities, office buildings, manufacturing facilities and computer facilities. The longstanding philosophy of Wischmeyer is to provide sound design based on logic, study and a comprehensive understanding of the client's needs.

Since its founding in 1951, the firm has maintained a size which is small enough to allow principals to be intimately involved with each client, yet large enough to facilitate the accumulation of knowledge in a time of a rapidly developing technology. The current staff of 25 includes architects, planners, designers and technical support personnel in three regional offices.

Tod Williams Billie Tsien and Associates

The work of Tod Williams Billie Tsien and Associates bridges across different worlds—across theory and practice; across architecture and the fine arts. Williams has a seasoned foundation in the practice of architecture with over six years as an associate in the office of Richard Meier before starting his own practice. Moreover, he maintains a foundation in theory, with a particular interest in the physical and philosophical nature of construction. Tsien brings to architecture a background in the Fine Arts and a keen interest in collaboration across disciplines. Together, Williams and Tsien have produced collaborative works with artists such as Jackie Ferrara, Mary Miss and Elyn Zimmerman.

Their built work, bordering on minimalism, pays careful attention to detail and the subtleties of context. The firm's project The Neurosciences Institute, completed in 1995 was termed a "magnificent piece of work" by *New York Times Architecture* critic Herbert Muschamp, and it has received a number of awards including an AIA national honour award.

Both architects maintain active teaching careers parallel to their practice. Tsien has taught at Parsons School of Design, SCI-ARC, Harvard and Yale. Billie Tsien received an appointment to the O'Neal Ford Chair at the University of Texas at Austin in 1995.

Williams has taught at the Cooper Union, SCI-ARC, Harvard, Yale and in 1994 was appointed to the Ruth Stapleton Carter Chair at the University of Texas at Austin.

Tonkin Design Limited

Tonkin Design Limited brings an original combination of poetry and practicality to the field of architecture and interior design. Combining functionalism with creativity it offers a unique approach to each client's need and aspiration.

Director Mike Tonkin received a first class honour degree in architecture from Leeds School of Architecture followed by an MA in Environmental design from the Royal College of Art in London. He qualified as an architect in 1989 and set up Tonkin Design in 1990. The company work load ranges from private houses and hotel projects through to shop, cinema and restaurants to corporate space and beyond into furniture and landscape.

Having received numerous awards for its work in Hong Kong, Tonkin Design has a growing reputation that has led to numerous commissions in Asia and Europe with the opening in 1997 of a new office in London, Tonkin Architects, in partnership with Paul Archer.

TRO/The Ritchie Organization

TRO/The Ritchie Organization (TRO), is an award-winning 170-person multi-disciplinary design firm headquartered in Newton, Massachusetts, with offices in Birmingham, Alabama and Sarasota, Florida. With services ranging from real estate asset management, to master planning, space programming, architectural and interior design and engineering, TRO's volume of work has encompassed over 400 clients throughout the world with construction projects totalling more than US$3.5 billion.

Together with its award-winning healthcare design, which has been a specialty for more than 45 years, TRO also provides innovative design solutions to educational and corporate clients.

TRO works with its clients to define a standard of excellence that responds to their needs with flexibility, imagination and the highest quality design services. The firm's measure of success is demonstrated by its record of repeat business—nearly 90%. Client relationships have spanned decades, some for over 40 continuous years, attesting to clients' utmost satisfaction with the firm's performance.

TSP Architects + Planners Pte Ltd

TSP Architects + Planners Pte Ltd is a long established regional practice with successful building, urban design and planning projects in Singapore, Malaysia, Indonesia, Brunei, Thailand and Hong Kong.

The practice was formed in 1946 under the name of E.J. Seow. In 1970, after 24 years of steady growth, the name was changed to SLH Partners. Upon retirement of E.J. Seow in 1974 the firm was renamed Timothy Seow & Partners. In 1988, the practice name was abbreviated to TSP Architects & Planners to reflect a more corporate image and in 1995, it became licensed corporate to facilitate a multi-disciplinary practice with an enhanced competitive edge.

Waro Kishi + K. Associates/Architects

Waro Kishi was born in Yokohama, Japan in 1950. He studied electronics at Kyoto University in 1973 and later received an architecture degree from the same university, in 1975.

After completing his graduate studies in 1978 he worked for the Atelier of Masayuki Kurokawa in Tokyo. Then in 1981, he commenced his own practice, eventually forming Waro Kishi + K. Associates/Architects in Kyoto in 1993. Presently he is an associate professor at Kyoto Institute of Technology.

In recognition of his talents and distinguished achievements he has received many awards: the 1987 SD Review Award for Event Zone of the World Historical Cities Exhibition in Kyoto; the 1995 annual Architectural Design Commendation from the Architectural Institute of Japan for the Sonobe SD Office in Kyoto; the 1993 (JIA) Japan Institute of Architects Award for the 'best young architect of the year'; the 1995 Kenneth F. Brown Asia Pacific Culture and Architecture Merit Award and in 1996 the great distinction of the Architecture Institute of Japan Prize for Design.

Westwork Architects

The work of Westwork Architects builds on the spirit of life in the high desert of New Mexico. Founded in 1979, Westwork has been recognised for its spirited response to regional form.

Westwork has completed over 100 public, private, and institutional projects and over 40 residential projects. Recognition of the firm's excellence in design has been reflected in both awards and publication of the firm's work. Projects designed by Westwork have appeared twice on the cover of *Architecture* magazine and numerous articles have been published on the firm's work in *Architectural Record, Architecture, New Mexico Magazine;* and several books. Westwork was named the 1993 Firm of the Year for the Western Mountain Region of the AIA as well as being named the 1996 Firm of the Year by AIA New Mexico.

The current principals in the firm are Glade Sperry, Jr. AIA and Cindy A. Terry AIA. Mr Sperry has resided in New Mexico since 1959. He attended the University of New Mexico where he received a Master of Architecture degree in 1972. He has been a member of several AIA committees and has lectured and authored articles on regional architecture and the work of the firm. He has also appeared on public television in a forum discussion of regional architecture and was a visiting instructor at the design studio at the University of New Mexico School of Architecture and Planning.

Ms Terry was born in Socorro, New Mexico in 1959 and graduated from Mc Murry University in Abeline, Texas with a BFA in Painting in 1981 and received her Masters in Architecture from the University of New Mexico in 1986.

William Kite Architects, Inc.

William L. Kite, Jr. AIA, is president of the architectural firm of William Kite Architects, Inc., a design oriented architectural and planning office located in Providence Rhode Island for almost 25 years. Mr Kite is a graduate of the Rhode Island School of Design with a B.S. in Architecture (1960) and Massachusetts Institute of Technology with a Masters in Architecture (1961). He is a registered architect in Rhode Island (447) and Massachusetts (4249) and holds NCARB accreditation.

William Kite has been the recipient of numerous design awards including first place in a national design competition and the first Career Award presented by the RI Chapter of the American Institute of Architects for "...longstanding, active participation and support of the AIA and the success of a career which has forwarded the profession as a whole." He has taught architectural design at the Rhode Island School of Design and continues to lecture and be an architectural critic at Roger Williams University. He has served on numerous Commissions and Design Review Committees, including the Providence Preservation Society and the Providence Historic District Commission. His work has been featured in national and internationally circulated publications such as *Architecture, Architectural Record, Urban Design International, Home Magazine, Custom Home,* and locally in *The Providence Journal, Rhode Island Monthly,* and *The Boston Globe.*

William Lim Associates Pte

The firm was founded by William S W Lim. Presently, the three partners are William S W Lim, Mok Wei Wei and Teh Joo Heng. The firm has nine architects with other supporting staff. The services provided by the offices includes planning and development economics; architecture and urban design; and interior architecture. Presently, the office is working on projects of various sizes in both Singapore and abroad.

The practice places great emphasis on the search for new design frontiers. The architects are employed based largely on their design capability. Teamwork is an important criterion for the generation of creative ideas. The firm attempts to continue producing innovative ideas and exciting design solutions within the necessary constraints of the clients' brief and market viability.

Recently the firm has received the following awards: Singapore Institute of Architects Architectural Design Award in the Individual Houses category for Reuter's House, Singapore (1991); Singapore Institute of Architects Honourable Mention in the Interior Architecture category for Mix Shop (Meridien), Singapore (1991); and Malaysian Institute of Architects Architecture Award in recognition of Design Excellence for Central Square at Jalan Hang Kasturi, Benteng, Malaysia (1991); and 1997 URA Architectural Heritage Award for 3A Chatsworth Park.

Zimmer Gunsul Frasca Partnership

Zimmer Gunsul Frasca Partnership (ZGF), is an architectural, planning and interior design firm based in Portland, Oregon with offices in Los Angeles, California; Seattle, Washington; and Washington, DC. Projects range from interiors commissions to building rehabilitations, museums, healthcare facilities, research laboratories, academic facilities, athletic clubs and office buildings, to city-wide urban design and transportation projects. Over 200 national, regional, and local design awards have been received by ZGF including the 1991 American Institute of Architects (AIA) Architecture Firm Award. The firm is also the recipient of two Lab of the Year Awards from *Research and Development* magazine, as well as two Federal Design Achievement Awards, GSA Design Awards, national AIA Honor Awards and Urban Design Awards.

Index

IMAGES wish to thank all participating firms for their valuable contribution to this publication and especially Helin & Siitonen Architects for the use of the cover photograph by Jussi Tiainen.

Every effort has been made to trace the original source of copyright material contained in this book. The publishers would be pleased to hear from copyright holders to rectify any errors or omissions.

The information and illustrations in this publication have been prepared and supplied by the entrants. While all reasonable efforts have been made to ensure accuracy, the publishers do not, under any circumstances, accept responsibility for errors, omissions and representations express or implied.